*The Sahibs and the Lotus*

By the same author

*A History of India*
*Asia in the European Age*
*British India 1772–1947*
*The Last Years of British India*
*Nehru: A Political Biography*
*The Myth of the Mahatma: Gandhi, the British and the Raj*

# THE SAHIBS
# AND THE LOTUS

*The British in India*

MICHAEL EDWARDES

CONSTABLE · LONDON

First published in Great Britain 1988
by Constable and Company Limited
10 Orange Street, London WC2H 7EG
Copyright © 1988 by Michael Edwardes
Set in Linotron Plantin 11 pt by
Rowland Phototypesetting Limited
Bury St Edmunds, Suffolk
Printed in Great Britain by
St Edmundsbury Press Limited
Bury St Edmunds, Suffolk

British Library CIP data
Edwardes, Michael, 1923–
The sahibs and the lotus
1. British – India – History
2. India – Social life and customs
I. Title
954'.00421    DS428

ISBN 0 09 467180 X

The sahib sits upon the lotus. The lotus sits upon the water. The sahib will get his feet wet and catch a chill and die. But like the ant who aspires to climb to the top of Mount Kailas, it will take a long time.

Itinerant storyteller overheard in a village near Patna. 1840

For Dorothy Balshaw

# CONTENTS

[7]

# ILLUSTRATIONS

'The Massacre at Cawnpore' 1857. Contemporary engraving

The Planter 'A farmer prince' from G. R. Aberigh-Mackay: *Twenty-One Days in India*, London 1910

Indigo Assistant's Bungalow. Lower Bengal. W. S. Reid, *The Cultivation of Indigo*, London 1870

The Travelling MP 'The British Lion Rampant' from G. R. Aberigh-Mackay: *Twenty-One Days in India*, London 1910

Meet of the Ootacamund Hunt 1896

'A House-warming at Simla', *Illustrated London News*, 22 September 1923

Viceregal Lodge, New Delhi, 1930 *Information Service of India, London*

The Last Viceroy, Lord Mountbatten. *Illustrated London News*, 23 April, 1947

# PREFACE

T HE story of British life in India from the seventeenth century
to the middle of the twentieth, resembles a sort of multi-
media production. There is melodrama, tragedy, circus acts,
high and low comedy, and Blood and Thunder, with *real* blood and
thunder. As one should expect from such a long-running production,
there are numerous changes of scenery, of actors – both principals
and supporting – as well as a variety of sound effects and incidental
music – sometimes played by a full orchestra and sometimes upon a
penny whistle. In a phrase, 'a panorama of human beings', in all their
diversity of character, ambitions, arrogance, cruelty, decency, stupidity, and ordinariness. Yes, ordinariness, for whatever the claims
to superiority of character, race, and insight, all the 'justifications'
made for the domination of one people over another, most of the
British who fought, ruled, died and survived in India were ordinary.
Above all, they were *of their times* – and if they are to be judged, they
must be in the terms of their times and not in those of ours, with its
differing but no less doubtful moralities.

The historian is, however, not a script-writer – though if he is so
inclined, he can certainly give to events a homogeneity that they did
not have; he can produce the Greek verities, a Grand Guignol, dim
the lights so that the action is obscure, increase the sound so that the
dialogue is, almost, inaudible. I have tried not to do any of those
things. I have also done nothing to correct an apparent imbalance in
the structure of the production. The Overture, though it covers in
time more than a hundred years, is short. But as all good overtures
should, it contains themes which will be developed into solo or

ensemble pieces in the following acts. Acts One and Two, and the Entr'acte which separates them, cover less than a century but are very long. This is simply because they contain the essence of the production, the greatest (and the hammiest) actors perform in them, the action is lively and the music loudest. Act Three was probably intended to be much longer than it turned out to be. The whole production, in fact, was closed-down rather precipitously, or so it seemed to many of the performers. The Epilogue, on the other hand, has no apparent end – except in this book.

Research for *The Sahibs and the Lotus* was mainly done in Britain, but the actual writing was carried out in a small town in northeastern Pennsylvania. For indispensable assistance in acquiring printed reference material, I am particularly grateful to Carol A. Tome; to the Osterhout Library of Wilkes-Barre, Pennsylvania, and to the highly efficient service of the Inter-Library Loan system. I also am grateful to my wife, Janet, who edited and typed the final manuscript.

Dallas, Pennsylvania February 1987

## A Note on Definitions

I have kept the jargon of 'Anglo-Indian' words and phrases to a minimum, explaining those that are used when they appear. But one or two that occur frequently need to be defined now. After 1900, 'Anglo-Indian' came to mean a person of mixed-blood, a Eurasian, but here it is used to mean a Briton in India, as it had done for more than a century. 'Civilian' is not simply the opposite of 'military', but, in the sense in which it was used by the British in India, a member of the civil service, and therefore distinct from such other Anglo-Indians as wives, businessmen, planters, and, of course, soldiers.

—— *OVERTURE* ——

# SHAKING THE PAGODA TREE

*Pagoda-tree* A slang phrase once current in England rather than in India, to express the openings to rapid fortune which at one time existed in India.

Hobson-Jobson
*A Glossary of Colloquial Anglo-Indian Words and Phrases*
new ed. 1903

. . . a Nabob of a couple of generations back, who had enriched himself when the pagoda tree was worth the shaking.

*Saturday Review* 3 September 1881

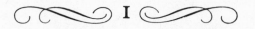

# I

## *A VISIT TO A FACTORY*

T HIS Factory does not make anything, except profit – at least
that is its sole purpose – for it is a place of trade, and the
merchants who work there and are now assembled for dinner
are known as Factors. The man at the head of the table is the Chief
Factor but is called the President or Governor. He is a person of
considerable consequence – and no little pretension. Such pretension
is good for trade. The President has to deal with Indian ambassadors
and other luminaries and ostentatious display helps to impress the
customer. And that is important, for the President's main function is
to make money for his masters – the Directors of the Honourable
East India Company, of Leadenhall Street in the City of London.

The Company has been in existence – though not without its ups
and downs, and even outs – since the first Queen Elizabeth granted it
a charter in 1601. Now at the beginning of the new century it is still
suffering, from disease, wars, the stupidity of some of its representatives, and the rivalry, both commercial and political, of other
European nations. At the present time the English are almost entirely
confined to the four main trading settlements of Madras, Calcutta,
Surat and Bombay. But as the century progresses there will be great
changes, not only in British society in India, but in the power
exercised by its members. As for the East India Company, it will have
moved from dividends to dominion.

But that is many years away. The President has arrived in the
dining room without ostentation though he never goes outside the
Factory unless accompanied by a large body of armed men, the two
flag bearers carrying large Union flags and a band of local musicians

who play with such enthusiasm and loudness as to 'frighten a stranger into belief the men were mad'. Inside the Factory he is less impressive. Most Presidents reached their high position not because of worth or superior expertise, but because a tough constitution has helped them survive, longer than others, the climate, disease, and the dietary habits they share with their fellow countrymen.

Even after reaching his exalted position, the President was by no means all-powerful. His decisions were subject to the approval of a council whose members he could not over-rule, as he had only a casting vote in the event of a tie. Members of Council could and not infrequently did report on the President behind his back to the Directors in London, an espionage encouraged by the Directors as a curb on the private enterprise of the President, and a reminder of where his primary loyalty lay. Such a reminder was undoubtedly needed, for everyone from the President downward was engaged in trade on his own account. The Company paid very low salaries on the assumption that its employees would keep themselves on the profits of private trade. Most did, but sometimes the Directors' parsimony led to hardship, especially amongst the lower echelons, the clerks or Writers, as they were called.

When the Factory kept a common table, as it did through the early years of the century, the writers occupied the bottom of the table, behaving, as young men did and do, with some gaiety and not a little noise. Their elders, arranged in seniority up to the Councillors and the President himself, were frequently no better behaved and often with less than good spirits. Quarrels broke out, which on occasion led to duels being fought. Where the President was weak in maintaining decorum, behaviour could be so bad that news of it reached the ears of the Honourable Directors in London, as it did in 1710, when they protested that things had come to a sorry state when it had been found necessary to send for 'Files of Musqueteers . . . for to keep the peace at dinner time.'

Many of the disturbances had their roots in jealousies inflamed by large quantities of liquor. European and Persian wines and spirits were imported in large quantities and many varieties: 'Mountain Wine, Rhenish, Syder, Galicia, Florence, Hock, Canary, Brandy, Claret, Ale, Beer, Shyrash (Shiraz) Wine' among them. There was always a great deal of food to be washed down, from the comparatively simple to the exotic: 'cabab' (kabab) and fowl stuffed with raisins and almonds and baked in butter to 'Deer and Antelopes, Peacocks, Hares and Partridges, and all kinds of Persian Fruits, Pistachioes, Plums, Apricots, Cherries, Etc.' It is little wonder that not only were tempers raised but mortality rates, too. It took some time for such medical opinion as there was in India to make a correlation between large, and largely meat meals – often eaten at the hottest time of the day, washed down with enormous quantities of alcohol – and general sickliness frequently leading to early death (see the Epilogue, Chapter 2). Indeed, physicians often recommended such 'native liquors' as arrack, made from the fermented sap of the coco-palm and described by one medical authority as 'good for the gripes.' Neri, another liquor, made this time from the sap of the areca-palm, was said to taste as sweet as milk. Unfortunately, the British were inclined to 'lose their lives by the immoderate use of these tempting liquors with which when once inflamed, they become so restless that no place is cool enough and therefore they lie down on the ground all night which occasions their being snatched away [i.e. die] in a very short time.'

The Directors made some attempt to encourage the drinking of tea among its employees in India. As the Company controlled the tea trade with China, (the tea plant was not cultivated in India until the 1840s) there was a commercial motive as well as a moral one. Tea was certainly drunk, and in quite large quantities, usually spiced and accompanied by preserved lemons and sugar candy. Tea was also considered of medicinal value but not, at least by the majority of Britons in India, as a substitute for wine and spirits.

The routines of the day invited recourse to the bottle – boredom and boozing are natural concomitants. Rising at 6.00 a.m. for prayers, the morning was given over to business, the writer to his clerkly duties in the counting house, the President with senior merchants in what was known as the consulting room, or examining newly-arrived merchandise in the godowns or warehouses, or supervising the assembly of cargoes to be shipped abroad.

Dinner – the largest meal of the day – was set for noon, the hottest time of the day. After a siesta, the junior merchants and writers might return to the office, but their seniors were free to relax either in a garden maintained by the Company or, if there was a convenient river, upon the water in a budgerow, a large native craft propelled by oars. The evening was usually the time for visiting. Supper at the common table was followed by prayers at 8 p.m. The gates of the Fort, inside which, at the beginning of the eighteenth century, everyone lived, were shut at 10 or 11 p.m., after which no one was allowed to leave except the guard. In Madras this consisted of 'one sergeant, one corporal and twelve men, half black, half white, who are to go from the barracks to the President's Garden House [i.e. country residence] outside the Fort from thence a sergeant and six men go at 11 o'clock round the suburbs to see if the boutiques are all shut, and that no disturbance is made in the streets through which they pass, to suppress gaming houses, to stop all persons suspected to be running of goods. And a corporal and six men go the same at two.'

For the men who had espoused the Protestant work-ethic – Whence do the merchant's profit come except from his own diligence and industry – Sunday was still a day of observance. In fact, the Directors were known to exhort their employees to a *strict* observance. However, as with most things in India, compliance was somewhat widely interpreted. Prayers were recited three times but the rest of the day was spent feasting and, naturally, drinking. Madras seems to have made something of a display of church-going, the President walking in procession with an honours guard of 200 soldiers lining the way. On his approach, 'the Organs strike up, and continue a Welcome till he is seated, when the Minister discharges the Duty of his Function, according to the Forms appointed by our prudent Ancestors of the Church of England'.

Apart from the sober excitements of the Anglican church service, there were the rarer pleasures of the seasonal arrival of vessels from England or from other English settlements in India. There would be new faces among the passengers, news from England, letters, often offensively phrased, from the Directors in London, and supplies of those necessities which become luxuries when one is far from home. These latter were sold by auction, an event of some importance in the exile's year.

Occasionally, there would be a state visit by some prince or important dignitary. On such occasions, the President and Council would put on a display. Troops lined the streets in their best uniforms. Guns would be fired from the Fort and perhaps from ships in the roads. Gifts would be offered and the guests feasted with as many as 600 dishes, and afterwards entertained by dancing girls. Other causes for celebration were the accession to the throne of a new monarch, the signing of a new charter for the Company, and a more regular, and recurring feature, the annual celebration of the king's birthday. It was all rather pleasant, even fun. A respite, certainly from the general boredom which could not be escaped. There was no such thing as leave, because there was nowhere to go, nowhere *safe* to go, outside the range of the Fort. Intellectual pursuits were hardly catered for, though there was a library consisting mainly of theological works and some secular ones of a generally uplifting nature. Few took advantage of what was there.

Sports offered no release. Strenuous ones were out of the question because of the climate. In time, as the merchants began to move outside the Fort and build country retreats, shooting became a common pastime, as did riding, and hunting with greyhounds. As the Forts became the nuclei of towns with paved streets, the driving of horse-chaises was added to the list of pastimes, though few could afford the cost. For those who could not, the writers and the junior factors, billiards and backgammon in a tavern were the usual games. Boredom in general led to gaming. Semi-professional gamblers appeared. In 1720, the Directors named a certain Captain Seton as making a 'trade of it to the stripping of several of the young men' in Madras. Any factor discovered gaming was supposed to be sent home to England but such punishment was rarely enforced.

A generally boring life in an alcoholic haze of varying opacity – no wonder the Directors were constantly complaining of bad handwriting and faulty book-keeping. A way out of dulling routine might have been social intercourse with the India surrounding the Fort, but on the whole the merchants only mixed with their own kind. This was not because of any racial prejudice – even if they had any, which they did not, display of it would not have been conducive to trade. The merchants had no objection to adopting the more appealing customs of the country such as the *zenana* or women's apartment. When

European women were few in number – and even after it had increased – the expatriate libido, and even the simple desire for the 'comforts of home' could be satisfied by installing one or more Indian females in a zenana. The size of that establishment varied according to the merchant's income.

Most merchants almost never bothered to even try to learn an Indian language, though they were happy to take Indian words and adapt them. But the language of their commerce was a demotic Portuguese which had been spread around the seaports by the first European nation to carry on trade in India. Failing this *lingua franca*, the English used Indian interpreters. The English were happy to wear comfortably loose Indian dress when they relaxed at home, perhaps drawing upon a hookah. This exotic pipe consisted of a bowl for tobacco, another at the base for water, and a long snake-like flexible tube ending in a mouthpiece. There were a variety of models available, including the 'Cream Can' named after the alleged inventor, Karim Khan Zend, the Ailloon, and the Hubble-Bubble. The latter was considered rather low class. Hoookah-smoking became something of a social necessity. Women were soon among its most devoted addicts, 'and the highest compliment they can pay a man is to give him preference by smoking his hookah. In this case it is a point of politeness to take off a mouthpiece he is using and substitute a fresh one, which he presents to the lady with his hookah . . .'

What might be called the stationary hookah, with its water bowl designed to take at least two quarts of water and a snake of some ten feet in length, was not convenient for travelling. A smaller version was therefore perfected for use while being carried in a palanquin. This form of transportation was used, by all who could afford one, for short journeys, from house to office, and even on long ones across country. Even after roads were constructed and horse-drawn carriages could be used, the palanquin was still favoured. The first palanquin had been a simple string bed about five feet long and two wide, covered with a bamboo frame draped with red cloth to keep out the sun and the gaze of the inquisitive. This was usually carried by four or more men. From this plain beginning, the palanquin developed luxuriously. The shape became first that of an oblong box, then an arched canopy was added, cushions placed inside, and adjustable side-curtains for even surer privacy. Later improvements were to include rigid sides with sliding doors and windows. Decoration became more extravagant with gold and silver bells, and richly embroidered curtains.

From the simple conveyance of a merchant to the conspicuous display of the empire-builder, the progress of the palanquin can be taken as symbolic of change in the status, and the pretensions of the British in India during the eighteenth century.

# 2

# DIPLOMATS, MERCENARIES,
# AND INDO-BRITONS

THOUGH the majority of the British were confined first to the Fort and then to the new towns that grew up around them, some penetrated the India that lay on the boundaries of the settlements. Most went on business – the Company's business – and some set up trading stations, subordinate Factories, for the purchase of locally-produced goods, mainly fine textiles, for onward transmissions to the Factory. The out-stations were models in miniature of the principal settlements and even more isolated. Cut off from the society of their fellow countrymen, the loneliness bred eccentricity. Some went native, 'gone Fantee' was the picturesque phrase. At least one merchant was so eccentric as to 'literally despise Money', something that hardly endeared him to his employers.

From the middle of the eighteenth century, more and more Europeans spread out across India. As the British acquired political power, diplomats, soldiers and other officials descended upon the out-stations, breaking their isolation and changing their character completely. Towards the end of the century, the Company encouraged the planting of indigo and another, and often violent element was added to the countryside.

The diplomats, when they were not concerned with single missions, were attached to the courts of Indian princes and were known as Residents. Many of those entrusted with delicate diplomatic affairs were 'characters'. Colonel John Collins, Resident at the court of the Maharaja Sindia, an important Maratha prince, in the first years of the nineteenth century, had an overbearing manner, without diplomacy or even cunning. He was known among the

[24]

British as 'King Collins'. He affected considerable state, and his camp was that of an Indian prince. When Collins travelled, he went accompanied by his zenana and a private brigade of artillery to fire salutes. Though his entourage was impressive, Collins was not, being small of stature and wizened of face. One visitor described him as 'dressed in an old-fashioned military coat, white breeches, sky blue stockings and large, glaring buckles in his shoes, having his highly-powdered wig, from which depended a pig-tail of no ordinary dimensions, surmounted by a small, round, black silk hat, ornamented with a single black feather, looking altogether not unlike a monkey dressed up for Bartholomew Fair.'

Collins may have looked odd, but he made up with an aggressive manner for what he lacked in presence. 'There was a fire in his small black eyes, shooting out from beneath a large, shaggy pent-house brow, which more than counterbalanced the ridicule that his first appearance naturally excited.' It was a pity that he did not impress Sindia, who refused to sign a treaty Collins was trying to get him to accept, and by 'his [Sindia's] insolent and hostile declaration to Colonel Collins' began a war which was to give the future Duke of Wellington some of his first experience of command.

The appointment of Resident was much sought after, as not infrequently, great profits could be made on the side. In Lucknow, for example, over a million pounds annually passed through the Resident's hands and some of it undoubtedly stuck. Even though many reforms took place at the end of the century, a British Resident was still in a position to make considerable private profit for himself. One who did was Henry Russell, Resident at the court of Hyderabad.

The ruler of Hyderabad was known as the Nizam and the founder of the state had once been a high official in the Mughal empire. In its decline, he had made himself the master of very substantial territories in central India. His successors had not been of the same calibre, and by the time Henry Russell had been appointed Resident early in the nineteenth century, the country had been constantly ravaged by more powerful Indian rulers. The Nizam made one attempt to resist Russell but failed. He then withdrew into a seclusion from which he rarely emerged. It was the Resident who appointed ministers, and Russell chose a Hindu (the Nizam was a Muslim) called Chandu Lal.

[25]

Under his benevolent administration, Hyderabad almost became a desert, without law or order. When the population rose up against the tax-collector, Russell suggested the sending in of a British military force *at the Nizam's expense!* This was done, and the rebellion quickly suppressed.

Having stripped the countryside bare, the problem facing Chandu Lal was how to raise revenue to pay, among other things, the absurdly high salaries of the officers commanding the military force which had stayed on after the end of the rebellion. Russell suggested the services of the banking house of William Palmer & Co., the head of which was the Eurasian son of an English general. Palmer agreed to lend the state the sum of six million rupees – though no actual money was to change hands. The interest on it was to be real enough, and was to be divided between Palmer & Co. and Chandu Lal! With the approval – and profit – of the Resident, Palmer & Co. almost became the actual rulers of Hyderabad, its agents collecting revenue and not infrequently besieging villages for payment.

As these activities took place outside *British* India, Russell, with the aid of powerful friends, was able to cover up what was happening for some time, and even when the scandal became obvious, and after he had been replaced as Resident, was very nearly successful in ruining the career of his successor, who was investigating the affair. The name of Russell's successor was Charles Metcalfe.

Metcalfe was a very different type to Russell, and was once described as displaying 'the Majesty of his Rectitude'. In 1811, five years after the British had captured the old Mughal city of Delhi, Metcalfe had been appointed Resident there. Delhi was then the frontier capital of British India, a watchtower surveying the marches, the centre of a great web of imperial diplomacy which stretched out into Punjab, Rajasthan, Nepal and beyond to the states of Central Asia. Its ruler, the Resident, was king in everything but name. Calcutta and higher authority were three months' journey away. The Resident was very much on his own, in a territory where precedent was useless, and decision was all. The British in Delhi, and there were very few of them, had to be many things – politicians, administrators, diplomats, judges, soldiers and spymasters. They were unfettered by regulations from higher authority, except in the most general outlines of policy. The Resident and his staff were left with a large discretion, and what virtually amounted to independence.

The Delhi Territory – the responsibility of the Resident – stretched from the river Jumna to the river Sutlej, from the city northwards to the foothills of the Himalayas. It had once been the centre of a vast empire, that of the Mughals, whose remains – buildings, sentiments, administrative systems – lay everywhere in whole or in partial decay. The Resident and his assistants operated in a kind of museum, in which many of the exhibits were still alive, and some dangerous. One of these was the king of Delhi, the last shadow of the Mughal emperors.

The city itself exercised a vivid hold on the imagination of the British. The source of its fascination was partly history, partly situation. History provided a vast assemblage of buildings, some in active use, most in the melancholy of ruin. Delhi provided all the elements of romance. Its relics of past empires inspired sentimentality. After the war that had given them control of the old imperial city, the British had not deposed the king. They considered him a pensioner, maintained out of sentiment and ignored out of policy. Such an attitude was quite alien to the Indian political consciousness. As long as the king remained in his palace – pensioner or not, with or without real power – the dignity of his position somehow remained untarnished. Such an attitude was fraught with potential dangers, dangers that were compounded over the years until finally they made the court of Delhi the focus of rebellion in the Mutiny of 1857.

But the terrible events of that year were over the horizon when Charles Metcalfe ruled Delhi, and the king the least of his problems. However, the past did influence his decisions. Metcalfe, riding on an elephant and surrounded by soldiers, had toured the whole territory to settle the land revenue. He found a system that worked, and decided to preserve it from outside interference. It was an astute move. To direct and control a traditional system – with the minimum of modification – was more than likely to endear the new government to the people. It was also cheaper. He also felt that Western laws were not suitable for India. He thought them easily corrupted. The British judge 'is the only part of them that is untainted'. Not that the judges themselves were above reproach, although inexperience was usually to blame. This criticism from a man who was only 26 years of age at the time of his appointment as Resident, when his own brother, who was President of the Civil Court, was in his early twenties, and the head of the criminal court even younger! British India was still very much a young man's world.

As Resident, Metcalfe was expected to display considerable state. It was essential to show who was the effective king of Delhi. He received a large grant for expenses, which he spent royally. Metcalfe's own financial arrangements demanded that he save as much of his salary as possible, so that he might be able, in twelve or fifteen years, 'to live at home [i.e., in England] in the plain manner in which I mean to live'. In Delhi, a 'plain manner', at least officially, was not possible. The Resident had frequent guests to entertain. Officials and even tourists put themselves up at the Residency, and expected, and were given, the best of welcomes. Metcalfe had found the Residency itself in a dilapidated state, lacking furniture and even basic equipment. As other Residencies were equipped at the government's expense, he assumed that he was justified in buying furniture and plate for which he would receive reimbursement. The Directors in London, however, found Metcalfe's expenses quite incredible, and he was informed that they expected him to pay a large part of the cost himself! Fortunately for Metcalfe, the decision was not enforced.

Though this was a relief, Metcalfe found himself becoming 'very unsociable and morose' and complained that he led a 'vexatious and joyless life'. It was certainly a full one. Nevertheless, he had an intimate, private face as well as a public mask. We know a great deal about the latter, but very little about the former. What we do know comes from the reports of spies employed by the native princes to keep a watchful eye on the activities of the great man.

The spies' reports still exist. Little escaped their constant espionage. Even if there were no European portraits and no European descriptions, we would still know exactly what Metcalfe looked like. He is a short, awkward, thickset, plain man, with a pimply complexion. A poor horseman, he prefers to travel on an elephant, not only for the sake of comfort, but because the slow-paced animal permits him to read while he is on the move. The spies note that he reads a great deal, even though much of his time is taken up with ceremonies and decision-making. There are always men who want help or are anxious to pay their respects to the man they call Muntazim-ud-daula, 'Administrator of the State'.

The spies report on the *nazars* (ceremonial presentations by an inferior to a superior) which are part of the protocol of authority in India. Sometimes, Metcalfe will touch the gift – a piece of brocade or a few gold coins – and return it to the giver. Other gifts he will accept, giving something in return. All are carefully catalogued by the spies, because quality and cost are symbols of status. To watchful eyes, the *nazars* may indicate some subtle change in the standing of a petty ruler in the eyes of the British.

Frequently, there are reports that Metcalfe has gone for a solitary walk, eaten his evening meal, and returned to study papers. He examines the tortuous accounts of the treasury and personally supervises the payment of salaries. On another occasion, hearing that two Europeans are lodged at an inn, he sends an elephant for them so that they may come and dine with him.

On one day, his spies report that this great English official, accompanied by his assistants, has paid a visit to the other king of Delhi, that shadowy puppet, in his great decaying palace. It is the anniversary of his accession to the throne, and the puppet-play demands that he be presented with gifts by the real ruler of the state, tokens of an allegiance that exists only in the imagination. On another day, the Hindu population of the city invites Muntazim-ud-daula to take part in the festival of Holi, a sort of bacchanalia in honour of the god Krishna. Many English officials are delighted to join in this heralding of spring, when coloured powders are scattered and obscene songs expressively sung. But not 'the Administrator of the State'. Metcalfe declines on the grounds that it is not an *English* festival. On a third day, the spies report that a horse has kicked a man and that Muntazim-ud-daula has decreed that the animal be put in jail until the owner can be found and tried instead.

But almost every day's report has the same ending. Muntazim-ud-daula goes to the Shalimar gardens, changes his clothing and retires, into privacy.

The Shalimar gardens are very beautiful and lie about six miles from the city. They occupy an important place in Indian history. The Mughal emperor, Shah Jahan, who built the Taj Mahal at Agra as a memorial to his love for his wife, beautified them with pavilions and pools. His son, Aurangzeb, the last of the great emperors, crowned himself in the shadow of their tall trees in 1658. When the British occupied Delhi, they found the Shalimar a wilderness, a tangle of palm and citrus trees, clogged with undergrowth, rustling with snakes, the air sharp-edged with the cry of parakeets, peacocks, and kingfishers. But they recognised its virtues as the emperors had done before them, and saw that the gardens would offer an escape into privacy and freedom after the formality and responsibility of the day. The undergrowth was partly cleared, the pools restocked with gold and silver fish, the old pavilions refurbished, their marble made clean and bright.

Metcalfe used Aurangzeb's pavilion for his private parties, but he has also built a house nearby. There he puts aside the formalities of his office, and the 'Majesty of his Rectitude'. There he settles down with his family. The house in the garden, unlike his official residence in the city, is simple though extremely comfortable, and in it lives a secret kept from posterity – Charles Metcalfe's Indian wife and half-caste family. As a concession to mid-Victorian prudery, all mention will be left out of his official biography when it is published more than forty years later, though one of his sons becomes a colonel, aide-de-camp to a governor-general, but almost nothing is known of their mother, not even her name. Something, however, can be deduced about her.

There seems no doubt that Metcalfe met his wife, who was probably a Sikh, at the court of Ranjit Singh, Maharaja of the Punjab, and may have been a member of the ruler's own family. She may not have been a concubine – many Englishmen kept them, including the first Lord Teignmouth, who is remembered, if at all, as one of the founders of the Bible Society. But in Metcalfe's case there is a tradition that he was married – though by what rites is obscure – and there is a faint perfume of a romantic story adhering to the tradition.

All that is known for certain is that at the end of a full day, Metcalfe's carriage was driven through the evening air along a sandy road to a house in a garden. The trees hid his life from view, and the spies returned to their garrets. There, by the light of an oil lamp, they prepared their reports on the things that really interested their masters: 'Today Muntazim-ud-daula pardoned a landlord sentenced to death . . . '

The wars between the British and the French in the middle years of the eighteenth century, and the gradual collapse of native powers attracted European mercenaries, military adventurers of many nationalities to sell their expertise to one or more of the Indian princes. It was a dangerous occupation for some, and profit frequently remained elusive . But a few lived well and were able and willing to return to Europe. Others settled into a semi-Indian way of life. Some allied themselves with important Muslim families, such as Major Hearsey, who married a daughter of the deposed ruler of Cambay, an ancestor of whom had been described by the seventeenth-century English poet, Samuel Butler, as having a somewhat unusual – and dangerous – taste in food:

> The prince of Cambay's daily food,
> Is asp and basilisk and toad,
> Which makes him have so strong a breath,
> Each night he stinks a queen to death.

There is no record of this facility descending in the family. Like other mercenaries, Hearsey went over to the British and took part in the Nepal war of 1814. He was supposed to be an expert on the country, and had reported that the Gurkhas were not particularly good fighters! After an engagement in which Hearsey was captured by the Gurkhas, his men 'hastened back to the plains with the utmost terror and expedition'.

It was not only the military adventurers who, when they could, adopted the luxuries of Indian ways. Some of the Company's servants did also. Perhaps the last of these, just as he was the first of the great soldier-administrators was David Ochterlony. Born in Boston, Massachusetts in 1759, his parents had fled to Canada at the time of the American War of Independence. Ochterlony arrived in India in 1778 at the beginning of a life spent between soldiering and the administration of the new territories acquired by the British in northern India after 1806. Reginald Heber, bishop of Calcutta, recorded a meeting with Ochterlony, then Resident in Delhi, in 1825. The bishop was on an overland journey from Calcutta to Bombay, and had heard many tales of the legendary Sir David. Of the great classical mansions he had built on various sites around Delhi; of his thirteen wives who, mounted upon the backs of thirteen elephants, took the air in the cool of the evening. The bishop had also heard that Sir David travelled like an oriental prince, accompanied by a retinue of servants, both European and Indian, and an escort of smartly-uniformed cavalry, his baggage transported on many elephants and camels. The private tents of his womenfolk were said to be set in a large enclosure hung round with red cloth, to inhibit the gaze of the profane.

In the harsh land of the Rajputs, where the countryside was naked and desolate, dotted only with a few mud-walled 'castles', the bishop saw approaching across the empty plain in the clear morning air a large number of horses, elephants and palanquins, as well as several covered carriages, two companies of infantry, a troop of regular cavalry, and about forty or fifty irregulars on horseback and foot, armed with spears and matchlocks. But the bishop – an unromantic man, though his journey across India at this period was the height of romanticism – was disappointed. The procession was undoubtedly very long; indeed, in Europe it might have passed for that of an Eastern prince. The bishop, however, felt that rumour had let him down. Sir David's caravan was by no means as large or as splendid as he had expected.

Ochterlony himself courteously descended from his carriage-and-four to greet the bishop. He was a tall, old man, so swaddled against the cold – which is severe in winter in Rajputana – with wraps and shawls, gold brocade and furred cap, that only his face was visible. The bishop observed that Sir David was infirm, and he was right. In a few months, Ochterlony would be dead.

There is no record of what the two men said to each other, surrounded by the restless throng of men and horses. But the bishop felt something symbolic in their meeting which had nothing to do with polite conversation. In his journal he wrote:

Within these few days, I have been reading Coxe's *Life of Marlborough*, and at this moment it struck me forcibly how little it would have seemed in the compass of possibility, to any of the warriors, statesmen, or divines of Queen Anne's time, that an English General and an English Bishop would ever shake hands on a desert plain in the heart of Rajpootana.

'Necessity is the Mother of Invention and Father of the Eurasian', the often quoted witticism, seriously explains the existence of what were, in the early days of the British in India, known by a variety of names, such as East Indian, Indo-Britons, or simply as half-castes. For most of the eighteenth century, there were few white women in India, and virtually no colour prejudice. Marriage with Indian women was not considered demeaning. Nor was there any discrimination against the offspring of such marriages. Indeed, the sons of such families were assumed to have a moral right to employment by the Company. The Portuguese, the first Europeans to form settlements in India, had intermarried freely and without prejudice. Indeed, it had been state policy to create a community of mixed-blood identified with Portugal, in order to sustain the Portuguese presence in Asia. The French, too, had not hesitated to take Indian wives. In 1790 it was said that only two French families in the principal settlement of Pondicherry were of pure French blood.

Liaisons of a temporary nature were common among ordinary soldiers, and the children born of these unions were often abandoned when their fathers moved on, a situation by no means unusual in our own times. The condition of these children was often deplorable, but orphan asylums were established in Calcutta and Madras, and towards the end of the eighteenth century a special establishment was set up in Calcutta for the children of officers, financed by deductions from the father's pay. There were problems when it came to getting work for the children. Officer's children could be apprenticed to business organisations, while those of ordinary soldiers were lucky to end up as drummers or fifers in some regiment of the Company's army. Girls either married European soldiers, became ladies' maids, or not infrequently, prostitutes.

As the Eurasian population increased, fears were expressed that it

[33]

might become dangerous. One course suggested was to make the fathers of half-caste children send them to Europe 'prohibiting their return in any capacity whatsoever'. The expense involved would 'operate as a check to the extension of zenanas which are now but too common among the Europeans.' It was an indication of how much prejudice had grown. The stereotypes of Victorian India were being formed. Soon the Eurasian community would find itself segregated from British society, and despised for failings few of its members actually possessed.

One of the later criticisms of Eurasians was that they would not make suitable army officers because Indian soldiers would despise them. In the late eighteenth century and afterwards, Eurasian officers in the Company's army as well as the forces of Indian princes, had been very successful. One of these was Colonel James Skinner, the son of a Scots father and a Rajput mother. Until his death in 1841, Skinner was the undoubted head of a group of aristocratic Eurasians living in Delhi. The group included men of French, German and Portuguese origins, as well as British. Their fathers had sometimes been military adventurers others had been officials of the Mughal government. Skinner had once been in the employ of one of the Maratha princes, then joined the British and been rewarded with a valuable estate and the Order of the Bath. He was described as 'very black', talking broken English, but nevertheless was one 'of those people whose lives ought to be written up for the particular amusement of succeeding generations'.

Colonel Skinner's English may have been faulty, but he spoke Persian with great fluency and wrote his memoirs in that language. He possessed houses on his estates outside Delhi, but he had a town mansion near the Kashmir gate of the city, built in the Classical style, with high colonnades. Inside were marble floors and marble baths, and behind were the women's quarters. Skinner gave lavish and much appreciated entertainments. In the cold weather season, he would arrange excursions into the Delhi countryside. Tents of oriental size and magnificence would be erected, and fine food and wines served to guests. Skinner was known to be a Christian, but his family seems to have remained Muslim by faith. He built a church, still standing, which looks like a small version of St Paul's Cathedral in London, with the dome painted bright pink. Opposite, he had constructed a mosque for the rest of his family to worship in.

# 3

## THE HEATHEN IN HIS BLINDNESS

THE British brought to India with the rest of their baggage of ideas and attitudes, the religious beliefs and practices of their age. At the opening of the eighteenth century, Puritan values still prevailed. The Directors of the East India Company were much concerned with the spiritual welfare of their employees, appointing chaplains for the Factories, and even for those of their trading vessels over 500 tons dead-weight. By the end of the century, a different form of Christianity possessed the British. Evangelicalism and its active partner, missionary zeal, had begun to set the tone. In between, religious observances became more formal than real, more display than piety. This was noted by Indians, especially Hindus, who came to the conclusion, according to one source, that they had nothing to fear from a religion whose leader (in this case, Bishop Heber of Calcutta) lived in a great mansion with many servants and carriages to ensure his physical comfort.

The ostentation of Sunday observance in the Factory has already been described, but it was a gaudiness covering a genuine faith. As the century progressed, the faith diminished until attendance at church became a social rather than a religious event, an opportunity to meet friends, size up new arrivals, and engage in flirtation. Even those aspects lost out, in time, to the race-course and the governor-general's levées, or balls at Government House. The Company's concern for the souls of its servants also declined, and for many years the Directors restricted the size of their trading vessels to 499 tons to avoid supplying them with a chaplain. On numerous occasions the Directors refused to appoint a clergyman to supervise the spiritual life of the Factories. In the early days, these chaplains were often the only men with any pretension to learning in the settlements, and they ranked second to the President or governor. They became responsible for the education of the children of the merchants, and were active in raising money for schools and orphanages. Though the Company forbade clergymen to engage in private trade, there is ample evidence that they did, though at the close of the century the Evangelical wave brought a certain asceticism, in which Mammon was considered an unworthy associate of a man of God.

With the wave of Evangelism came a new interest in missions. Before this they had been left to Danes and Germans, and English Baptists living and working outside the territorial jurisdiction of the Company. At the beginning of the eighteenth century, the only Christian missionaries had been Roman Catholic, among them the Jesuits, who had made a remarkable attempt to Indianise Christianity, until their methods had been condemned by the Pope in 1704. Before that, they had permitted their converts to maintain Hindu caste divisions, even refusing the Mass to those of low caste in churches reserved for the highest! The priest assumed the garb and demeanour of a Hindu *guru* and the practice of the two highest castes of wearing a sacred thread was transformed into a Christian symbol, a triple gold cord representing the Trinity, and two silver ones the human and divine natures of Christ. It is interesting that a similar attempt to Hinduise Christianity, at least superficially, is being attempted in India today.

None of this worried the Company's servants, who had to live with the Portuguese and their converts, sometimes married them, and certainly did business with them. The Directors, on the other hand, were intolerant, and frequently castigated their servants for their easy-going attitudes. In 1751 they instructed the Governor at Madras that a Roman Catholic church, 'in the very heart of the settlement has been very injurious to us' and that it must be torn down, 'and not retained on any pretense.'

The Company's attitude to Catholic missions was partly political. The French, who in the eighteenth century threatened the growth of British power, were, of course, Roman Catholic, but that antagonism was now balanced by the Company's support of Protestant missions about which it had been initially neutral. As British rule in India expanded, the Company's government practised the sensible policy of interfering as little as possible in the religious life of its new subjects. Though conscious of their growing power, the British were equally conscious that it depended on the acceptance of the large mass of the people who did not particularly care who governed them, as long as their customs were not challenged. The Company tried to sustain a sense of continuity, and its basic religious policy was not to give offence. This was taken to such lengths that until 1831 the Company prohibited the employment of Indian Christians in its judicial services nor were they permitted to practise as lawyers in the Company's courts. In contrast, the Company not only tolerated Hindu and Muslim festivals, but allowed the Company's troops and military bands to participate in them. In 1802, as a thanksgiving for the Treaty of Amiens between Britain and France, an official government party went in procession with armed soldiers and military music to the principal shrine of the Hindu goddess Kali in Calcutta, and presented the goddess with a considerable sum of money in the name of the Company!

In 1808, the Directors in London were so concerned about the possible consequences in India of Christian proselytism, that it instructed the governor-general that

it will be your bounden duty vigilantly to guard the public tranquility from interruption [by Christian missions] and will impress upon the minds of the inhabitants of India, that the British faith, upon which they rely for the free exercise of their religion, will be inviolably maintained.

But the Company was fighting something of a rearguard action. Powerful supporters of missionising were becoming more and more influential in English political life, and the Company depended upon the renewal of its charter by the British parliament for its very existence. By the Charter Act of 1813 it found itself forced to allow some Christian missionary activity within the territories it controlled, but it did what it could to impede it.

The Company as a ruling power had inherited the responsibilities of the governments it succeeded in relation to religious endowments and buildings and the control of the pilgrim traffic to the many shrines of Hinduism. A Regulation of 1817 authorised the government to take over the administration of a large number of Hindu temples and their funds. The pilgrim taxes levied by the Company were to be used for the repair and upkeep of temples. In fact, the government's involvement left its servants wide open to the criticism of supporting idolatry and acting, in the picturesque language of one observer, as 'dry-nurse to Vishnu'. As late as 1833, the government of Madras was still responsible for the administration of some 7,500 temples and their funds, and British officials played an intimate role in the material life of the temples, assessing and ordering repairs, and even, on occasion, press-ganging men to pull the cars used to carry images of the gods.

The Charter Act of 1833 was to put an end to this, at least officially, though it was many years before the effect was felt and it was not until thirty years later that government finally separated itself from the administration of religious endowments. Many Indians were to look upon this dissociation from what was one of the traditional functions of Indian rulers, as an abdication of responsibility and the deliberate repudiation of a duty incumbent upon all rulers, whatever religion they professed. More important still, it was to appear as an act of withdrawal, separating the government from the people and dramatising for Indian society the uniquely alien nature of British rule.

In the early years of the nineteenth century as the British in India ceased to be merchants by profession and became empire-builders by conviction, their concern for the spiritual life of the people they conquered lost compassion and acquired contempt. The missionaries themselves *hated* the heathenism they were battling against. 'This is Mohammedanism to murder as infidels the children of God, and to live without prayer' said one Henry Martyn, who also found that 'never did such sounds [the cymbals of a Hindu temple] go through my heart with such horror in my life . . . I shivered at being in the neighbourhood of Hell, my heart was ready to burst at the dreadful state to which the Devil had brought my poor fellow creatures.'

Henry Martyn, whose diatribes against the Muslims and the

Hindus were recorded in his Journal, which was not published until nearly fifty years after his death, arrived in India as a chaplain in 1806. The only house that could be found for him was an old pagoda on the banks of the river Hugli at Calcutta. Martyn was not particularly concerned about his creature comforts. He lived the simplest of lives, walking instead of riding, to the disgust of some of his fellow Britons. He did, however, take the trouble to learn an Indian language and translated the whole of the New Testament into Urdu. His acquaintance with actual life in India was not shared by others who equalled the violence of his denunciations of Indian religions. William Wilberforce, whose name will ever be associated with the abolition of the slave trade, dismissed the faiths of India as 'one grand abomination.'

The missionary endeavour released by such contempt produced something that might be considered a secular blessing, for it opened the door to the introduction of Western ideas of education in India. The Evangelicals believed that the relation of God and man was entirely personal and that access to this relationship could only be achieved through His revealed word. Education would be, they maintained, the key to conversion; the ability to read, a passport to Heaven. The missionaries had been prepared to translate the revealed word of the Bible into Indian vernaculars. The Baptist William Carey not only translated the Bible into many languages, but cut the typefaces and printed them at the Baptist Mission Press in the then Danish territory of Serampur, near Calcutta. But the new men were anglicizers, who believed, in effect, that English was the language of God.

The Evangelicals in Britain managed to have a clause inserted into the Charter Act of 1813 to the effect that 'it shall be lawful for the governor-general-in-council to direct that . . . a sum of not less than one lakh [100,000] rupees in each year shall be set apart and applied to the revival and improvement of literature [they meant *in English*] and the encouragement of the learned natives of India . . .' English education in the English language was to be the means through which Indians 'now engaged in the degrading and polluting worship of idols shall be brought to the knowledge of the true God and Jesus Christ whom He has sent.'

But:

> In vain with lavish kindness,
> The gifts of God are strown;
> The heathen in his blindness
> Bows down to wood and stone.

The majority of Indians continued in their faith, but at least a minority of them would be able to read the works of William Shakespeare in the original English.

# 4

# NABOBS AND NAUTCHES

THE commercial-minded employees of the East India Company in the first century of its activity hoped to make money for themselves as well as their employers, and by the same means – reasonably honest trade. For the three decades following the battle at Plassey in 1757, which resulted in the territorial acquisition of Bengal by the Company, to the coming of Lord Cornwallis in 1786, the real profits were to come from extortion and corrupt practices. It was the era of the 'Nabob', the Englishman behaving like an Indian prince – 'with an immense fortune, a tawny complexion, a bad liver and worse heart.'

Robert Clive – the subject of that pithy description by Macaulay – is certainly the archetype of the 'nabob', but he was motivated by much more than greed. A merchant turned soldier by the demands of the wars with the French in southern India, Clive found himself, at the ripe age of 32, the conqueror of the rich province of Bengal. It was basically a conquest by conspiracy, and one originated by others. In 1756, the Company's settlement at Calcutta had been captured by the Nawab of Bengal in response to the insolence of the British and their refusal to dismantle the Fort. Clive and a fleet of ships sent from Madras recaptured the Fort and town after the briefest of bombardments in January 1757. Clive then went on to capture the French settlement at Chandernagore.

About this time Clive learned that a conspiracy existed to overthrow the Muslim Nawab. Hindu merchants and bankers were at the heart of it, and Clive was approached with requests for his cooperation. An elderly Muslim general, Mir Jafar, was to be placed on the throne and there would be large disbursements of money for every-body, out of the State Treasury, which was rumoured to hold more than £40 million in gold bullion and jewels. It was suggested to Clive that there would be profit for both himself as well as the Company, should the conspiracy be successful.

The conspiracy came to a head in the renowned, but slightly ridiculous battle of Plassey. Clive's forces numbered less than 3,000, the Nawab's more than 50,000, but most of the troops opposing Clive were commanded by men who were involved in the conspiracy. The battle on 23 June 1757, which founded the British Empire in India, consisted of two parts: a cannonade in the morning followed by an immense downpour of monsoon rain which damaged the Nawab's ammunition, but not that of the British, who had the presence of mind to throw tarpaulins over theirs. This was followed by an attack precipitated by the over-enthusiasm of an English officer, which ended in complete victory at a cost to the British of 63 casualties. Even the losers were the poorer only by some 500 killed and wounded.

However, there was nothing minor about the *consequences* of Plassey. Clive was now a kingmaker, and the plunder of Bengal lay there for the taking. Clive placed Mir Jafar upon the throne, and then with his colleagues collected their rewards. Though the Nawab's Treasury turned out not to contain the fabulous sums everyone had believed – or had been led to believe – those that remained were still substantial. The Company became the landlord of some 880 square miles, mostly south of Calcutta, with rents estimated at £150,000 per annum. Clive received £234,000 in cash and the senior English merchants between £8,000 and £50,000 each. Together the Company and private individuals netted more than £3 million, the equivalent today of at least forty times that sum. It was clear to all that engineering a revolution was a most profitable game. A lust for gold inflamed the British, and Bengal was to have little peace until they had bled it white.

Clive took a rather superior view of the whole business. Other people were avaricious, he himself had merely accepted his just deserts.

[43]

He told a Committee of the British Parliament which in 1772 sought to criticise his behaviour: Consider the situation in which the battle of Plassey had placed me. A great prince was dependent on my pleasure; an opulent city lay at my mercy; its richest bankers bid against each other for my smiles. I walked through vaults which were open to me alone, piled on either hand with gold and jewels. Mr Chairman, at this moment, I stand astonished at my own moderation!

Clive's claim had some justification, especially at a time when corruption and self-seeking was the norm rather than the exception in British political life. Clive's motivation was not merely personal aggrandisement, as so many of those who profited from the consequences of his actions in Bengal. One of the concessions extracted by Clive from the puppet nawab, Mir Jafar, was an exemption from river tolls, one of the lucrative sources of the state's revenues, for the Company's merchants. The opportunity such exemption offered attracted a number of adventurers, French, Dutch, German and American, as well as British. With forged passes and employing Indians dressed as Company's soldiers and carrying the British flag, they bullied Indian merchants into buying goods at vastly inflated prices. Their depredations were finally stopped in 1772.

The period immediately following the battle of Plassey has been characterised as one of 'magnificence and disorder'. The growing wealth of the British in India was amply demonstrated in the magnificence of new town and country mansions, the disorder by the general lack of distinction in their surroundings and the absence of even the vaguest of town planning in their siting. A similar disorder reigned in the Company's administration. When the British found themselves the principal power in Bengal, they were faced with a series of dilemmas. The first was how to rule without revealing that the British had neither the capacity nor the manpower to operate the government. Clive's solution was the concept of 'dual government', by which native officials continued to function as they had done before, while the British remained in the background. This was primarily a matter of expediency, but what was actually a puppet government appealed to the British, as their first interest was undoubtedly profit. They considered themselves not as innovators, new brooms sweeping away the past, but as inheritors, and they hoped to make the inheritance work for them.

The lack of experienced men was even seen in the Company's own much-expanded affairs. Clive reported to the Directors in London in 1766 that the business of one of the most important departments was 'committed to a youth of three years standing in your service' and that 'the important trusts of Military Storekeeper, Naval Store-keeper, and Storekeeper of the Works, were bestowed when last vacant, upon Writers [the equivalent of junior officeworkers].' A similarly inexperienced youth 'held the post of Paymaster to the Army, at a period when nearly [20 million] rupees had been deposited for months together in his hands.' The Writer's inexperience was not confined to the expertise of the counting house. His ignorance of the language brought reliance upon Banians, Indian brokers, who 'became the principals in the several departments; the affairs of the Company flowed through a new and unnatural channel, and your most secret concerns were publicly known in the bazaar.'

The use of political and military power in the pursuit of private profit was by no means confined to Bengal. In Madras, a former ruler of the Carnatic, known as the Nawab of Arcot, was at the centre of political and financial intrigue. In 1776, when one of his sons planned a restoration, the Nawab borrowed large sums of money from some of the English merchants and members of the Madras Council. A quarrel between the governor, Lord Pigot, and members of the Council over the matter led to the governor's arrest and imprisonment. He was still in custody when he died on 11 May 1777. This sad event not unnaturally resulted in an enquiry, ordered by the Directors, to find out what bribes had been given by the Nawab to members of Council. On investigation these were found to total more than 1 million rupees.

The Nawab kept an agent in London and it was rumoured several members of the British parliament were in his pay. In the end, the scandal of his debts and the sea of corruption which enveloped them was dispelled by the action of the government in taking over the debt. Until then the Nawab would find himself besieged by European creditors. He would turn them away courteously – and empty-handed – with promises that his situation would very soon improve. Despite the fact that the Nawab's life was occupied in fending-off creditors, submitting petitions and complaining to Council, he was popular with the British. Some made profit from him and others hoped to do so, but he also appealed to the British through his dignity and good manners and his generosity, even if his creditors paid, and paid dearly, for the last. If the Nawab was nothing more – he was a gentleman.

The word 'gentleman' offers a vital clue to the social as well as financial aspirations of the Company's employees. From the very beginning the Directors of the East India Company had been against the employment of 'gentlemen'. They felt that they would have personal interests which could not be easily, if at all, reconciled with those of the Company; in effect, that trade and gentle birth did not mix. On the whole then, the Company's employees were men of bourgeois origins and were happy to remain within their class. Before 1750, those who amassed fortunes during their stay in India returned to England, bought some land and generally behaved as their fellow merchants who had never left England did: i.e., lived comfortably without any particular display of wealth.

After Plassey, however, when the merchant found himself a ruler, his horizons widened. As a plain merchant he had had little inter-course with the Indian aristocracy. A trader's main connection was with other traders. But everything changed with the exercise of political power. The merchants-turned-administrators came into contact as never before with the local gentry, the nawabs and landowners, and acquired from them the 'oriental' tastes and habits which were to characterise the 'Nabob' of late eighteenth-century England. No longer did the merchant desire only to be a country landowner. He wanted titles and deference to go with his property, prestige and social standing to go with his wealth. With the election of 1768, large numbers of 'nabobs' entered the British parliament becoming both a force in British politics and the subject of satire.

In India, the 'nabobising' of the merchants could be seen in the adoption of such Indian pleasures as the zenana and the nautch. Even after the number of European women increased in the settlements and it was possible to indulge in European dancing, the attachment to the nautch was scarcely diminished. A sort of Indian ballet, combining singing with dancing, the nautch was a common form of entertainment in the mansions of the new rulers of Bengal and the other parts of India. There seems to have been no discrimination against European women *attending* the performances, though there is an occasional expression of the opinion that the contortions of the dancers were not quite 'decent'. By the end of the century the attitude had changed, and the nautch was more frequently condemned than praised. Nevertheless, the nautch was still considered a suitable entertainment to give a visiting notable. Edward, Prince of Wales was given one in 1875, and so was his eldest son fifteen years later. At this time the Bishop of Calcutta forwarded a memorial to the then Viceroy alleging that the performance had an 'immoral character'. The Viceroy's rejection of the memorial caused a considerable furore, and the next royal visitor was not offered a nautch as part of the official entertainment!

Another Indian 'luxury' which increasing wealth sustained, was that of the zenana. What had begun as an understandable acceptance of an Indian solution to the sexual isolation of the English merchant was now seen as a symbol of status as well. It also reflected a growing racialism. Many of the new men who came to India at the end of the eighteenth century considered marriage with any but European women out of the question. When the numbers of marriageable English women increased, the zenana declined. But by the end of the century, the monthly expenses of keeping a zenana were still included in a semi-official guide for the young recruit to the Company's service.

Existing side by side with these 'oriental' elements in the society of the British in India were the European ones which would ultimately prevail. With growing numbers of British settlers, the character of the settlements changed. The idea of turning them into replicas of English towns came into fashion. English amusements called for a concert hall and a theatre. The architecture of these buildings was, of course, that of the best that *Europe* could provide. The new rulers erected buildings in the classical style, not only for public purposes, but for private residence – the outward show of the governing classes back in Britain. Houses in India, even if they were only of one storey, had a classical portico. On the whole, classical architecture transplanted well, being an exotic product itself, brought to Britain from Italy by aristocratic travellers making the European Grand Tour. But some adaptation had to be made to suit an intemperate climate. Lofty classical 'piazzas' – as they were called at the time – with their pillars rising to the full height of the house, let in the harsh sun of the early afternoon. They were therefore filled with immense venetian blinds. The outside was finished off with *chunam*, a sort of stucco made with powdered sea-shells and lime which produced a brilliant white effect. By the end of the century the blinding white had been softened by the addition of sand, the white being applied only to the cornices and capitals.

The interiors of the houses were sparsely furnished: high raftered rooms with a rich Persian carpet upon the floor and very little furniture, and fewer pictures. There was, however, a large staff of servants and a great deal of expensive entertaining to keep them busy. The owner of such an establishment would rise at dawn and ride before breakfast, which was served at eight or nine o'clock, after which he would go to his office. This, if he was a merchant, would be next to the house; if a government official, some distance away. The principal meal of the day was dinner at two or three o'clock in the afternoon, a change of time from the one o'clock of the earlier settlers. Soon the dinner time would move to five or six, and finally to around half past seven or eight in the evening. After dinner was the time for a siesta so that at five tea could be taken, and then a ride or a drive. The evening was the time for paying formal calls or attending entertainments. Supper was at ten.

A day in the life of one of the British in Bengal lacked privacy. The moment he was ready to rise from his bed, an army of servants, clerks, petitioners and tradesmen awaited the opportunity to rush in upon him. In half an hour, 'a clean shirt, breeches, stockings, and slippers are put upon his body, thighs, legs and feet, without any greater exertion than if he was a statue.' Another servant brings water and pours it upon his master's hands and face, and a barber shaves him, cuts his nails and cleans his ears. A waistcoat is held for him, and after it has been put on to his satisfaction, he proceeds in semi-state to the breakfast room for the ritual serving of tea and toast.

[48]

A hairdresser begins to arrange the great man's hair while the servant whose sole responsibility is to attend to his master's hookah, slips the mouthpiece into his hand. 'While the hairdresser is doing his duty, the gentleman is eating, sipping, and smoking by turns.'

At a moment decided upon by his personal clerk, some of the petitioners are allowed to approach the master. If they are of sufficient importance, they will be given a chair; others must remain respectfully standing, hoping to catch the great man's eye. At around ten o'clock, the ceremony is ended by the master entering his palanquin and, surrounded by servants and hangers-on, leaves for his office or upon such visits that have been previously arranged. At two he will sit down to dinner with a party of friends, each of whom will have brought with him a personal servant to look after his needs. At the end of the meal – whether there are ladies present or not – each gentleman will be given his hookah. At four o'clock 'they begin to withdraw without ceremony, and step into their palanquins; so that in a few minutes, the man is left to go into his bedroom, when he is instantly undressed to his shirt.' He sleeps to about seven or eight o'clock when the ceremony that took place at his rising is repeated. After tea he may make some visits, returning no later than ten for supper. Guests may stay until midnight or one in the morning. After they leave, the master is conducted to his bedroom 'where he finds a female companion to amuse him' until next morning. 'With no greater exertions than these do the Company's servants amass the most splendid fortunes.'

This description by a visitor is true in the generality if not in the particular. Some of the Company's servants did indeed live very similar lives to those described. Many of the most important did not. Among them was Warren Hastings, one of the most interesting and influential figures in the whole of British Indian history: if Robert Clive dug the foundations of the Raj, Hastings erected the scaffolding inside which this immense structure was built.

Hastings first arrived in India in 1750, and apart from a few years back in Britain remained there until 1785, his last appointment being as the first governor-general-in-Bengal with authority over the rest of British India. Privately, he lived the most unostentatious of lives, being famous for his plain green coat and general lack of vulgar display. He would rise early and ride eight miles before breakfasting and taking a cold bath. Tea or plain water were his favourite beverages. He did not indulge in supper, and liked to be in bed by ten. When the situation demanded it, however, the unassuming and friendly Mr Hastings could assume the hauteur, the pomp, and occasional imperiousness of His Excellency the Governor-General. But he had an understanding of India and its ways that no other ruler of British India had before or since. He encouraged 'oriental' learning, partly as a means of avoiding too much government interference in the lives of the people: 'The people of this country,' he maintained, 'do not require our aid to furnish them with a rule for their conduct or a standard for their property.'

Hastings' interest in Indian culture was more than merely that of an alien administration looking for ways to avoid antagonising its new subjects. He encouraged the work of a number of scholars, including Sir William Jones who was appointed to the Supreme Court in Calcutta in 1783, and assisted Hastings in the founding of the Asiatic Society of Bengal in the following year. Jones's translation of the Sanskrit drama *Sakuntala* by the fifth-century playwright Kalidasa was to have a profound influence upon the Romantic movement in European literature.

Another member of the hierarchy, Sir John Shore, later Lord Teignmouth, who was governor-general from 1793 to 1798, and had been a colleague of Warren Hastings, also lived a simple life. In a letter dated 21 January 1787 he described his normal routine:

I rise early, ride seven to ten miles, and breakfast by eight o'clock: after that, business occupies my time until the hour of dinner, which is three. Our meals here are short: and in the evening, when the weather permits, which at this season of the year is daily, I walk out. The remaining time between that and ten o'clock, which is my hour of rest, I spend with my friends; as I make it a rule not to attend to business of the evening. Suppers are by no means agreeable to me. At present we have balls every week; but I am not fond of them; and indeed have been at one private ball only . . . nor yet have I attended one play.

As he was writing to his wife, Shore naturally did not mention the zenana that was attached to his house!

For the first fifty years of their rule in India, the British never felt wholly secure or even convinced of the permanence of their dominion. They were often critical of what they saw around them, but they were careful not to allow those feelings to influence their actions in case it aroused opposition which they might not be in a position to resist. At the same time they had some respect for Indian culture, or at least certain aspects of it. There was considerable intercourse between the British and the Muslim aristocracy. Many British officials spoke Persian, the language of the Indian upper classes. Some of them even regarded themselves as Indian rulers. On one level those British who had no intellectual interests enjoyed the superficial luxuries of Indian aristocratic life. English women, because they were few in a profoundly masculine society, generally accepted the men's opinions. They, too, enjoyed the luxuries. They were not in the least worried at attending balls and dinners given by Indians, though Indian women were not present, except as dancers.

However, towards the end of the eighteenth century, the British were becoming conscious of a sense of racial superiority. The easy social relations, the relations essentially of equals, they had had with Indians began to decline, though at first only in Calcutta. In other parts of India, where English society was numerically small and fashionable attitudes slow to arrive, the old relations with Indians continued.

The change in the social atmosphere began with the arrival in 1786 of Lord Cornwallis, whose defeat by the American colonists at Yorktown five years earlier had barely interrupted his career. His purpose in India was to reform the administration, to clean up corruption and abolish nepotism among the British in India. But in his reasonable desire to create a body of honest officials, he also excluded Indians from the higher posts in government: 'Every native of Hindustan,' he said, 'I verily believe is corrupt'. Cornwallis was convinced that the way to stamp out corruption among the British was to pay them salaries high enough to satisfy or at least mollify aspirations. He did not think that similar methods might reduce Indian corruption, too. Instead, he replaced Indian judges with

English judges. He abandoned almost entirely the traditional etiquette of diplomatic relations. Cornwallis succeeded in forcing the old Indian governing classes into isolation, leaving behind only the Indian servant, the clerk, the merchant and the banker, as representatives of India and Indian culture.

Not unnaturally, the rest of the British community took its lead from senior officials and, in particular, the governor-general. As they withdrew from contact, so did lesser beings. By 1810, a visitor to Calcutta was able to report that 'every Briton appears to pride himself on being outrageously a John Bull'.

—— *ACT ONE* ——

# *THIS SPLENDID EMPIRE*

On a small island in another quarter of the globe, in a narrow street,
where the rays of the sun are seldom able to penetrate the thick smoke,
a company of peaceable merchants meet; these are the conquerors of
India; these are the absolute sovereigns of this splendid empire.

Count Bjornstjerna, 1840

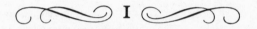

# HER MAJESTY'S INDIAN
# DOMINIONS

WHEN the eighteen-year-old Queen Victoria succeeded to the throne in 1837, Britain's Indian dominion was little older than she was herself. The East India Company, of course, had been in India since the beginning of the seventeenth century, first as traders, and then as conquerors. Robert Clive had really set things moving by making himself ruler of the vast province of Bengal in the middle of the eighteenth century. From then onwards, great proconsuls had pushed out the boundaries of conquest. For more than half a century, it had been a soldier's world – of defence and attack, victory, defeat and stalemate. In fact, the British had never been sure of their dominion. Some had never even been sure that they wanted it, either. And it was not until 1818, with the final defeat of the one native power which might have thrown the British into the sea, that a sense of permanence appeared.

With permanence came change. Change in attitudes, change in ideas, concerning Britain's purpose in India, concerning Indians themselves. The British began to think of their conquest as something of a miracle, or, at the very least, as a sign from divine providence that it was their destiny to rule India. But Britain's expansion in India had had another, strictly worldly causation. Those politicians in Britain who had supported the conquerors in India had not been dreamers of empire, but believers in the potential profits of conquest. Progressively, they broke the East India Company's monopolies in the interests of a rapidly industrialising Britain, avid for markets. The Company remained sovereign, but on an eroding sufferance.

Why the British conquered India is fairly straightforward. How they were able to do it – and against what appeared to be great odds – is not. The 'philosophers' of empire who were to proliferate in the last decades of the queen's reign produced their reasons, of which the most generally accepted (because the most stimulating) was a belief in the superiority of the white man over the coloured. It is true that there were some remarkable men among the conquerors who made India into Britain's back yard, but, on balance, there was no more leadership of an exceptional order on the British side than there was on the Indian. In fact, quite a number of Indian leaders were the equals of their British contemporaries, a few were distinctly superior. The clue lies in the competitive nature of Indian leadership. Ambitious Indians were concerned with establishing their own sovereignty and maintaining it against all comers, their own supporters (adventurers like themselves) included. The contrast between the Indian leaders and the British was a contrast between ambition uncontrolled and ambition disciplined. What gave the British their supreme feeling of confidence was the knowledge that, in times of crisis, *they* could rely on the support of their fellows.

The British had no more military expertise than their opponents. Some of the European-trained armies of the Indian princes were quite as good as the Company's forces, just as well armed, and frequently better generalled. But these armies were usually led by mercenaries whose main aim was to satisfy their own ambitions, even if it meant changing sides or using their strength to set themselves up as independent rulers. The British, when they fought, were out to win not just one battle but a whole campaign. For them, defeat was merely a passing setback, whose effect could be cancelled out in the next engagement. It was this belief that no single defeat would be final which gave victory to small British forces faced with what seemed to be outrageous odds. Once a number of such victories had been won, the British became convinced that even the most powerful of their enemies could be crushed – in the end.

It was also greatly to the advantage of the British that they could not only concentrate resources upon some given area, but could also replenish them once they were exhausted. This was a matter both of economics and of maritime mobility. The British could move re-inforcements, human and material, by sea from Britain or around the coasts of India. If things went badly in one place they could compensate from another. Not so the Indian rulers. They had nothing to draw on, for their defeat was someone else's gain. Furthermore, the revenues of the Indian princes were constantly decreasing. The Indian economy, in general, was contracting, while the British – in the first flood of the industrial revolution – possessed a rapidly expanding commerce.

The British, therefore, were equipped for conquest. They also had their sense of solidarity, and a belief that their actions not only satisfied personal ambition and the commercial interests of their employers, but were also to the general advantage of the British nation.

Against such nationalism, racial identity, or what you will, Indians had little defence. Community was divided from community by caste, and men of one religion from those of another by that sharpest of barbed wire, tradition and custom. Some particular hatred might momentarily unite the antagonists, but when it was removed their prejudices revived with even greater intensity. All this made it possible for the British to conquer India, piecemeal. It also made their conquest acceptable – because they were foreign, detached, almost irrelevant to the bitter infighting which preoccupied the Indian rulers. Those who knew intimately the realities of power, felt no shame at acknowledging the rule of men who were capable of exercising it, as long as the capability remained, and as long as it was made evident.

This was the task of the Company's army, a substantial force, only a sixth of whom were Europeans. The British had conquered India with Indian soldiers, and that was how they intended to hold on to it. The European population was very small – about 41,000 in 1837. Approximately 37,000 of these were soldiers, either in the Company's own European regiments or in those of the queen, on loan to the Company. 6,000 were officers. The civil service accounted for 1,000 of the remaining Europeans, and, of those not in the services, there were about 2,000 in Bengal and 500 each in Bombay and Madras. In a limbo, neither European nor Indian, lay the Eurasians

who numbered around 30,000. The native population was somewhere in the region of 150,000,000.

Until 1833, the Company had exercised strict control over European immigration. The authorities did not approve of 'non-officials'
such as missionaries, businessmen, and indigo planters, and used
their powers of deportation frequently against people whom they
regarded as undesirable. Most Europeans in India approved of this.
'Many of the adventurers who come hither from Europe,' wrote
Bishop Heber in 1824, 'are the greatest profligates the sun ever saw;
men whom nothing but despotism can manage, and who, unless they
are really under a despotic rule, would insult, beat and plunder the
natives without shame or pity.' Deportation, he went on, was 'the
only control which the Company possesses over the tradesmen and
ship-builders in Calcutta and the indigo planter up the country'. The
Charter Act of 1833 put a stop to that, and the country became wide
open to all – even missionaries.

If anything, the opening up of the Company's dominions to
unrestricted immigration intensified the disdain with which the army
and the civil service looked upon the other members of English
society in India. As in England, people engaged in trade were beyond
the pale. That paragon of Victorian chivalry, Henry Lawrence,
summed up the view in a note in his journal about a Calcutta chemist
and his wife, who were fellow-passengers on Lawrence's first journey
home. The man, he said, was 'a forward, vulgar, ignorant, malicious
and pertinaceously obstinate fellow', and his wife was 'much of a
muchness . . . Of course, they were in no society in Calcutta'.
Eurasians were regarded with as little favour, having the additional –
and insulting – disability of mixed parentage and guilty liaisons.
Thirty years before, no one would have thought much about it. A
new spirit of morality, however, partly compounded of racial arrogance and partly of a stricter Christian faith, now frowned not only
on any new liaison, but on the product of earlier ones. This meant
that higher appointments in the Company's service were no longer
open to Eurasians, so, instead, they practically monopolised the
positions of clerk and bookkeeper both in government and private
offices.

There was, of course, no doubt about who were the leaders of society. Whatever it said in public, the army (on which British dominion depended) never had any doubt in its heart that it was 'infinitely inferior in every respect' to the civil service in rank and rewards. The advice Henry Lawrence, himself a soldier, gave to his brother John was simply that the civil service offered 'the greater field for ability, vigour, and for usefulness.'

On the whole, the civilians had no firm ground for their superiority. Few really bothered to learn the language of the people they ruled with any fluency, and they were thus heavily dependent on their native clerks, who had taken the trouble to learn the language of their conquerors and were, in many cases, not at all unwilling to use their masters' ignorance to their own advantage. British rule in India had, in fact, very early become a tyranny of interpreters. 'I have heard,' wrote Colonel Sleeman in the late 1830s, 'some of our highest diplomatic characters talking, without the slightest feeling of shame or embarrassment to native princes on the most ordinary subjects in a language which no human being but themselves could understand!'

The average civilian was promoted according to a fairly routine pattern. He started work as an assistant to the Commissioners of Revenue and Circuit, spending one day in one department and the next in the other. If he was drawn by opportunity or inclination towards the law, he became first an assistant, then a joint magistrate, then full magistrate, then, if he was lucky, a judge or commissioner. This stage was usually only achieved after eighteen or twenty years' service. A young man who leant towards the revenue side would follow a roughly parallel course of seniority until, in due process, he might become a Collector or even a Commissioner of Revenue and Circuit himself.

Between the army and the civil service, there lay a strange ill-defined region in which military men acted as administrators, and civilians claimed the right to direct military operations. Among the soldier-administrators there were many great names, and, on the whole, when educated military officers were appointed to difficult situations and wild regions they contributed an expertise which no civilian could match. There were young men like Captain Kennedy, an ex-artillery officer in charge of a district in the Himalayas, who not only commanded a regiment of mountain chasseurs but also discharged, according to Victor Jacquemont, 'the functions of a collector, acting as judge over his own subjects and, what is more, those of the neighbouring rajas, Hindu, Tartar, and Tibetan, sending them to prison, fining them, and even hanging them when he thinks fit'. It was from such men as Kennedy, Jacquemont said, that he learned most 'about the affairs of the land'.

That civilians were placed in positions of such authority as to be able to interfere with the operations of an army in the field was the result of campaigns in north-west India and Afghanistan which began within a couple of years of the queen's accession and continued for the rest of her reign, and afterwards. A new species of civilian, called the 'political officer', came into existence. He was usually skilled in languages, given control of wild frontier areas inhabited by warlike tribes, and entrusted with emergency powers which were basically undefined but included authority to make use of military forces in his area. Relations between himself and the local military commander were often strained. His actions were almost invariably high-handed and independent, lacking in precedent, and – given the unavoidable delays in communication – without the endorsement of 'higher authority'. When the British occupied the Punjab in the forties, it was young men with military training but civilian duties who established a pioneer administration – assuming wide responsibilities, taking unconventional action, and disregarding the formalities of discipline.

Such freedom led, not infrequently, to folly and disaster, as in the first Afghan war. In 1849, the then governor-general, Lord Dalhousie, blasted the pretensions of over-enterprising political officers when he wrote to Henry Lawrence about one of his subordinates, Major Herbert Edwardes:

From the tone of your letter, I perceive it is not necessary to say that you should pull up Major Edwardes – at once. But I further wish to repeat what I said before, that there are more than Major Edwardes . . . who appear to consider themselves nowadays as governor-general at least. The sooner you set about disenchanting their minds of this illusion, the better for your comfort and their own. I don't doubt you will find bit and martingale for them speedily. For I repeat, I will not stand it in quieter times for half an hour, and will come down unmistakeably upon any of them who may try it on, from Major Edwardes, C.B., down to the latest enlisted General-Ensign-Plenipotentiary in the establishment.

Concerning the men who had neither the inclination nor the patronage to leave the army for the better paid – and more often exciting – work of a political officer, there was not a great deal to say. The training given to officers in the Company's army scarcely fitted them either for efficiency or for heroism. And like his civilian counterpart, the young cadet soon found himself in debt. At the larger stations, too, social conditions invited him to waste his time. In Europe, said Colonel Sleeman,

there are separate classes of people who subsist by catering for the amusements of the higher classes of society, in theatres, operas, concerts, balls, etc., etc.; but in India this duty devolves entirely upon the young civil and military officers of the government, and at large stations it really is a very laborious one, which often takes up the whole of a young man's time. The ladies must have amusement; and the officers must find it for them, because there are no other persons to undertake the arduous duty. The consequence is that they often become entirely alienated from their men, and betray signs of the greatest impatience while they listen to the necessary reports of their native officers, as they come on or go off duty.

Even without the social demands of a large station, an officer's military duties were scarcely arduous. The same Herbert Edwardes who later incurred the wrath of the governor-general described the routine of his life in 1841 to a friend in England. 'Well, a black rascal makes an oration by my bed every morning about half an hour before daylight. I wake, and see him salaaming with a cup of hot coffee in his hand. I sit on a chair and wash the teaspoon till the spoon is hot and the fluid cold, while he introduces me gradually into an ambush of pantaloons and wellingtons – if there is a parade. I am shut up in a red coat, and a glazed lid set upon my head, and thus, carefully packed,

[61]

exhibit my reluctance to do what I am going to do – to wit, my *duty* –
by *riding* a couple of hundred yards to the parade.

'Here two or three hundred very cold people, in same condition,
are assembled. We all agree to keep ourselves warm with a game of
soldiers, whereupon a very funny scene ensues, and we run about the
plain, and wheel about and turn about, till the sun gets up to come
and see what all the row is about; and then, like frightened children,
we all scamper off and make the best of our way home. Then the
packing-case is all taken off again and I resume my nap . . . This, if
there is a parade; if not, I take a gallop with the dogs.'

The army had an oriental extravagance about its arrangements.
When the Bengal army moved from its base at Firozpur in 1838, it
numbered 95,000 combatants, and 38,000 camp followers. One of
the officers excelled his fellows by having a train of four horses, eight
camels and elephants, and twenty personal servants. Even in actual
battle conditions, three elephants carrying, for the use of one officer,
a number of double-sided tents with glass doors, was thought to be
only slightly eccentric. And so it was, for the commissariat and
transport arrangements for the rest of the army were a great deal less
than efficient. In the Afghan war of 1839–41, the British army
suffered one of the most shameful defeats it ever had to bear, from an
enemy who carried their commissariat on their backs and their
weapons in their hands.

In its fitness for war, of course, an army depends on the mental and
physical fitness of its officer corps. But in the British army in India,
all chances of promotion were seriously hedged by the tendency of
officers to hang on till they dropped (or were killed). The younger
officer, avid for promotion, had little chance unless disease weeded
out some of his seniors. Even so, a youth joining the army at
seventeen could hope for no more than to become a lieutenant at
twenty-one, a captain at twenty-nine, a major at forty-four, and –
with luck – a lieutenant-colonel at fifty-four. As one soldier who
deserted the army for political work put it, when war came the army
would be led by 'gallant veterans, who during health and strength
were never trusted with command, and whose only guarantee of
efficiency was old age – whose very existence was often a token of
their never having earned command'. It was as well for the British

that, when their own leadership was at its worst, Indian leadership was virtually non-existent.

Because European society in India was divided into hermetically sealed compartments, it is easy to overlook the fact that the majority of the European population in the larger towns and stations consisted of common soldiers and seamen. The latter were constantly changing as vessels arrived and departed, but the European soldiers of the Company's military establishment remained in India for an indefinite period – which was, in actual fact, assumed to be twenty-one years if death or disease did not intervene. They usually did. The mortality rate among common soldiers was extremely high. Indeed, the life expectancy of a European soldier in India was less than half what it was in England. The only compensation was that the rate of pay was higher than in Her Majesty's forces and, if the soldier survived, he received a reasonable pension. But the odds against survival were high. Apart from the natural stresses of an abrasive climate, the soldier's lot was not enviable. Discipline was extremely harsh and, though flogging had been abolished in the native army, white soldiers could still face sentences of from five hundred to a thousand lashes. Such sentences were by no means rare. Three out of every four men in the Company's forces – and the queen's men were no different – could show the stigmata of a back scarred by the lash into lumps of thick calloused flesh and hideous weals. Men often died in their early twenties from the effects of the lash. Flogging depended very much on the whim of the commanding officer, but even this brutal and infinitely degrading punishment was considered merciful when the alternative was a court martial which wielded the power of life and death. A military execution (and they were alarmingly frequent) was a ceremonial occasion. The soldiers were paraded to form three sides of a square, the fourth being the stage for the condemned man and his executioners. From the guard room came a procession moving to the strains of the Dead March, played by the regimental band. The Provost Marshal rode in front, followed by two files of soldiers with their arms reversed. Then came the parson and the prisoner and, bringing up the rear, the execution squad of twelve privates with a corporal and a sergeant in charge. After the procession had made a circuit of the square, it stopped before a coffin, and the parson prayed. Hysteria moved through the rigid ranks; some soldiers wept and others fainted as the condemned man, eyes bound, stood to attention to hear the death warrant read out once again.

Outside the bounds of this harsh and unmerciful discipline, the common soldier had ample leisure in which to do nothing. There was, in fact, nothing for him to do. Drunkenness and fornication were his principal activities. No attempt was made to control the soldiers' relations with Indian women, and some settled down into permanent relationships which contributed not only to the man's happiness but to the Eurasian population. There were even some English wives, whose morals were notoriously lax. But it was

only just to notice the temptations, restraints and miseries to which this class of women are subject, in a country so little calculated to cherish their better feelings, or to provide them with necessary occupation, or common comfort. Unable, from extreme heat, to move out of the little room allotted to them in the 'married men's quarters', during the day, and provided, for two rupees a month, with a Portuguese 'cook boy' who relieves them from the toil of domestic duties, the only resource of the soldiers' wives is in mischievous associations, discontented murmurings, and habits of dissipated indulgence. Strolling in the evenings through the dirty bazaars of a native town, probably under the auspices of an ayah who may have picked up a smattering of the English language, these unhappy women purchase liquor, to conciliate their careless husbands. On returning late to the barracks, the truant wife frequently finds her partner already in a state of intoxication; mutual recrimination follows, and then succeeds a scene for which we may well weep, that humanity has such.

The children were, more often then not, neglected. Indeed, the child of a European soldier had very little chance of reaching maturity. It was not until 1846 that a scheme was begun to provide schools in the hills for such children, neglected both by their parents and by the army.

For a year or two of Queen Victoria's reign, there was another class

Warren Hastings (1732–1818)
First Governor-General of the British possessions in India.

*Above :* Bombay Green 1767. A few buildings around an open space for military drill or for just enjoying the air. *Below :* Bombay Green 1811. No longer casual, the government of Bombay has assumed a Classical face. On right, the Office of the Secretary to the Government and in the centre, the Supreme Court.

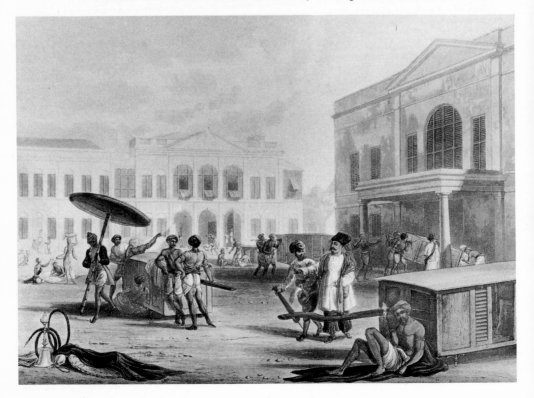

*Above :* The Poona Durbar 1790. A British envoy squats at the court of an Indian prince. Such deference to Indian etiquette will not survive the century. *Below :* Poona 1808. Nine years after the date of this view, the British annexed Poona and turned it into that refuge from the heat of the Plains : A Hill-station.

Lord Cornwallis (1739–1805). Succeeded Warren Hastings as Governor-General in 1786. Unlike his predecessor, a conditional Indophile, Cornwallis thought Indians corrupt and sought to Anglicize the administration as much as possible.

Rocket Corps and Dromedary Corps. An exotic section of the army – mostly Indian – with which the British conquered, and maintained their rule.

Part of the South Park Street Cemetery, Calcutta. The necropolis of empire. The inscriptions are a record of the dangers to life in India.

The Missionary as Educator (c.1820). William Carey, who translated the Bible into a number of Indian languages and also cut the type with which to print them.

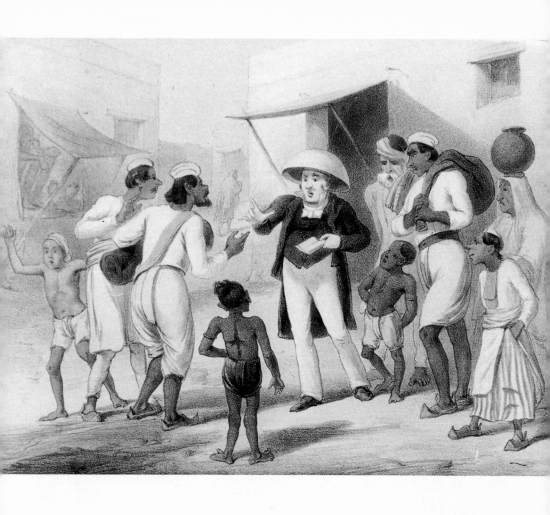

The Missionary in the Front-line, preaching to the Heathen, sometimes with success.

The Official Church. It was not until after 1813 that missionaries were allowed into British India, but the Church Established, i.e., the Church of England was, at least symbolically, a part of the power-structure. A church in Calcutta, c.1790.

of European soldier in India – the military adventurer. While the Punjab remained an independent native state, its army included a number of European officers. The most important of these were not British – Generals Allard and Court came from France, and Avitabile was a Neapolitan. But quite a few of the smaller units in the Sikh forces were led by British officers who had once served in the Company's army but who had left for one of a number of reasons, ranging from dismissal for misconduct to a desire for the higher, and probably more dangerous, rewards offered by employment in the service of a native prince. Some of these men were Eurasians, who could rise to a position denied them in the Company's service. The majority, however, were deserters, and most were Irish, though they very often tried to conceal their origins by calling themselves Americans. One, Alexander Gardiner, traced his 'ancestry' through a father who had settled on the shores of Lake Superior, 'just where the Mississippi breaks out of it'!

The lives of many of these men might have been lifted from an Elizabethan play, and there is a terrible uniformity in the tragedy of their deaths. But some passed into the British service when the Punjab was annexed and were given respect by those who might otherwise have despised them.

And what of relations between the British, this tiny ruling minority, and the immensely fecund majority – the 'natives'? On the highest level, governors-general dealt with princes, with much pomp and ceremony. On occasion, their meetings took on all the attributes of an oriental Field of Cloth of Gold. But it was always a meeting of superficialities, and though a few men – usually political Residents at some native court – did establish relations of mutual respect and understanding with both princes and peasants, they had always been rare and became even more so in Victoria's reign. As a rule, ordinary Englishmen were aloof and often arrogant. Bishop Heber, with his sharply discerning eye, had noticed during his travels in 1825 that the old free and unselfconscious relationship between Indians and British was rapidly disappearing. The English had an 'exclusive and intolerant spirit' which made them wherever they went, 'a caste by themselves, disliking and disliked by all their neighbours. Of this foolish, surly, national pride, I see but too many instances daily, and

[65]

I am convinced it does us much harm in this country. We are not guilty of injustice or wilful oppression, but we shut out the natives from our society, and a bullying, insolent manner is continually assumed in speaking to them.'

The attitude of the British to their native subordinates in the civil administration oscillated between the poles of indifference and abuse. Little or no encouragement was given to those who worked well and hard. As for servants, perhaps the best description of their treatment by the majority of their masters and mistresses is implicit in the reason given by Emily Eden for the devotion of Government House domestic servants – it was, she said, 'one of the few houses in Calcutta where they were not beaten'.

Whether the British had indeed a purpose in India had begun to occupy men's minds some time before the Victorian era began. Some of the men who had consolidated British rule had had their doubts. 'We have ceased,' wrote Charles Metcalfe, who had done much to establish the empire in the first decades of the century, 'to be the wonder that we were to the natives; the charm that once accompanied us has been dissolved, and our subjects have had time to enquire why they have been subdued.' But others had no doubts. There seemed to be no point in morbid speculation about the future. The present was there to be faced – and dominated. 'To fear God and to have no other fear is a maxim of religion, but the truth of it and the wisdom of it was proved day by day in politics.' It was a suitable motto for the militant Christians of early Victorian India, representing the aggressive side of their attitudes, and achievements. It also explained much of their popular appeal in a period constantly in need of heroes and in which enthusiasm was easily aroused – for here were men creating a splendid empire with neither doubt nor fear, not content to allow circumstances to control them, men who compelled the world to shape itself to suit their vision.

# 2

# DUCKS, MULLS AND QUI-HIS

THE newcomer to India found it a land of nicknames. It was the British way of putting everyone in his place, a carefully considered – and highly effective – system of caste. The English who lived and worked in Bengal were known as 'Qui-his', from the usual manner of summoning servants in that presidency (*koi hai* = is there anyone there?). The English in Madras were called 'Mulls', a contraction of 'mulligatawny', the hot pepper soup supposed to be drunk by everyone in the area. The English of Bombay had to carry the name of 'Ducks', presumably by association with the strong-smelling bummelo, a dried fish better known as Bombay Duck. It was just as well that when a civilian was appointed to serve in one of the presidencies he usually stayed there for the whole of his official life. A Duck would never have felt comfortable in Bengal, and a Mull was always considered outside Madras as a pretty low form of life.

Bombay had always been something of a backwater. In 1825, in fact, the Directors described it as 'of little importance to the Company'. But the opening of the overland route was to give it importance, though old habits took a long time to change. It was many years before Bombay had a decent hotel or boarding house. According to a local belief, this was simply because no hotel could have a chance of financial success as long as private hospitality was so lavish. It was just too bad if a visitor had no friends in Bombay and no letters of introduction. 'The Victoria Hotel solicits the patronage of travellers; but, as it is situated in the very dirtiest and very narrowest street of the fort, the additional annoyances of flights of mosquitoes, a billiard table, coffee and a tap room, place it without the pale of respectable support. The Sanitarium affords shelter to invalids, and is delightfully situated, where the smooth sands and fine sea breeze render it a tempting locality for the convalescent; but the rooms are far too small for family accommodation. In this dilemma, visitors usually pitch tents on the esplanade; and if in the hot season, cause them to be *chuppered in*, as the phrase is, or a false roof erected with bamboos and date leaves, to secure them equally from the intense heat of the mid-day sun, and the evil effect of the evening dews'. On the whole, a tent was quite the thing. If comfortably furnished and provided with a small retinue of servants, the expense was 'not greater than will be incurred at the hotel, and with the advantage of perfect seclusion and independence'.

The new civilian or cadet, of course, had no need to worry. He was met, and his accommodation arranged. A cadet would invariably receive 'an invitation from the regiment quartered in the town, or Fort George barracks, to accept the hospitalities of the mess, and is put into appropriate apartments by the barrack-master'.

When a newcomer had settled in, it was time to see the town. Those who had been led to believe that everywhere in India was like Calcutta, a city of palaces, were immediately disillusioned. Bombay was no new Rome; it was more like an English country town transferred to the Orient. Only the Town Hall, an elegant neo-Classical building, had any distinction. The European houses were usually of one storey, 'with an overhanging thatched roof', and looked to the disappointed eye of a new arrival 'for all the world like a comfortable English cow-house'. Fortunately, the interior was more impressive: 'We stepped direct, without any intervening hall or passage, into a large and elegant drawing room, supported on pillars of faultless proportion. A large screen of red silk divided this apartment from a spacious dining room.'

An unusual feature (to the visitor's eye) was the wide verandah, its shady overhanging roof supported on low arches and open to the garden. The trouble was that, once you had seen one Bombay bungalow, you had seen them all. Even the furniture all seemed to have been supplied from the same emporium, the only difference being that the more affluent bungalows had mahogany furniture

[68]

instead of jackwood, and silk or damask on the couches in place of chintz.

As time went on, of course, and Bombay became more affluent, so too did the houses of the upper levels of English society there. By 1851, the bungalow, however substantial, was not thought good enough for senior members of the civil service. Their houses became 'lofty and stately-looking mansions, with facades adorned with spacious porticos supported on pillars of sufficient width to admit two carriages abreast, thus insuring to the occupants a sheltered mode of ingress and egress, equally essential during the heat of the fair season and the damp of the monsoon'. Inside, the ground floor contained dining and breakfast rooms, a library, and one or two suites of guest rooms. 'The staircases are generally wide and handsome, conducting to the reception and family room; and not infrequently, a charming withdrawing room is found on the flat top of the porch by surrounding it with a balustrade, which also serves as a support to a light veranda-like roof'.

Bombay had a pleasant tradition in 'hot weather houses'. During the hot season, the Bombay esplanade was 'adorned with pretty, cool, temporary residences, erected near the sea; their chuppered roofs and rustic porches half concealed by the flowering creepers and luxuriant shrubs, which shade them from the midday glare'. Standing in a line along the sea front, the bungalows were made of 'bamboo and plaster, lined with strained dungaree, dyed a pale straw colour; the offices are placed at a short distance from the bungalow; and the whole is enclosed with a pretty compound, filled with fine plants, arranged in tubs, round the trellised verandahs; in this situation the shrubs flourish well, despite their vicinity to the sea, usually considered so inimical to the labours of horticulturists'. Inside, there was an agreeable simplicity and cool China matting. 'The clean smooth China matting which covers the floors; the numerous lamps shedding their equal light from the snowy ceilings; the sweet perfume of the surrounding plants, and the fresh sea breeze, blowing through the trellis-worked verandahs, render them delightful retreats after the heat and lassitude endured throughout the day. Elegance combines with comfort, making these pretty abodes so truly pleasant; and a fine-toned piano, and a good billiard table, are the usual additions to varied articles of luxury and convenience.' On the whole, the writer decided it was 'difficult to imagine anything more agreeable than a late dinner in an esplanade bungalow after returning from the evening drive'.

In the cool of the evening, the ladies and their escorts would venture to take the air. The usual mode of travel was at first a palanquin. Very few people had their own, so they were usually rented by the hour. The palanquin bearers were, however, something of a trial as they had a habit of putting down the conveyance at some spot suitably distant from the passenger's destination and striking for more pay. Palanquins began to disappear in the early years of the young queen's reign, although they were not finally frowned upon until the 1860s.

The more fashionable way of taking the air was in a carriage, and there was a wide variety of styles to choose from. On the esplanade, during the hour of the promenade, 'there may be seen the English landau fresh from Longacre; the smart dennet [a two-wheeled gig] of the military aspirant marked by its high cushions; the roomy buggy of the mercantile Parsee, adorned with green and gold; the richly gilt chariot of a high caste Hindu, with its silken reins and emblazoned panels'.

There was very little else to do in the hot weather and at the time of the monsoon rains. There would be a band playing on the esplanade, each music stand lit by a lamp – for the dark came down quickly in Bombay. The only other lights were on the carriages, drawn up for a moment so that their occupants might listen to the music. The ladies did not descend and walk about, but the gentlemen 'flitted about from carriage to carriage, paying their *devoirs* to the fair occupants, who were just recovering from the unusual and overpowering heat of the day'. The European children either rode their own ponies or were drawn by servants in little carriages of their own. They were, however, encouraged to take a stroll and were 'led by their own servants round and round the band-stand, which', thought one observer, 'would give the little things a decided taste, or dislike, for music in future years'.

The hot weather *was* particularly trying. Mentally and physically, no one was at his best. 'A few sickly attempts at dinner-parties' took

[70]

place, but it was 'impossible to conceive anything more ludicrously forlorn than the pallid faces of both hosts and guests exhibited upon these occasions. Though struggling convulsively to repress the yawns of weariness and languour, every one was haunted by the same insane notion that something was expected of him in the way of conversation, whilst the mind was totally incapable of forming two connected ideas; and even the recognised "beaux esprits" of society, trembling for their laurels, were obliged to succumb to the leaden influence of the weather, and lapse into the universal dreamless silence'. And even though everyone hoped for a shower of rain to bring some relief, when the monsoon actually broke, things were hardly better – if certainly different. 'Nothing short of perfect health, and an easy conscience, could enable one to bear up cheerfully through the intense gloom of a season, which may be described as consisting of one uninterrupted succession of thunder, torrents, and tedium'.

The rainy season usually began early in June, and for the first ten days or so brought a welcome change from the stifling heat of the preceding weeks. 'But beyond that, human nature cannot be expected to endure, without the relief of a grumble; and the natural consequence is, that faces become blue as the sky continues black'. Fortunately, even the monsoon had an occasional break, with fair weather, and even some sunshine which 'coming "like angels' visits, few and far between", are rapturously hailed, acting as a sufficient stimulant upon our fainting spirits, to enable them in a measure to hold out during the four mortal months of the monsoon. These "breaks", as they are called, are eagerly taken advantage of for the purposes of sociability, and many a pleasant dinner-party, and sometimes even a "soiree dansante" will be given by spirited individuals who are determined to brave all the risks of the sudden storms, and defalcations of guests, rather than endure any longer the monotony of total seclusion'.

For those who were not compelled to stay in Bombay during the hot season – and that usually meant wives and children – there were the hill stations of Poona and Mahableshwar. Everyone was rather more relaxed in these pleasant airy places, and the rigid protocol of Bombay was put aside in favour of an 'increased spirit of sociability

. . . The little unostentatious dinner, and even tea parties go briskly round, bringing the good folks together on a footing of intimacy which might never be attained in Bombay'.

Poona was a pleasant station, even in the rains, but Mahableshwar had to be evacuated when the rains came – the roads became impassable and rivers swollen so that they could not be crossed. The little bungalows, which had given so much pleasure by their simplicity were now 'completely encased in a most comfortable greatcoat, consisting of large screens of thatch, fastened to frames of poles, and so contrived that they cover up each face of the cottage, and prevent the rain from reaching the walls. The chimney is taken care of in the same manner; the bungalow has no longer any shape whatever; it looks much like the figures of ladies in the loose "polka" greatcoat, which has been the fashion of late years, more useful than graceful!'

Still, throughout all that the worst seasons could produce, the men at least had work to do. Whatever their various responsibilities, their lives followed much the same pattern. From March until October, the months which comprise the hot and rainy seasons, a man would wear a 'light cotton jacket, like a barber's or a footman's, in the morning'. After rising at an early hour, and whatever the season, he would go for a ride (unless it was raining). In the cold weather he might even join the local hunt. In the hot weather, however, he would hasten home before the sun rose; then 'he usually undresses, puts on his pajamas (the loose Turkish trouser), drinks iced soda-water, lies down on the couch, novel or newspaper in hand, and in all human probability goes to sleep'. Rising again, he would bathe and dress for breakfast at ten. This, whatever the season, consisted of rice, fried fish, eggs, omelette, preserves, tea or coffee – 'more in the fashion of a Scotch than an English matutinal recreation'. Suitably defended against hunger, the civilian then left for his office, where he worked until four or five o'clock. After that, it was time for bathing and dressing again as a preliminary to the evening drive, an occupation which had 'no recommendation beyond that of passing the most disagreeable hour of the day in inhaling coolish air, for you meet the same faces, the same equipages, and receive and make the same formal bows, almost every evening'. This was quite understandable, for the entire European population of Bombay did not exceed 450.

[72]

While the men were at works, the married ladies either visited each other or settled down to the writing of chits. The writing and answering of these notes, which were sent by the hand of a special class of servant, was one of the great preoccupations of European society. One authority held that 'every lady of *ton* has to write on an average two thousand chits per annum'. The chit system was greatly dependent on the servants who carried these missives. Very often, they delivered them to the wrong person – with interesting consequences, if they contained gossip and scandal, as they often did. Even shopping was carried out by chit. An answer was always required, except perhaps in the case of a simple invitation to dinner, when the word *salaam*, sent by the messenger to his master, 'serves the several purposes of an acknowledgement of, or a receipt for, the chit, and an acquiescence in the request it contained'.

Chit-writing was mainly a hot weather occupation, as people were too fatigued by the weather to venture out of doors. In the cold weather, Bombay society came to life. 'Our fashionables flock in from all the adjacent parts, to take possession of their handsome winter quarters; and every gradation of sociability from the snug, round-table dinner party to the crowded ball is in full requisition'. For the gentlemen, the day's routine remained the same, but the ladies had a constant round of visits to make and visitors to receive. Morning was the usual time for these, after ten o'clock and before two, when the family took its midday meal, the sacred Anglo-Indian ritual of tiffin. This was no longer the vast meal of the eighteenth century, however, when 'hecatombs of slaughtered animals' graced the table, but a fairly light collation. There might be guests, but it was considered 'an act of glaring impropriety in a lady, to invite any gentleman to stay and partake of this meal, who is not either a relative, or an intimate friend of the family'. This curious though presumably moral attitude could be very hard on the poor visitor who was neither relative nor close friend. Even in the cold weather, the sun can be warm, and a round of visits during which no refreshment was offered could be very frustrating. 'At the last house', one such visitor recorded, 'we actually listened, with parched throats, to the jingling of glasses and plates, which betokened the preparation of the tiffin table in an adjoining room, without these sounds producing any

[73]

other effect upon the lady of the house than giving us, by suddenly dropping the conversation, a pretty significant hint to decamp; and accordingly in a state of utter exhaustion we made our parting bows'.

Conversation at these morning visits was often dull. Lady Falkland, wife of the governor of Bombay in the late 'forties, found her guests with little more to talk about than their health and the weather – hardly to be wondered at, as they had driven six miles at the hottest time of the day in the hottest month of the Bombay year for the privilege of attending her ladyship's morning reception. No wonder the Englishwomen in India had a 'washed out look'. In the cold weather, their conversation may have been more lively.

The new overland route, fully functioning by 1838, had made quite a difference to the intellectual climate of Bombay. 'The present rapid communication with Europe', wrote a lady resident in that year, 'has introduced a very superior class of ideas and interests; and among other advantages, are many of a literary kind – reviews, papers, periodicals, and books, arrive before their novelty is dimmed in Europe; thus all intelligence of interest is discussed, and every means of gaining information easily acquired'.

Certainly, rapid transit of goods had made quite a difference to the elegance of the ladies' dresses, which were now only as far behind the latest London and Paris fashions as the time it took for the patterns to reach Bombay and the tailor to make them up.

The cold weather was the time for fine clothes to match the gaiety of release from the rains. Colourful bonnets and gowns were brought out from the cases of camphorwood and tin where they had laid protected from the damp and insects. Vessels arrived from Europe, almost every day, it seemed, with 'their interminable cargoes of millinery and haberdashery; whilst almost every lady is anxiously on the look-out for some particular ship, conveying to her that most coveted of all acquisitions – a box of new finery, selected by her friends at home'. And ladies for whom there was no parcel would besiege the shop of a Parsee entrepreneur called Muncherjee and buy up his entire stock in an afternoon.

Afternoon shopping was only indulged in as a matter of necessity. The morning was the more favoured time. Opinions differed widely on the shops' standards, according perhaps to the sophistication of the traveller or the length of time the resident had been away from England. The invaluable *Handbook of India* was much concerned over 'high charges and paucity of supplies'. One visit was enough to show 'how inefficient they are to gratify taste, or to satisfy the numerous wants of civilised life':

The Parsee master, attired in a white cotton garment and pointed head-dress of glazed chintz, meets the visitor at the door, and with something more grave than a nod, yet scarcely graceful enough to be called a bow, ushers him along between a double row of glass cases; less, certainly, but of the same form as those which English gardeners use for raising cucumbers. These are locked; but as soon as the article sought for is supposed to be seen, the Parsee produces from a large pocket in the side of his dress a small bunch of keys, when something remembered to be in fashion or invented ten years ago is laid before the purchaser. Nothing of the kind can carry disappointment farther than a Parsee shop, where, in lieu of the improvements of modern times, where the highest degree of convenience is the object desired by the manufacturer, are to be found articles only of the most cumbrous kind; the mechanism, where any exists, totally deranged, and the intrinsic value consequently lost. The poor Parsee, however, knows little of all this, and prices his various goods with amusing inconsistency making all pay for his bad debts and damaged wares.

But there was at least one establishment which gave the lie to the *Handbook*. This was the emporium of Jangerjee Nasserawanjee, where the walls were 'surrounded with glass cases, filled with fine French china, bijouterie, gold lace, sauces, brandied fruits, riding whips . . . A central avenue is flanked with cases containing jewellery, French clocks, and all descriptions of knicknackery. On the floor have subsided Cheshire and Gruyere cheeses, hams, cases of sardine, salmon and other edibles; and from the ceiling depend bird cages, lamps, and coloured French lithographs in handsome frames'.

There was a good chemist's shop where supplies of soda water – which, when iced, was considered a great blessing – could be obtained. But for many years the main lack was of a good bootmaker.

[75]

Instead, there were a number of Chinese tradesmen who went from house to house 'with white coats, red slippers, straw hats, flat features, and long plaited hair, holding in their hands little bundles, containing silk and satin shoes intended to fit everybody, and consequently fitting nobody. These worthy Crispins receive orders, and with bad leather, coarse linen, and paste in abundance, essay their execution, the result being that the public pay for their want of skill in the penalty of uneasy or distorted feet'.

There were quite a number of travelling merchants, though their numbers decreased as time went on and more and more 'Europe shops' opened in the bazaar. Most of these merchants – 'box-wallahs', they were called – were Muslims, hereditary traders and money-lenders. Part of their stock would be made up of Kashmir shawls and Delhi scarves, chintzes, calicos, crapes and woollens, fine muslins, and silks from China. In a small mahogany box they might carry a blaze of jewels, rubies, emeralds, diamonds and sapphires, some well cut, some only roughly cut. The box-wallahs, however, dealt not only in fine cloths and jewels but also in 'chow-chow', bits and pieces, commonplace things like soap and pickles, vinegar, cotton socks, eau de cologne, and orange marmalade which was allegedly Scottish but actually made in Surat.

The box-wallah dismissed, the visitors gone, tiffin over, the afternoon was spent decorously at home unless there was the sudden need to besiege a merchant for the latest thing from Europe, just that moment landed. It seems that by the late 'forties the habit of taking a siesta had become unfashionable on the grounds that this 'pernicious habit' enervated the system and induced a tendency to fever. Instead, the hours were 'most agreeably filled up by the undisturbed exercise of music, working and reading'. At last, five o'clock came and the carriages were ready for the evening drive along the esplanade.

Afterwards, it was time for entertainment. This took the form either of private dinners or functions at Government House. There was a theatre, but it was seldom open. A concert was a very rare occurrence. No great singer ever thought of appearing in Bombay, 'and when a mediocre one arrives, very little encouragement is given, because he or she may not be a Mario or a Jenny Lind'. Apart from the races, the only public amusement in Bombay consisted of a series of subscription balls which were carried on 'with tolerable spirit and liberality throughout the season; all arrangements being under the control of a selected number of gentlemen stewards'.

A dinner and ball at Government House displayed clearly the stratification of Anglo-Indian society. There was a really very simple division 'between those who belong to the service and those who do not'. The services, of course, had their own hierarchies, while the ladies were 'more tenacious of their rank than we are in England'. The women, said Lady Falkland, 'going into and leaving the dining room, take precedence according to the rank of their husbands, as they do in Europe: but I was, at first, surprised that at the end of the evening no one moved to go away till she whose husband held the highest official position rose to depart'. This preoccupation with protocol could lead to uncomfortable situations. Lady Falkland 'once saw a lady, far from well, after a dinner-party at Government House, and wishing very much to go home; who, on my urging her to do so, hesitated, because another person in the company – the wife of higher official rank than her own husband – did not seem disposed to move. I took the opportunity of impressing on the poor sufferer, that the sooner this custom was broken through, the better. However, she did not like to infringe it, and so she sat on'. Lady Falkland consoled herself that, whatever the ladies' social position might be in Bombay, 'they would be but "small folk" in London'.

If the dinner was something of a state occasion, then there would be as many as two hundred guests at Government House at Parell. The building had originally been a Portuguese church, but there was no sign of its ancestry in the spacious rooms. On such occasions, the governor's aides-de-camp were greatly taxed by problems of precedence. The names of partners were very carefully selected beforehand, rigorously adjusted 'with the nicest regard to the distinctions of rank'. This method usually allotted the most charming woman in the room 'to some prosy old civilian or mumbling colonel whose sole merit was his length of service'. Fortunately, there were few elderly Europeans in India. But neither were there many pretty women. Most of the really elderly were army officers. 'There was one old general of the queen's forces who had been appointed to a senior command in Bombay even though he was nearly blind and deaf, and

[77]

his aides-de-camp were for ever occupied in preventing his falling over the footstools in the drawing-room, when he went out to dinner'.

Acceptance of the non-official Englishmen took some time. The wealthier merchants and businessmen continued to be looked down upon by the official services, though they were not denied entry to Government House. The lawyers of Bombay were something of a class by themselves, being part of the system of British law, and yet mainly concerned with the litigation of the native population, and making a great deal of money out of it, too.

Still, the majority of those seen at Government House and at private parties were the younger military men, adding a touch of exotic colour with their elegant uniforms, and easily outdoing the civilians whose plain coats were relieved only by flowing cravats. The most welcome of guests were, naturally, the ladies, even though most of them were married. The cold weather, however, usually brought out a few unmarried girls to flutter the hearts of the bachelors. As Lady Falkland noted, 'the arrival of a cargo (if I dare term it so) of young damsels from England, is one of the exciting events that mark the advent of the cold season. It can be well imagined that their age, height, features, dress, and manners become topics of conversation, and as they bring the last fashions from Europe, they are objects of interest to their own sex'. But there was very little chance for the bachelors unless a girl's parents, or the relatives to whom she had been consigned, approved of a suitor – and everyone in India always knew just who each young man was, his prospects, and his family background.

A young girl had to be protected from military men, especially from any young ensign with whom she might have come to an 'understanding' on the voyage out. The best catch of all for her was undoubtedly the civilian, known as a 'three hundred a year dead or alive' man because when he joined the service he received a salary of £300 a year, and had to subscribe to a fund which, after a number of years' service, would guarantee his widow a pension of £300 a year.

Failing marriage, a man's opportunities for a healthy sexual life seemed to have been restricted. Gone for ever were the free and easy liaisons with Indian women which had aroused no criticism in the early part of the century, and which still occurred in the remoter inland stations. A young man might invite some courtesan to his bungalow, but he would have to be excessively discreet if he wished to maintain his position in 'civilised society'. Bombay, if the majority of travellers are to be believed, was a remarkably moral place, perhaps because of the difficulty of keeping any irregularities secret in a tiny and intimate community. Perhaps, too, as a result of lack of opportunity. 'There are none of those lures and haunts which prove so attractive and fatal to the young Londoner', maintained the *Handbook of India.* 'His Indian contemporary *must* spend his evenings in a decorous manner, for not only would he soon become marked if he frequented such scenes of debauchery as there are, which are of the very lowest description, and where common soldiers, sailors, and the absolute blackguards of the place resort; but there is not that field for a "lark" which tempts the London spruce apprentice, and youths of higher degree, to take to the streets in search of such adventures'. Even drinking was frowned upon, not apparently because it was a vice and might wreck a man's health, but because this 'sad propensity risks the degradation of the English character in the eyes of the native community'.

In fact, many of the attitudes which later came to be associated exclusively with Victorian England were already present in India. But Anglo-Indian society had distinct advantages over society in England. Anglo-India had neither '"parvenus" nor "nouveaux riches" . . . to shock one with their upstart airs', and 'with very few exceptions, no one comes to this country without either having laid the foundation, or completed the accomplishment, of a gentleman's education'. Indeed, 'the man of cultivated mind will perhaps meet with less to shock his fastidious tastes than in the necessarily mixed society of England, where the aristocracy of birth, and the aristocracy of wealth, alike struggle for eminence'.

★  ★  ★

The Calcutta-bound traveller missed Bombay even if he came by the overland route, for the steamer from Aden made directly for Ceylon and went on from there to Madras, capital of what the rest of Anglo-India knew as 'the benighted province'. Once it had been the

[79]

most important of the Company's territories, its tenure menaced alike by Indian rulers and French rivals, but by the time Victoria came to the throne it ranked low in the scale, 'for the very satisfactory reason', wrote Mr Stocqueler, the Baedeker of early Victorian India, 'that the country which formed its limits is in a settled state, abundantly fertile, and making a pleasant progress towards civilisation'. It was called 'benighted' because it had become a backwater and young men believed, with reason, that the future held more adventure in the north.

Madras was difficult to land at because a heavy swell rolled onto the shore. Ships had to stand off in the roads and transfer goods and passengers to boats which carried them over the surf. There were plans for a pier and a harbour, but it was to be the end of the queen's reign before they were built.

The Madras roads were full of ships and boats of every kind and shape. 'But none can compare to the catamarans, and the wonderful people that manage them. Fancy a raft of only three logs of wood, tied together at each end when they go out to sea, and untied and left to dry on the beach when they come in again. Each catamaran has one, two, or three men to manage it: they sit crouched upon their heels, throwing their paddles about very dextrously, but remarkably unlike rowing'. To a newcomer, the first sight of a catamaran could be almost unnerving. 'I perceived to my astonishment, a naked figure walking apparently on the surface of the sea, and rapidly approaching us. This was a catamaran man, the bearer of a dispatch from the shore'. As well as official messages, these intrepid boatmen carried the inevitable chits from 'hospitable residents, whose doors are open to the introduced stranger'.

Whether introduced or lacking in credentials, passengers still had to reach the shore. For that often exciting passage there was the masoolah boat:

Imagine a huge affair, something in shape like one of those paper cock-boats which children make for amusement, or an old-fashioned tureen, or the transverse section of a pear or pumpkin, stem and stern alike, composed of light and flexible planks, sewn together with coir, and riding buoyant as a gull on the heaving wave, the sides rising six feet or so above its surface, the huge empty shell crossed by narrow planks or benches, on which, when seated, or rather roosted, your legs dangle in air several feet from the bottom: further, picture in the fore-part, a dozen or more spare black creatures, each working an unwieldy pole-like paddle to a dismal and monotonous chant – and you may have some idea of a masoolah boat and its equipage. This rather crude affair was what the visitor to Madras had to commit himself to if he were going to land at all.

On approaching the surf, the boatmen's monotonous chant quickened to a wild *ulluloo* . . . I looked astern, and there, at some distance, but in full chase, advanced a curling mountain-billow, opening its vast concave jaws, as to devour us. On, on it came, '*Ullee! Ullee! Ullee!*' shouted the rowers; smash came the wave; up flew the stern, down went the prow; squall went the ladies, over canted the major . . . while those more fortunate in retaining their seats held on with all the energy of alarm with one hand and dashed the brine from their habilments with the other. The wave passed, and order a little restored, the boatsmen pulled again with re-doubled energy, to make as much way as they could before the next should overtake us. It soon came, roaring like so many fiends, and with nearly similar results. Another and another followed, till, at last, the unwieldy bark, amidst an awful bobbery, swung high and dry on the shelving beach; and out we all sprung, right glad once more to feel ourselves on terra firma.

When the travellers recovered themselves, those possessed of letters of introduction left for their friends' houses. Other gentlemen were strongly advised to present themselves at the Madras club and seek election as members. 'This club is an admirable institution. Without insisting upon an aristocratic exclusiveness, it is neverthe-less strictly an asylum for gentlemen. It is well and liberally con-ducted, and the charges come within the means of most persons in the upper circle of society'. There was no alternative, in fact, as the hotels were 'wretched places, affording but little accommodation, and abounding with dirt, bad viands, and worse wines'.

The most striking parts of Madras were the Fort and the Black

Town. The first housed some of the offices of government and the latter, as its name precisely states, 'contained the residences of the natives, and the shops of Europeans and natives'. The best European houses were along the Mount Road, 'six miles in length, bordered by trees and villas'. In one of these the traveller with an introduction would find himself a guest. The houses were usually of one storey, with a flat roof and an elegant portico in the neo-Classical style. The hostess would probably be young, though the host was in all likelihood much older – for the man of substance and position had more than an advantage over a young man who still had his way to make. 'India is the paradise of middle-aged gentlemen. When they are young they are thought nothing of; but at about forty when they are "high in the service", rather yellow and somewhat grey, they begin to be taken notice of and called "young men". These respectable persons do all the flirtation too in a solemn sort of way' – and, of course, most of the marrying.

In the pleasant bungalow on the Mount Road, the old style of Anglo-Indian hospitality – a style which never really died out – probably still reigned. Its main constituents were 'absence of unnecessary restraint, abundance of good cheer, and the most unaffected and cordial welcome'.

Guests who were not new to the country followed the custom of taking their own servants with them when staying with friends. At least this meant no extra trouble for the hostess, or (rather more important) her servants. 'The servants fend for themselves in a most curious way. They seem to me to sleep nowhere, and eat nothing – that is to say, in our houses, or of our goods. They have mats on the steps, and live upon rice'. Since the Indian social order was strictly classified by function, each servant had his or her separate work. A lady would have an ayah, a maid, and a tailor. Her husband would have a 'boy'. In addition, there was one man to sweep out the rooms and another to carry water. Another laid the table, and another brought in dinner. There was one servant whose sole duty appeared to be to light the candles, and others who served the meals. Each horse had not only a groom but a grasscutter who, in Madras, was usually a woman. Every dog, too, had his 'boy'. One visitor enquired 'whether the cat had any servants, but I found that she was allowed to wait upon herself; and, as she seemed the only person in the establishment capable of so doing, I respected her accordingly.'

Each servant seemed to have an assistant 'who does all the work that can be put off upon him without being found out by the master and mistress'. Of course, a great many servants were needed, not only to uphold the standing of the establishment, but to be on constant call for those attentions which were considered necessary to civilised life in India. Ladies who had been in India for any length of time had learned never to raise a finger if they could avoid it. They 'lie on a sofa, and, if they drop their handkerchief, they just lower their voices and say "Boy!" in a very gentle tone, and then creeps in, perhaps, some old wizen, skinny brownie, looking like a superannu-ated thread-paper, who twiddles after them for a little while, and then creeps out again as softly as a black cat, and sits down cross-legged in the verandah till "Mistress please to call again"'.

The trouble with servants, warned the *Indian Domestic Economy and Receipt Book* on its very first page, was that 'laziness, dishonesty, falsehood, with a host of other vices, seem to be inherent in them', which was not surprising 'when we consider the way in which they are brought up'. But the master and mistress had to take some part of the blame. In the first place, they had a distressing habit of taking servants into their employ 'merely on the recommendation of a written character'. This was a very foolish thing to do, 'as most of them were written for the occasion, by a class of persons who earn their bread by writing characters for any applicant who will give them a few annas, or agree to pay a percentage should he succeed in getting the place'. But having found a good servant, the master and mistress might be unable to keep him; in Anglo-India a servant's slightest fault was 'often visited with blows and such abuse as no respectable man will bear, very often too for no other fault than that of not understanding what the master has said, who has given his directions in some unintelligible stuff, from ignorance of the lan-guage, that no one could understand'. It was, in fact, surprising that the servants understood anything, for their masters and mistresses spoke to them in a peculiar jargon which one lady christened 'John Company's English'. She herself began to learn the Tamil lan-guage, but found it fearfully ugly, 'clattering, twittering, chirping, sputtering – like a whole poultry-yard let lose upon one', and soon relapsed into John Company's English again.

Newcomers found that even the barest civility to servants might not be understood. 'One day I said to my ayah (a very elegant lady in white muslin), "Ayah, bring me a glass of toast-and-water if you please". She crept to the door and then came back again, looking extremely perplexed, and whined out, "What Mistress tell? I don't know". "I told you to bring me some toast-and-water." "Toast-water I know very well, but Mistress tell *if you please*; I don't know *if you please*"'.

Inseparable from the servant problem was the upbringing of children, who spent so much of their life in the servants' charge before being packed off to England (or 'Home'). The children were able to command the widest devotion from the servants, but nurses were not above using a pill of opium to keep them quiet. Often, it kept them permanently so, and the European cemeteries held many graves of children dead in early infancy. If the children survived the combined assault of their nurses and of disease, it was necessary in the interests of their education as well as their health to send them to England. There were even one or two over-Christian mothers who felt that their children were in the gravest moral danger in India from the moment of birth. Think, wrote one of them, 'of our children hearing a language which they generally understand better than their parents, and of our lessons respecting a holy and spiritual God, being mingled in their minds with the silly and abominable fables and images of the surrounding idols!' It was a terrible thought that English children might grow up influenced by heathens, and it was no satisfactory answer to maintain, as most sensible mothers did: 'It is very sad but it can't be helped; and a year at Home will set them all to rights'.

Whatever the religious attitude of the parents, it is fair to say that children in India were 'peculiarly objects of passionate love', not only because death or departure for England threatened permanent or temporary separation, but because in the circumstances of an Anglo-Indian household children somehow became 'actually more attractive . . . Unshackled by the discipline of an English nursery, and the tyranny of a head nurse, both of which tend to engender a spirit of reserve and even cunning, they roam at will through every part of the house, prattling with all the artlessness of fearless childhood, and effectually twining themselves round the affections of every member of the family, and visitors to the house'.

If Anglo-Indian children were seen and heard with more tolerance than they would have been in England, the prevalence of servants kept them out of their parents' way when other entertainment offered. Not that such entertainment was in any way exciting. At dinner parties, the food was mediocre to say the least, and the conversation afterwards positively crushing. 'After dinner the company all sit round in the middle of the great gallery-like rooms, talk in whispers, and scratch their mosquito bites'.

There was more likelihood of entertainment at the home of some native acquaintance, though most Anglo-Indians do not seem to have had such acquaintances outside the way of business. One senior lady, asked what she had seen of the natives during her years in India, replied: 'Oh, nothing! Thank goodness, I know nothing at all about them, nor I don't wish to: really, I think the less one sees and knows of them the better!' The entertainment in an Indian house would, of course, be regarded as 'interesting' rather than enjoyable. A musician might play the vina, 'an instrument like a large mandoline', but the music that emerged was 'just a mixture of twang and whine'. The dancing girls, too, were a disappointment; though 'graceful creatures . . . sailing about like queens', in spite of their grace and their gorgeous jewellery they were 'tame'. And when they began to sing, it was like the 'bawling of bad street-singers – a most fearful noise and no tune'. These comments, however, came from a woman; perhaps things were more lively when the audience was male. The lady was no more impressed by the food than she had been by the entertainment, or by the house itself (which reminded her of a French *pension*). Most of the dishes were heavy with cayenne pepper, though otherwise quite good, 'but among the Hindoo messes I at last came to something so queer, slimy and oily, that I was obliged to stop'. On the whole Indian India was more amusing at a distance, in letters, for example, written in 'the true Fudge style' and containing such delightful phrases as 'hoping to have the honour of throwing myself at your goodness's philanthropic feet'!

[85]

Compared with some of the smaller stations to which a civilian might be sent, Madras was moderately sophisticated. In a small station, there might be only three or four Europeans, who had to rely on travellers or local eccentrics to vary the routine of their lives. Scattered around the country, outside the web of Anglo-Indian society, occasional Europeans were to be found – ex-soldiers of the Company's army, perhaps, pensioners who had settled in the Indian countryside because they knew they would not be happy at 'Home'. (The word 'Home', incidentally, always meant England; 'nobody calls India home – not even those who have been here thirty years and are never likely to return to Europe'). At Rajahmundry, several hundred miles north of Madras, there was 'an old Englishman living as barrack-sergeant – a sinecure for long service. He has been in the place these ten years, and is a very respectable old man. He has a half-caste, dropsical wife, and a sickly nigger-looking child, but seems quiet and contented'.

English soldiers travelling to join their regiments might provide some diversion for the residents of the smaller stations, and give them the opportunity of indulging in good works. A magistrate in a remote district one day discovered seven such, resting on their journey, and tried to find out if there was anything he could possibly give them. The greatest treat he could possibly give them, they said, 'would be a little tea and sugar to make themselves "a cup of English tea", which was a thing "they had not tasted they did not know when"'. With their tea they were given some tracts, but when asked whether they had a Bible, they replied that 'they set such store by it they seldom let it see the light'. So they were presented with another one for general use.

Naturally, common soldiers could not be invited to stay in one's house. Other travellers could, however. Some were welcome, like the young ensign of seventeen, travelling with a company of sepoys who were guarding a consignment of treasure; it was 'a pleasure to see a creature so innocently important and happy'. Others were less welcome and less innocent – travellers who inflicted themselves on some poor official and became a positive nuisance, borrowing a favourite horse, perhaps, or (even worse) going off and leaving all their luggage in their host's spare room until they chose to return, uninvited as before, to claim it. The trouble was that the government would not spend money on travellers' bungalows, making the excuse that 'the residents can always receive travellers'.

The civilian in any station, but particularly in a remote one, had to receive and sometimes return visits from the local aristocracy, great landlords and petty rajas. Conversation on these occasions was often rather stilted, consisting of a series of high-flown compliments and enquiries about His-Honour-the-civilian's health. But occasionally it widened a little. Queen Victoria's accession at least aroused some interest in the native mind. Queens regnant were rarities in India. How was the queen to get *men* to agree to obey her? It proved impossible to explain.

Indians of lower rank were constantly petitioning for appointments on the civilian's staff. There was a routine for this. It was not even necessary to make the petition in words. All that was needed was for the applicant to hang about the gate of the bungalow, displaying some part of the official trappings for the relevant appointment – writing material if the man aspired to be a clerk, a dagger if he hoped to become a messenger. Others insisted on having an audience with the great man, sometimes as often as twice a week if they were the determined kind. On these occasions, the dialogue might be expected to take the following course:

*Visitor*: Salaam, great chief!
*Civilian*: Salaam to you.
*Visitor*: Your Excellency is my father and my mother.
*Civilian*: I am much obliged to you.
*Visitor*: Sar, I am come to behold your honourable face.
*Civilian*: Thank you. Have you anything to say to me?
*Visitor*: Nothing, great chief!
*Civilian*: Neither have I anything to say, so good morning, enough for today.
*Visitor*: Enough; good morning, sar: great chief, salaam!

Even when the visitors were more acceptable there was no great likelihood of interesting conversation. If they were civilians, most of

[87]

the talk was of promotion, or, as one impatient blue-stocking of a magistrate's wife put it (apropos of the post of Collector, who was head of the district administration in certain parts of India); 'They sit and conjugate the verb "to collect": "I am a collector – He was a collector – We shall be collectors – You ought to be a collector – They would have been collectors"'.

With civilian ladies, it was very hard work to keep any conversation going, even about promotion. They were 'generally very quiet, rather languid, speaking in almost a whisper, simply dressed, almost always ladylike and *comme-il-faut*, not pretty, but pleasant and nice-looking'. Military wives, on the other hand, were always 'quite young, pretty, noisy, affected, showily dressed with a great many ornaments . . . [and] chatter incessantly from the moment they enter the house'. Their conversation matched their personalities. 'While they are alone with me after dinner, they talk about suckling their babies, the disadvantages of scandal, "the Officers", and "the Regiment"'. When the gentlemen reappeared, they flirted 'most furiously'.

As well as wild animals, hyenas, snakes, and whole martyrdoms of objectionable insects, there were other strange creatures in the countryside around the civilians' bungalows. Among them were the missionaries and their converts – who were usually known by the self-explanatory name of 'curry-and-rice Christians'.

The missionaries' unsubtle evangelism could often undo the more ingenious religious propaganda of others. The civilian official in an out-station would often set up a school and slip in tracts and versions of the Bible in local languages among the textbooks. But missionaries openly attacked the Hindu religion, and their aggression frequently put the town in a ferment and resulted in children being taken away from the school.

★ ★ ★

The approaches to Calcutta, the first city of British India, were depressing. Unlike Bombay and Madras, which the traveller could observe while still at sea, Calcutta was a hundred miles up a particularly forbidding estuary. The journey up-river might, of course, take place partly at night, which at least spared the traveller a view of the flat, seemingly endless, and featureless plains which bounded the river. But Calcutta from the water was not a sight to be missed, and Garden Reach gave the first indication that the city might be worth the boredom of a journey by daylight. On the left was the Botanical Garden, hidden behind a screen of cypress trees, on the right a long succession of villas 'situated amidst verdant lawns and park-like pleasure grounds, sloping gently down to the water's edge'. Once past the Reach, the great pile of Fort William came into sight, with a forest of masts in the river before it. There would be merchant ships flying the flags of many countries. Lean, well-trimmed American vessels which brought great blocks of ice in their holds. Chinese ships, with an eye painted either side, so that the vessels could see their way. Great awkward country boats laden with produce; the green, goose-shaped budgerows used by Europeans for river travel; the 'airy little bauleahs, with their light venetian'd rooms, which seemed fitted for the water-bowers of lovers on some of the lakes of those sunny isles which poets are wont to sing of, and where the breezes are never stronger than can be borne by silken sails'. Behind all these, the 'lines of stately mansions reposing under the still calm sky, like some Grecian capital of old, bespoke the City of Palaces, the proud metropolis of British India'.

This was no static picture, no elegant aquatint world without movement or smell. On the contrary, Calcutta was famous for its stenches. The newcomer was frequently shocked to find a loathsome half-decayed corpse banging against the anchor cable. The Hindus burned their dead – but only if they could afford the fuel. The poor usually left partially burned bodies by the side of the river until they were borne away by the tide. So many bodies infested the river that the police kept a fleet of boats and men whose job was 'to remove, by sinking, all offensive objects found floating in the river, which they do possibly after the spectacle has passed through the whole fleet'. If the winds were blowing off the land, then newcomers were also greeted with the smell of the open drains which helped to make Calcutta one of the most unhealthy places in India.

But there were thousands of small boats dashing in and out amongst the anchored ships and the landing stage (the *ghat*) was crowded with the most colourful people. 'Females bearing pots or

[89]

jars on their heads, and children, resembling little black monkeys astride on their hips; bhisties, or water-carriers, filling their bags from the turbid tide, well seasoned with coconut husks, defunct Brahmins, dead dogs, etc.; puckalls, or bullocks, bearing huge skins of the same pure element; palankeen [palanquin] bearers, gabbling (to me) unintelligible abuse, in eager competition, pushing into the very river, and banging their portable boxes one against the other in their struggle to secure fares amongst the frequent arrivals from the shipping; baboos, parroquet-venders, chattah-bearers, sailors, lascars, and adjutant-birds' – all were there. In fact, Europe and India 'commingled . . . in confusion'.

The newcomer was known in Anglo-India as a 'griff' or 'griffin'. If he had not been met, he would find himself besieged by potential servants brandishing a variety of testimonials from long-dead or non-existent Englishmen. Certainly, a new arrival needed servants, but he was well advised to wait a little.

An army man would be given accommodation in Fort William if he applied to the Town Major. The Fort itself had no architectural pretensions, though it had been built according to all the best tenets of military engineering. It remained a fort in the strict sense, and it was said to be large enough to shelter the 'whole Christian population' if it ever came to the crunch. The only trouble was that there was no water supply inside the fort. Water for the 'whole Christian population' would have to be brought from a tank (or pond) *outside* the ramparts. The fort, however, was amply stocked with weapons and powder. Mounted on its walls, against the unlikely possibility of attack, were some 600 guns of various calibres. The arsenal held a floating stock of 60,000 firearms and 20,000 swords, and the magazines, which were alleged to be 'bomb-proof', could accommodate 5,000 barrels of gunpowder. Unfortunately, the principal powder depots were not in the fort itself, but outside the town, and most of the magazine space within the fort was given over to millions of rounds of small-arms ammunition.

The griff's quarters inside the fort were hardly luxurious by anybody's standards – except perhaps those of a traveller who has been cooped up on board ship for weeks or months. The barrack allotted to unmarried officers consisted of a single corridor with rooms leading off it. These were small, but each was designed to act as parlour, bedroom and bath.

For the latter indispensable accessory to an Indian toilet, provision had been made, by enclosing a corner of the room with a parapet a foot high, and by piercing the outer wall to let the water off. Naked and comfortless as any quarter in England, the appearance of this one was not rendered more prepossessing by the circumstances of the walls being adorned with sundry deep indentations, stains of suspicious colour, and a profuse sprinkling of ink, all of which told of the choleric temperament of a former occupant, probably some 'jolly cadet', who . . . impatient of the stupidity of a bearer, or *khidmutgar*, for being ignorant of *his* language, had perchance striven to render himself intelligible by hurling, in rapid succession, at the head of his domestic, an empty brandy bottle, a boot-jack, and an inkstand.

The barracks were exceptionally noisy. 'The passage was sounding and reverberating, and each occupant of a quarter had much of the benefit of his neighbour's flute, fiddle or French horn, whether "i' the vein" for harmony or not; shoe brushings, occasional yells of servants undergoing the discipline of fists or horsewhips [and] whistling' – all served to contribute to the clamour. Visually, too, there was considerable variety and disorder. 'On the ground might be seen a goodly display of trays with egg-shells, fish-bones, rice, muffin, and other wrecks of breakfast; sweepers – certain degraded menials . . . – squatting near and waiting for the said remnants, hookahs . . . in course of preparation for those who indulged in the luxury of smoking'.

Fort William was not considered a healthy station. A young soldier arriving there in 1852 wrote in his memoirs forty years later: 'The men were crowded into small badly-ventilated buildings and the sanitary arrangements were as deplorable as the state of the water supply. The only efficient scavengers were the huge birds of prey called adjutants, and so great was the dependence placed upon the exertions of these unclean creatures that the young cadets were

[91]

warned that any injury done to them would be treated as gross misconduct'.

The traveller did, however, have an alternative to this kind of accommodation. Unlike Bombay and Madras, Calcutta had a number of quite reasonable hotels and boarding houses. Spence's, near Government House, was said to be the best, though there were differing opinions as to its merits. In 1842, a German traveller found its comfort and service pleasant and its charges not too high. Ten years later, the future Lord Roberts found it dreary – although this may have been because he discovered that, by staying there instead of going directly to the artillery depot he had lost not only a day's pay but a day's seniority!

Another hotel, the Auckland, was described by the great war correspondent, William Howard Russell of the London *Times*, as a large house in which there had been made an attempt to combine:

> a tailor's, a milliner's and dressmaker's, a haberdasher's, a confectioner's, a hardwareman's, a woolen merchant's, a perfumer's, a grocer's, a coffee-house keeper's establishment, with an hotel, and with a variety of other trades and callings. I should say from my own experience, the hotel suffers in the amalgamation; but it is a great advantage to have at your feet all you want, although, I must confess, I could not manage to get a chop one morning for breakfast below stairs. Mr D. Wilson, who created this establishment by his energy, ability and industry, has made a large fortune; and judging from the zeal with which he advertises all over India, is bent on making it larger.

But the traveller's best solution, failing a private house, was a club. In Calcutta, the finest was undoubtedly the Bengal Club. This had been founded in 1827 and had occupied a number of houses in the centre of the city before it moved to its final premises in 1845. The Bengal Club had not been the first club to open in Calcutta, but it was the one which most closely resembled the great London clubs. Before its final move to the Chowringee, the principal thoroughfare of British Calcutta, it had occupied a building on the esplanade overlooking the port and its shipping. There it had contained reading rooms, a library, and dining rooms all of which were 'fitted up in the most convenient and elegant manner'. The new building was even more luxurious and impressive. In fact, all the great houses along the Chowringee and the adjacent roads looked like palaces. They were built in the style of the Classical mansion, which the aristocracy of Europe had elevated into a symbol of power and success. Palladio inspired it, and lesser architects adapted his plans to suit the availability of materials and the demands of the tropics.

Unfortunately, on closer inspection, the great palaces of the men who ruled India had their flaws. The houses were too close together, for one thing. In an open park, each would have had its special grandeur, but the fact of their being close together and surrounded by high walls seemed to detract from their elegance. It did not improve matters to find next to these great mansions a 'batch of miserable native huts, which are about as much out of place as a row of pigsties would be in the middle of Regent Street'. Even the ambience was decidedly vulgar. 'Instead of the caparisoned elephant, and the golden umbrella, and the decorated palankeen with its liveried out-runners, we see the primitive-looking native bullock-cart, as it creaks along the dusty road – the wretched, dilapidated *carhanchy*, or hack-carriage of Bengal filled with some half dozen fat natives, and drawn by a pair of lean and wall-eyed ponies, threatening every moment to part with at least one of its wheels, and groaning beneath the mass of flesh that it carries'. On foot, there were none of the gorgeous creatures artists insisted on putting in their illustrations of 'Life in India', no princes in 'jewelled turbans and silken raiment'. It was something of a let-down. Could this really be the 'city of palaces'?

Even when night fell, there was little glamour added to the scene, for Calcutta was most wretchedly lighted – at least at the beginning of the queen's reign – and it took a long time for it to improve. The only street lighting was from 'sordid oil-lamps, supplied with material of so inferior a description that even the inside of the lamp is scarcely illuminated, and placed at the respectable distances of the corners of streets, or other wide intervals, which make them appear as few and far between as did the angels' visits of the poet's illustration'.

The streets were not patrolled by watchmen, nor were they paved.

The open drains were 'execrable', and helped Calcutta maintain its reputation for all-the-year-round unhealthiness. According to one well-worn saying, the capital of British India was 'bad for new arrivals in the hot weather, in the rains for old Indians (i.e. Anglo-Indians], and in the cold weather for everybody'.

For part of the year the great mansions might be shining white, having been coated with a layer of *chunam*, or lime. But in the monsoon, they had 'a somewhat desolate aspect of uninhabited grandeur; for the walls and the pillars were black and weather-stained, large patches of green stain were visible about the base, and down the sides of the house you might trace the course of the water, that had been, almost incessantly for the last two months, streaming down from the conduits on the roof. The house, too, was shut up; between the pillars of the spacious verandah . . . large green blinds, made of thin pieces of split and painted bamboo, were let down to exclude the glare'.

Indoors, the houses had magnificent rooms. The reception room was invariably hung with chandeliers, which were usually protected by great bags of some red material. 'Besides these, were suspended from the beams two large punkahs, most elaborately moulded and gilt, with deep fringes attached to the bottom, and semi-circular spaces cut at the top of them, to give a clear berth to the above-described chandeliers, which would otherwise have been smashed to atoms at the first swing of these formidable ventilators'. The furniture was, as a rule, heavy and expensively luxurious, with lots of marble tables, mahogany-framed sofas covered in damask, writing tables, an alabaster cupid or two, and at least one bronze stag. There would also be a piano and numerous elegant-looking albums, some of music, others with such titles as *The Book of Beauty* or *The Book of Royalty*. Just to indicate that the household was by no means frivolous, there would also be a volume of the *Calcutta Christian Observer* – though the first 'very favourable impression of the religious character of the lady of the house' which this conveyed was often belied by the fact that it bore the 'most unequivocal symptoms of having been unread'. In other words, the pages would still be uncut.

The governor-general's house was a real palace, although foreign visitors were inclined to find it unpretentious. The approach was 'up a colossal flight of steps, so spacious that a large number of the inhabitants of the town can assemble in it to greet an arriving [governor-general]. Immediately on entering you find yourself in the great marble banqueting hall, capable of holding with ease more than a hundred guests, and so lofty that palm trees are frequently introduced on the occasion of great entertainments, and the tables of the guests are laid beneath their spreading branches. There are white pillars down the whole length of this noble chamber; and at the end of the vista, an admirable finish to the general effect, is the throne room.

'But the marble hall is only the vestibule to an apartment of greater dimensions – the ballroom, where as many as two thousand guests are sometimes received, and the general look of which is that of a Royal state room. The plan of the whole house is curious, and is exactly suited to an Indian climate. From four corners of a central block of buildings, in which are the reception rooms just mentioned, and others of lesser magnitude, long corridors radiate, communicating at a considerable distance with four wings, each of which virtually constitutes a separate and detached house. Each of these wings is so built that from whatever side the wind comes – north, south, east, or west – a thorough draught can be obtained through every room.

'In one of these wings the [governor-general] has his own establishment, his private rooms, and offices of state. In the same wing, and immediately adjoining it, are the political secretary's room, the aide-de-camp's room, and waiting room; while on the floor below are the private secretary's office, and rooms for the staff of under-secretaries and clerks, whose services are in perpetual requisition to deal with the mountains of papers which daily come before the governor-general. So far as its ornaments and fittings are concerned, the whole house is a curious miscellany of trophies and historical associations. The council room and some of the corridors are lined with portraits of . . . Warren Hastings, Wellesley and others. The marble hall abounds with busts of Roman emperors, the busts captured from a French man-of-war and ranged along the walls; while chandeliers of rare beauty hang in each of the principal apartments, also some taken from the French'.

[95]

Such was Government House when Lord Auckland announced the accession of Queen Victoria, but it had changed – and not for the better – when a new governor-general arrived eleven years later. 'I find the house superb', wrote Lord Dalhousie, 'the furniture disgraceful; an ADC's bed absolutely broke down to the ground with him the other day from sheer age; the plate and table equipage very poor. I can't afford to spend money on plate, but I think the deficiency in plate and in the inferiority of table decoration would be very much remedied, if I had the means of setting off the table with plants, as is done at Buckingham Palace and elsewhere in London'. However, he noted regretfully that 'at present John Company has no more cash than his neighbours, and I can't ask much at present'.

At least the governor-general's yacht was in better condition. 'Nothing can be more luxurious', Dalhousie was pleased to say, 'than this style of travelling, in a yacht, all green and gilding, with no crew, towed by a steamer, with sofas and punkahs, and bedrooms and luxuries of all sorts; one sits as much at ease as in a room, with the advantage of catching every breath of air which can find its way to you in this incipient frying-pan'. The yacht was the governor-general's usual means of transport to Barrackpore, his weekend retreat about fifteen miles from Calcutta where the air was believed to be somewhat cooler than in the capital. It was certainly more salubrious.

The Barrackpore house was genuinely unpretentious. Though the rooms were large, the house itself was small, so that governor-general's family could have it very much to themselves. The aides-de-camp, secretaries, and other essential supports of the Company's ruler, slept in small thatched cottages built around the park. Even guests were accommodated away from the main house, in separate guest bungalows. Lord Dalhousie found that the furniture was still 'not smart', but at least it was 'not so scandalous and blackguard as that at Government House' in Calcutta. Obviously no improvement had been made since Emily Eden, some years before, wrote in her journal that the furniture and hangings were shabby, and the furniture 'worse than that of an average London hotel'. The governor-general and his family did not suffer over-much, however. A vast fleet of boats accompanied his yacht from Calcutta, and four hundred servants were thought an adequate number to sustain him in the manner to which he was accustomed.

The park surrounding the Barrackpore house was – almost – like home, 'a pretty pleasure-ground, beautiful garden, an aviary, a menagerie, and all situated on the bank of the river, and surrounded by a park quite home-like in its character, and as English as anything can be, where you have banains [fig] and cocoanuts and palms, and mangoes, for oaks and elms, larch, and beech'.

Calcutta, despite all strictures, was an impressive city. Well-travelled visitors frequently likened it to St Petersburg, and with reason. The public buildings, taken as a whole, *were* elegant – architecturally, at least – and they were often kept in better condition than some of the private mansions. The native city was avoided as much as possible, though it was interesting enough to drive through if only the crowds had not made it difficult for the horses to pursue their way. For the romantic visitor or the newly-arrived resident, there were always a few natives with 'wild, handsome countenances', or perhaps a Chinese with 'twinkling eyes and yellow face and satin dress' stalking among 'these black, naked creatures'.

Some of the richer Indians lived in houses outside Calcutta. Dwarkanath Tagore, perhaps the first Western-style Indian capitalist (who had visited England and been received by the queen), owned a villa in the English style five miles from the city. It stood isolated in a small park which was also in the English style, and was apparently 'a favourite resort of young married couples, who are often invited by the hospitable owner to spend the honeymoon there'. The furnishings of the two-storeyed house were entirely European in taste. So, too, was the owner, for his dinner-table held 'the richest wines and even roasted joints of the sacred animal' – the cow. When Captain von Orlich visited the house in 1843, however, musicians and nautch girls arrived to entertain the guests after dinner. Their dancing was not much admired, but the Captain, who had an eye for a pretty figure, noted that they had delicate feet and hands, and a 'fine contour'. But soon 'their movements became so offensive, that we requested that the dance might be concluded'. It was very regrettable, the Captain felt, that 'the notions of morality and decorum entertained by the Indians, even when they have acquired that degree of refinement which our host undoubtedly possessed, are still so different from ours, that they are quite insensible to that impropriety which so much shocked us'.

It was not the first time that a visit to Dwarkanath Tagore's villa had been productive of moralising. Before Captain Orlich's experience, the governor-general, Lord Auckland, accompanied by his sisters, had accepted an invitation there and had found elephants on the lawn and ices in the summerhouse. On the whole, the party had had a most enjoyable time. The trouble came afterwards. Much of Calcutta society did not approve of their governor-general hobnobbing with the natives.

Life in Calcutta was not particularly exciting. There were balls at Government House, of course, and many private dances and dinners, for Anglo-Indian society was a gregarious society. People who did not mix were regarded as odd (or worse) and did not stand much chance of promotion. If they were old and distinguished, however, any anti-social tendencies – as long as they were not too bizarre – were considered as merely eccentric.

Members of Anglo-Indian society liked to be assured that it was still alive, for death had a habit of coming very swiftly. And yet death was treated with a certain calculated indifference. When, for example, a communication arrived at one of the great mansions on the Chowringee, announcing the death of a certain Mr Collingwood, an exchange such as the following might ensue:

'Mr Collingwood', returned Mrs Parkinson; 'it really is quite shocking; he dined with us the day before yesterday – cholera, I suppose – dreadful!' And Mrs Parkinson endeavoured to look quite overcome, but was not particularly successful.

But Mrs Poggleton pretended nothing at all: she leant forward, held out her hand for the undertaker's circular, looked rather pleased than otherwise, and said, 'Dear me! if it is not the gentleman with that pretty carriage, I declare!'

'Small use to him a pretty carriage now', said Mrs Parkinson, 'the only carriage that he needs is a hearse'.

'Oh but', exclaimed Mrs Poggleton, with more eagerness than she had manifested throughout the conversation, 'I have been dying a long time for that carriage, and now I shall be able to get it. What a nice thing to be sure!'

Upon this Mrs Parkinson lifted up her hands, and pretended to be immeasurably shocked, muttering to herself, but quite loud enough for everybody to hear, that life was a span, and death hanging over us, and that the world might be destroyed tomorrow, for anything she knew to the contrary, with sundry other moral reflections of this kind, equally original, and expressive of virtuous emotion.

Though society was close-knit, it was by no means free from hatreds. These even blew up into duels, though duelling was no longer the approved way of settling points of honour. Attempts had been made to stop duelling in the royal armed forces by lobbyists of the Association for the Discouragement of Duelling, who presented a memorial to the queen in 1843. Within a year, the Articles of War had been so amended that any officer accepting, sending, or carrying a challenge was liable to be cashiered; the seconds suffered in proportion. These regulations had some effect, if not all that had been intended, but they were slow to influence quick-tempered men in India.

The ladies, who had little to occupy their hands but embroidery, had less to occupy their minds. Cultural life in Calcutta was not at its height during the first twenty years of the queen's reign. Books were scarce, and greatly over-priced for many years – a novel, at one time, cost three guineas a copy. The books which new residents inherited, left behind by some nabob of the previous century, were usually books which had not excited the nabob, either. They scarcely offered light reading, for they all seemed to be sermons, or commentaries on the Gospels. Fortunately, the Americans brought in the holds of their ships not only bags of ice, but cheap (pirated) editions of English books. Their range was not very wide, but there were many novels, and even such a bluestocking as Emily Eden insisted: 'the more trash the better'.

There were newspapers, fortunately, and they had been freed from censorship in 1835. Mostly, they were mouthpieces of the various special-interest groups (particularly merchants) who owned them, but they also willingly gave space to disgruntled members of the civil service or the army who wished to attack the government, or even specific persons. Though the person attacked had no anonymity granted to him, his attackers hid behind such high-sounding pseudonyms as 'Brutus' and other Classical personalities. Herbert Edwardes, however, caused something of a sensation in the 1850s by contributing a series of letters under the name of 'Brahminy Bull'. In 1847 members of the civil service were ordered not to contribute to newspapers, but this order had little effect. Scandal and abuse always make news, especially in such a small society as that of Anglo-India.

Scandal, in fact, was the lubricant of much of the social mechanism, particularly for the women. 'In other parts of the world they talk about things, here they talk about people. The conversation is all personal, and, as such, you may be sure tolerably abusive.' What did they find to say about one another? 'The veriest trifles in the world. Nothing is so insignificant as the staple of Calcutta conversation. What Mr This said to Miss That and what Miss That did to Mr This; and then all the interminable gossip about marriages and no-marriages, and will-be marriages and ought-to-be marriages, and gentlemen's attention and ladies' flirtings, dress, reunions, and the last burrakhana [big dinner]'

Calcutta did offer more European-style diversions than the other cities of Anglo-India. There was a theatre, an elegant building opened in 1840 and called the Sans Souci. There were visiting companies, and even an operatic performance or two – though according to mentions in diaries and letters they never seem to have been very good. There was racing round the course in front of Fort William. Racing began very early in the day, at sunrise, in fact, and the meetings were usually over by ten o'clock, 'thus enabling all classes to attend and enjoy the sport without trenching upon their daily avocations'. The horses were usually Arabs from the Persian Gulf, with an occasional entry from New South Wales: later, Australia came to supply most of the mounts. The men also went shooting outside the city, or hunting. For the less bloodthirsty, there were cricket and racquets.

For all its gossiping and scandal-mongering, Calcutta society was really very moral. Emily Eden had already found it so in the early years of Victoria's reign. 'People are very domestic in their habits, and there are no idle men. Every man without exception is employed in his office all day, and in the evening drives. Husbands and wives are always in the same carriage. It is not considered possible for one to come without the other; it is quite out of the question. If Mr Jones is ill, everybody knows that Mrs Jones cannot go out, so she is not expected'.

There were a number of men who had grown old in the service and who chose not to keep up with the new-fangled protocol of society. They lived as they had always been accustomed to, richly – even grossly – and to hell with everybody. But even men of the older generation kept their old-fashioned outspoken manners for the time *after* the ladies had left the table. Then, 'all was grossness and sensuality'. William Knighton, writing in 1855 of just such an old Anglo-Indian (whom he called Ducklet), was greatly relieved 'when he moved an adjournment to the drawing-room, where we found Mrs Ducklet dozing over a volume of sermons, and the fascinating Julia performing sacred pieces on the piano. It was now half-past ten o'clock, and we had sat down to dinner at half-past seven!'

Within twenty years of Victoria's accession, the old men had long died or gone Home. William Howard Russell noted that 'the good old hookah days are past; cheroots and pipes have now usurped the place of the aristocratic silver bowl, the cut-glass goblets, and the twisted glistening snake with silver or amber mouthpiece . . . The race of Eurasians is not so freely supplied with recruits . . . There is now no bee-bee's house – a sort of European zenana'. Had things changed for the better? 'There are now European rivals to those ladies [the native kept women] at some stations. It was the topic of conversation the other day at mess that the colonel of a regiment had thought it right to prohibit one of his officers from appearing publicly with an unauthorised companion at the band parade; and the general opinion was that he had no right to interfere. But the society of the station does interfere in such cases, and though it does not mind bee-bees or their friends, it rightly taboos him who entertains their white rivals'.

But that, of course, was 'up the country'.

# 3

# UP THE COUNTRY
# AND UNTO THE HILLS

OUTSIDE the great centres of Anglo-Indian life there remained the wild and lonely places, where perhaps one British official would rule a vast area and great numbers of people, without seeing a fellow-Englishman for months. The new frontiers still dominated much of British India.

In the less remote districts there were large colonies of civilians and soldiers, known simply as 'the station'. For displaying Anglo-Indian society, this was the ideal frame – but the visitor had to get there first.

There were a number of ways of travelling 'up the country'; by land, by river, or by a combination of the two. In the early 'fifties, it was just becoming possible to make part of the journey by rail. But this had its disadvantages. One was the possibility of being set on fire by sparks from the engine; the fuel was wood, not coal. In fact, the danger was so acute that, on one occasion 'as a detachment of Sikh soldiers were going up country, one of them had his clothes set on fire by the embers. All his comrades were dressed in cotton-quilted tunics, with their pouches full of ammunition, and in their alarm they adopted the notable device of pitching the man out of the window in order to get rid of the danger to which they were exposed'.

It was usual for civilians or single officers to travel by land. A regiment of soldiers, however, customarily went by river which was a very slow and tedious journey. The land traveller could ride his own horse, and usually did so for at least part of the journey. For the rest, there was the palanquin, or the *palki-garee*, a palanquin on wheels – rather like a coffin on springs – which could turn out to be very comfortable, for with the doors closed and a lamp beside one's head it was possible to have a pleasant hour or two's reading before sleep.

Travel needed forethought and careful arrangement. The post office was responsible for the travel service from about 1843 on-wards. To organise a journey, or 'lay a dak' (the word 'dak' means 'post'), it was necessary to inform the head postmaster well in advance, so that he could make arrangements with postal officials up the country for the supply of bearers at authorised stopping places along the route. Unfortunately, the post office was organised to handle only a small number of the most frequented routes. Travellers elsewhere had to try and arrange matters for themselves. The usual thing was to buy a palanquin and have it fitted up as comfortably as one's means would allow. The cost of a palanquin was about £10 – a substantial sum in terms of the time – but it could usually be resold at not too much of a loss at the end of the journey. 'Fitting up' usually consisted of a minimum furnishing of books, plus 'shaving and washing apparatus, a canister of biscuits, a bottle and glass, a drinking cup, a little additional night clothing . . . The clothes of the traveller and such articles as he does not immediately require, are carried in tin boxes, or wicker baskets, called pettarahs, by separate bearers, who run ahead or alongside of the palanquin; and these pettarahs may be procured in any number at the chief towns and stations at a very slight cost.'

The traveller was advised, as far as money was concerned, to take only silver, and particularly 'a considerable number of the smaller coins of eight and four annas, as gratuities to boatmen who ferry you across the small nullahs or rivers, and to the palanquin-bearers . . . at each stage; for in many parts of the country these latter people are paid so irregularly, or kept so much in arrears, that their very subsistence depends upon the bounty of the dak traveller'. The usual number of long-distance palanquin-bearers was eleven; two pettarah-bearers and a torch-bearer were also needed, for much of the journey was made at night to avoid the heats of the day. The torch-bearer fed his flambeau 'every now and then with oil which he poured out of a bamboo, shaped like a quill toothpick'.

Mrs Colin Mackenzie, who made such an up-country journey in 1847, found it delightful. 'Whenever we woke there was something to see or hear; sometimes a jackal prowling near, sometimes the merry chatter of the bearers, and sometimes the wild, but not unmusical, shout in chorus, by which they give notice of their arrival at the chouki [stopping place].' But Captain Richard Burton, later to become famous for his translation of the *Arabian Nights* – and the *Kama sutra* – was not so enthusiastic. 'After a day or two', he said, 'you will hesitate which to hate most, your bearers' monotonous, melancholy grunting, groaning chaunt, when fresh, or their jolting, jerking, shambling, staggering gait, when tired. In a perpetual state of low fever you cannot eat, drink, or sleep; your mouth burns, your head throbs, your back aches, and your temper borders on the ferocious. At night, when sinking into a temporary oblivion of your ills, the wretches are sure to awaken you for the purpose of begging a few pice, to swear that they dare not proceed because there is no oil for the torch, or to let you and your vehicle fall heavily upon the ground, because the foremost bearer very nearly trod upon a snake. Of course you scramble as well as you can out of your cage, and administer discipline to the offenders. And what is the result? They all run away and leave you to pass the night'.

In northern India, part of the journey (at least as far as Cawnpore) could be made in flats pulled by steam vessels. These flats had sixteen cabins, ranged on either side, and were divided by size into three classes. The journey to Cawnpore took about three weeks and, in the cold weather, could be most enjoyable. But at Cawnpore the service ceased, and there was no alternative but horse or palanquin.

As most travelling, particularly in the hot weather, was done at night, it was essential to have somewhere to rest during the hours of sunlight. Along the principal routes, at regular intervals, a benevolent government supplied rest-houses, or dak bungalows. On the whole, the government's benevolence was strictly limited to erecting a building. For other comforts, all depended on the person in charge. Young Lieutenant Roberts found the *khansamah*, or steward in charge, like 'mine host' at Home. He 'declared himself at the outset prepared to provide everything the heart of man could desire; when, however, the traveller was safely cornered for the rest of the day, the menu invariably dwindled down to the elementary and universal "sudden death", which meant a wretchedly thin chicken, caught, decapitated, grilled, and served up within twenty minutes of the meal being ordered. At dinner, a variety was made by the chicken being curried, accompanied by an unlimited supply of rice and chutney'.

In between times, there was no surcease for the traveller's pains. 'The hours lag long and wearily; the punkah, of limited dimensions, with a deranged flounce and with unsymmetrical ropes, waggles with a quaint and threatening aspect, and affords but little mitigation of the burning heat . . . We lie recumbent on the cot, which has the authorised and popular number of legs, of which the chairs cannot be said to boast; – we have dozed; – we have read the regulations that hang upon the walls forty times at least; – we have drunk tepid beer, and warm soda-water has allayed our thirst; – we have recorded our names in the book of fate and of the Bungalow'. It was almost a relief when the sound of the palanquin-bearers was heard outside. The sun had set and it was time to journey on.

All dak bungalows were not quite such temporary purgatories for empire-builders. In some, the khansamah had made such an impression on the catering, that satisfied travellers even left written testimonials behind, which were carefully preserved. The khansamah in charge of the dak bungalow at Krishnaghur in Bengal, for example, had received such encomiums as 'Peter is a brick'. Better still, there was 'a very poetical effusion' from Mr Cadet Brown:

> So I will praise Peter wherever I go,
> And always speak well of his Dak bungalow;
> If I always gets food just as good as he gives,
> In time I shall get jolly fat – if I lives!

This was rare praise indeed. So were stewards of Peter's quality.

Some people, of course, were able to travel in considerable state. When the governor-general, Lord Auckland, made his tremendous journey across upper India – which lasted from October 1837 until March 1840 – he moved with an armed camp as vast as a city. But he was the governor-general, after all, and had to make an impression on the natives. There were lesser figures, however, who still moved in some style. A collector, with his wife and child, considered it modest to travel with an elephant, ten palki-garees, two palanquins, six horses, and sixty house-servants, as well as about eighty porters and palanquin-bearers.

When a traveller finally reached the up-country station, he found that it presented a very different appearance from Calcutta and the other great urban centres on the coast. It was usually placed a few miles from some native city, so as to overawe it and not be dominated by it. The layout of the little town was much the same everywhere. There were bungalows, naturally, and 'that square white-washed edifice, with an excrescence at one end, looking for all the world like an extinguisher on a three-dozen chest – what is it? You may well ask. It is the church! A regular protestant building! protesting against everything architectural, aesthetic, ornamental, or useful; designed and built according to a Government prescription. Next to it is our assembly-room and theatre; just beyond you see the hospitals; then comes the raquet-court, and to the left is the well-stocked burial ground. This is the course, where the live splendours of the station resort when shades of evening close upon us. There is the bandstand, and this is the station bath. On the extreme right are the barracks, for you must know that Europeans man the guns of our battery that is quartered here. That is the artillery-mess and opposite lives Sticker-doss, who sells Europe-goods, and can accommodate you with anything from a baby's bottle to a bolster'.

The bungalows were only faintly reminiscent of Calcutta's great mansions. They were white-washed and had columns holding up the projecting verandah. But their roofs were high and thatched; sometimes they had a double roof to give extra protection from the sun. In the hot weather, the doorways would be filled in with grass curtains which, when doused with water, produced a slightly cooled breeze. To help keep down the temperature, there was a remarkable device known as a thermantidote. This was an enormous machine, made of wood. About 7 feet high, 4 or 5 feet wide, and between 9 and 11 feet long, it was hollow, and circular in shape, ending in a funnel fixed to the window of the house. Inside the cylinder there were four large fans, fixed to an axle which was driven from outside. When the fans revolved, air was driven into the house. The air was cooled in the cylinder; a circle about 4 feet in diameter was cut out of each side of the thermantidote and filled with a mat made from a grass called khas-khas, which gave off a fragrant smell when wet. The mats were kept wet by means of a perforated trough above, which it was a servant's duty to keep filled with water. On a simpler level, there was also a device rather like a paddle-wheel which could be used to direct air on to the wet grass screens in the doorways.

A low wall surrounded each bungalow, enclosing what was known in the special language of Anglo-India as 'the compound'. Inside the compound, as well as the bungalow there were the servants' quarters, the stables, and a cow-house. There was also the garden, to which a great deal of attention was devoted. Water was drawn from a well (of which there would usually be two). Irrigating the ground was a rather complex piece of engineering. The water was raised by bullock power and then emptied into a channel which, in turn, fed many smaller channels all over the garden, each flower and vegetable bed having its own. Because of the plants and trees, the fact that it was an *Indian* garden could never be disguised, but it was always possible to grow roses which reminded one pleasantly of Home. The trouble was that the very English desire for a garden could have its disadvantages, even lethal ones. The gardener and his assistants often flooded the flower-beds, and the water that remained there became a splendid breeding ground for mosquitoes.

Inside, the typical bungalow was very sparsely furnished. There would be a few basket chairs from the bazaar; perhaps, too, a vaguely Sheraton one made up by some local carpenter or purchased – as most of the fittings of an Anglo-Indian bungalow were – from the effects of someone who had died. Clothes were kept in tin boxes, to defend them against the avid white ants which ate practically everything and were particularly fond of cloth. In the hot weather, there would be no carpet on the floor. The punkah was kept going all the time, except when the punkah-puller fell asleep, the rope fastened to his big toe. The bed was no splendid fourposter, but only a string frame on four short legs.

The Anglo-Indian household everywhere woke early. The civilian took his exercise before breakfast, and the soldier made his first and only appearance on the parade-ground. After breakfast, the civilian departed for his office or the court, while the officer usually spent the rest of the day in the most pleasant form of idleness he could achieve.

Some devoted their days to music or drawing, 'which of course they prefer in the society of ladies'. Military men also spent a great deal of time in gaming for very high stakes, though as time went on this came to be frowned upon as un-Christian – which did not make a great deal of difference. The hot, dull vacancy of everyday life demanded compensation.

Unfortunately, there were few compensations. For the majority of people, the petty dissipations of society formed the only resort. 'These are the men who drink but are not drunkards, bet and play cards but do not gamble ruinously; eat and drink and sleep and gossip and shilly-shally through their day, trying with all the singleness of purpose they possess to steer a dexterous course between the burden of existence on the one hand, and the vacuum of literally doing nothing on the other'.

The army mess was usually on its best behaviour when there were guests, but at other times its manners could be pretty coarse. 'I had always thought of a mess as the abode of luxurious refinement', wrote one rather naive young man in the 1850s:

I find it a bad tavern. I had not expected to hear literary conversation at a mess-table, but still less such appalling ribaldry as I did hear in the fortnight during which I belonged to the mess. I am not likely to be prudish in these matters; I have spent all my life at Winchester and Oxford, and at both places have been in company with boys and men who were noted for this style of conversation; but I am quite certain that a man saying, at a wine party, such things as are common at the 81st mess, would have been kicked out of the room as a gross offender – I do not say against morality, but against gentlemanly behaviour. They pride themselves on a very subtle distinction between dinner· and after-dinner. A man is supposed to be reasonably decent while the cloth is on the table, but may compensate himself by the utmost licence of blackguardism directly it is off. I stayed in the mess for a fortnight, but could not stand it any longer; so now I live alone.

The up-country station often displayed the tension between the two types of Englishmen who now ruled India. The militant

Christians were now growing in numbers and they did not reserve their criticism just for the heathen. On the contrary, it was more often directed at their fellow-countrymen and their standards of behaviour. The white man's burden was slowly being gathered together, and those whose backs appeared too weak to take the strain – or who were obviously unwilling to shoulder the load – became the target for abuse. A man who kept a native mistress was not only beyond the pale on moral grounds; 'when a man in office is under the power of a native woman, she invariably takes bribes, and he gets the credit for doing so; for she of course gives out that the Sahib shares in her extortions . . . Now, putting the principles of morality out of the question, it is evident that an officer who thus places himself into the hands of a Heathen woman, is wholly unfit for any situation of authority'. As far as drinking was concerned, Mrs Colonel Mackenzie (who was very much a muscular Christian) exclaimed: 'How many are as fit for work, as clear-headed, as even-tempered, as fit for meditation and prayer, after dinner as before! . . . I have long thought we should abstain from wine and beer (for many ladies in India drink both) in order to redeem the time – to keep our bodies in *subjection*, and . . . be able to minister more largely to the wants of others'.

This preoccupation with other people's souls did not inhibit the Anglo-Indian vice of retailing scandal. Except for the possibility of converting the heathen, there was nothing else to do. Most of the gossip derived from the women servants, who met frequently to exchange intelligence about what was served at the last dinner to which their mistresses had not been invited, or what the judge's wife was up to, or how the doctor was able to afford such expensive dresses for his wife. These tales and more suitably embroidered or even invented, served to fill the time while the memsahib was having her hair brushed or her feet shampooed.

Later in the morning there were more serious, or at least more practical matters awaiting the memsahib's attention. The provision cupboards had to be inspected, because servants could *never* be trusted. Inventories of stores had to be checked. Everything that could be weighed had to be weighed. The level of the liquid in wine bottles had to be marked, as menservants were known to have a penchant for the sahib's brandy. The routines of the household had to be observed and tours of inspection carried out. The kitchen had to be visited.

Only the most determined and conscientious of wives carried through this programme. The weaker ones, clearly, did not. Many were so overcome by their first sight of the kitchen where their food was prepared that they never summoned up the courage to enter it a second time:

If your eyes are not instantly blinded with the smoke, and if your sight can penetrate into the darkness, enter that hovel, and witness the preparation of your dinner. The table and the dresser, you observe, are Mother Earth . . . The preparation for your dinner must therefore be performed in the earth's broad lap, like everything else in this Eastern land. As a matter of course, you will have curry, the standing dish of the East. There are the slaves, busy at its preparation. The chase for the fowls has terminated in a speedy capture. Already the feathers are being stripped, and the mixture of the spicy condiments is in course of preparation . . . Simplicity is the prevailing feature in an Indian kitchen. A spit, two native saucepans, a ladle, and a knife, comprise all the requirements of an Eastern cook. His grate is extemporised at a moment's warning with a lump of mud and a cruse of water.

The Indian cook had a talent for extemporising, and as long as one did not see him stirring the rice pudding with his fingers or straining the soup through his turban-cloth, the results were reasonably satisfactory. If a London chef had been set down in an Indian kitchen

and there told to prepare a dinner, consisting of every delicacy in fish, flesh, and pudding, for twenty people, by seven o'clock p.m., his first emotion would have a direct tendency to suicide . . . Nothing that he would call a spit, a grate, an oven, or any one convenience would meet his withered eye; and he might as well go to the Highlands to look for knee-buckles, as there to search for a dripping-pan, or a roller, sieves, dredgers, cullenders and such like would be just as plentiful as blackberries are in Hyde Park, and even a dishclout would be very difficult to procure. Yet the indigenous cook will, out of this nettle, deficiency, pluck the flower, good dinner.

The ordeals of inspection did not take up the whole of a mem-sahib's day by any means. The lady with intellectual pretensions might read instructive works, though they often turned out to be only 'improving' in the precise Victorian sense – formidable books with formidable titles, like *The Fulfilment of the Scriptural Prophecies*, or collections of sermons. Books were expensive in Calcutta, and even more so in the outstations. Anyone who came into possession of a novel had to keep the fact secret if she was not to be subjected to constant importuning. Most bungalows boasted a book or two of poems, prominently displayed. Bulwer-Lytton became quite popular and Lord Byron, strangely enough, retained a considerable following. Anglo-Indians were much given to writing verses, though these were seldom published in book form. They were usually used to bulk out the enormous letters that everyone wrote. Most of them had a fashionable touch of melancholy, for one of the continuing themes of Anglo-Indian poetry was exile, a terrible nostalgia for the green fields, simple flowers, and soft rain of England.

As well as reading, and writing poetry, the Anglo-Indian wrote endless letters. There were always relatives at Home anxiously awaiting a really long screed, full of information about everything from local scandal to descriptions (usually inaccurate) of native customs.

Some ladies newly arrived in India took up natural history with uncritical devotion. Young women always seem to have been told before they left England that the insects of India were either not properly classified or totally unknown. In their boredom with life, they determined to rectify the situation. It was 'impossible to go "*à la chasse*" oneself, so I employed the beggar-boys, who at first liked the amusement and brought me a great many'. But they had a habit of becoming tired of collecting *rare* insects and either gave up altogether or only brought horrifying beetles, instead of the beautiful insects that were constantly appearing at dinner and settling in the soup.

It was often a little difficult for the amateur coleopterist to take a purely scientific, and therefore detached, attitude to what were, after all, pests. 'Attracted by the lights, they fly into the room in countless numbers. There is every variety. The long, graceful green mantis alights on the table, and begins stretching out its arms as in an imploring attitude. There are myriads of moths, with wings which seem made of delicate gold and silver tissue; some look inlaid with mother-of-pearl'. These were intriguing, but unfortunately there were also likely to be a 'long, dark, yellow, hornet-shaped insect, with no end of joints, which makes you shudder as it flies by; blister flies, with either ruby or emerald-coloured bodies; large beetles, "armed to the teeth" in black, strong, shining armour, and with horns like formidable spears. These beetles are so strong that, when placed under a wine-glass, they move it before them as they advance along the table'.

The men had some latitude in their choice of entertainment, even if the choice was limited. Women seldom indulged in any kind of sport. Though it was not entirely unknown for a lady to accompany the gentlemen on a tiger hunt, it was still thought to be a little 'fast'. But it could be a most delightful experience. In the cold weather, the jungles were quite beautiful, the trees covered with creepers and blossoms of different colours. Peacocks could not only be heard, giving their peculiar shrieking call, but would actually be seen in great numbers. In front of the hunter's elephants, herds of spotted deer would start out of the undergrowth. But such enjoyment of nature could have its disturbances. A lady might be distracted from admiring the wild roses when a great wild hog appeared and charged the elephant. When the gentlemen shot it and the elephant trampled it to death, it was a disgusting sight which quite marred the day.

After their morning ride, most of the men on the station gathered at the coffee shop for a cup of steaming coffee and a good gossip. Their subjects were usually very much the same as those which occupied the ladies in their bungalows. They might discuss the authentic revelation that the 'prime York ham' which had been presented with such a flourish at the judge's dinner the other night came not from York, but from a ravine near the local river; the native vendor of swine had actually been seen handing over his produce to Mrs Judge on her verandah. Even more entertaining was an eye-witness account of the dance at the Collector's, when the heat was so great that 'Mrs Chunam, who, as it is declared, has elevenpence out of the shilling of Hindoo blood floating in her veins, and who delights to veneer as much of herself as is exposed to public view, for the purpose of the whitening of her otherwise shady complexion – the heat, we understand, was so great that the veneer cracked and peeled off in flakes; and further, that her dress happening to subside from off her shoulders, a lovely olive rim, where the veneer had not been applied, became visible for the general edification'. Or the gentlemen might agree that one of the ladies danced like a 'paviour's rammer', or argue over the song which another of the ladies had favoured the company with. It was all about a 'bonnie coo', and the man who had been present maintained that it was 'a hymn, or at any rate a roundelay' – although one of his hearers immediately placed a bet that it was, in fact, 'a Caledonian melody of an agricultural character'.

Whatever laughter the dinner-parties might afterwards raise in the coffee shop, they were the foundation of social life in the station, especially when some visiting notable passed through. The senior civilians competed strongly for the honour of his presence at table. The district magistrate might be the most expert at catching travellers of renown. 'A governor was once entrapped in his snare, to his unlimited satisfaction; while last year, he skilfully made capture of a bishop, but for whose appropriation popular rumour avows that he betokened symptoms of repentance'. But visitors of any tolerable rank were made more than welcome, if only because they had unfamiliar faces and, perhaps, brought news from Calcutta and the great world outside the station. Travellers were advised to avoid embarrassment for themselves and any friends they might have at a particular station by warning their friends in advance, so as 'literally to give them the start of the three-cornered billets which come tumbling down' on any new arrival.

At dinner parties there was a ritual which was seldom contravened. The host and hostess occupied the centre of the table. At either end were the unfortunate young men who, as the most junior among those present, had to carve the ritual dishes of turkey and ham. It was not unknown for the unhappy dissector of the turkey to consign 'a pound and a half of stuffing into the lap of the adjoining Mrs Koofter'. Greater disasters than that were possible, too. 'The flounce of the punkah becomes partially disengaged and, after flapping about remorselessly like an unreefed sail in a gale of wind, succeeds in whisking off the protecting wire-gauze top of the lamp, and launching it on the apex of Miss Goley's head, occasioning the blowing-out of the lamp, and the consequent oleaginous effluvium that proceeds from the expiring wick . . . Then the punkah has to be stopped to undergo reparation; and frantic and awful is the heat that is engendered thereby.

'Then, after an interregnum of considerable duration, the second course is produced, succeeded by a pause "more fearful than before".

'The sweets have vanished, and at last the dessert, indicative of a concluding climax; the decanters are circulated, and the fair hostess telegraphs . . . the signal for departure and a move (in the right direction) is made.

'Then the gentlemen are doomed to a further session, which terminates in the production of coffee, when the gong tells its tale of midnight. The piano is heard in the adjoining room: some faint voice warbles a doleful strain, the "Burra Beebee" [senior lady] rises, and a general dispersion ensues'.

The dinner would have included iced wines, and probably an iced pudding. Only Calcutta and the coastal cities could make use of the ice imported from America but, inland, there was a traditional method of manufacture which was used to the full. During the cold weather, 'small earthenware vessels of shallow build, resembling saucers in shape, are filled with water, and placed in an open field, upon a low bed of straw. At dawn of day there is a coating of ice upon each vessel, of about the thickness of a shilling. This is collected by men, women and children . . . who receive for each morning's, or hour's work, a sum of money, in cowries, equal to about half of a farthing. When collected, it is carried to an ice-pit, and there stored.

'The expenses are borne by a subscription, and the amount for each ticket depends entirely on the number of subscribers. In some large stations, an ice-ticket for the hot season costs only three pounds. In smaller stations it will cost six pounds. The amount of ice received by each ticket-holder is about four pounds, and is brought away each morning at daylight, in a canvas bag, enveloped in a thick blanket, by the ticket-holder's own servant.

'It is then deposited in a basket made expressly for the purpose. In this basket is placed the wine, beer, water, butter, and fruit. The bag of solid ice is in the centre of all these, and imparts to each an equal coldness. These four pounds of ice, if properly managed, and the air kept out of the basket, will cool an inconceivable quantity of fluids, and will last for twenty-four hours – that is to say, there will be some ice remaining when the fresh bag is brought in'.

If the station included a regiment – not all stations did – there would be amateur theatricals, put on by the junior officers. Among the more puritanical Christians, a strong disapproval of this type of entertainment developed, though no such disapproval was felt when another type of contemporary distraction was offered – a Thug's demonstration of the methods he had used to murder innocent travellers. This may have been because the British were justifiably proud of having stamped out the terrible cult whose adherents robbed and killed in the name of the Hindu goddess, Kali. By the time Victoria came to the throne, the campaign against the Thugs had been going on for twelve years, with considerable success. But there were still many Thugs around, sheltering from the British in the native states, who had to be persuaded to move against them. It was always possible that a local jail might contain a few Thugs awaiting transport to another district.

The Thugs used a scarf to strangle their victims, and were quite happy to demonstrate how they did it to anyone who cared to watch. 'Some of them pretended to be travellers, and the others joined them and flattered them, and asked them to sit down and smoke, and then pointed up to the sun, or a bird; and when the traveller looked up, the noose was round his neck in an instant, and of course, as a *real* traveller, he would have been buried in five minutes'.

In a highly formal society – formal at least in its public face – the worship of God had a special significance. Church attendance was not only a social duty but an expression of solidarity. This was, however, scarcely the solidarity of Christians as Christians, nor was the church a meeting place for men and women of all colours united in worship.

[115]

When William Howard Russell enquired as to the identity of a man riding in a very smart carriage, complete with liveried servants, he was told: 'That is the chaplain of the station, who marries, and baptises, and performs services for the Europeans.' 'Does he go among the natives?' 'Not he; he leaves that to the missionaries, of whom there are lots here.'

More often than not, the chaplain was quite a decent fellow, and if you visited him in his bungalow you would probably find 'a hearty welcome and some excellent bitter beer. His sanctum will recall your college days – gowns, guns and hunting-whips promiscuously combine: here a MS sermon lies complacently by a cookery-book and a *Bell's Life*; while there a packet of letters and a prospectus of the races, with the hospital report and a receipt for milk-punch'.

The inhabitants of the station had as little as possible to do with the natives, but contact could not be entirely avoided. The civilian had his court to contend with, the officer his sepoys. Others managed to avoid encounters even if they were supposed to have a duty to the natives. The station doctor, for example, often treated only Europeans, though he was paid 'head money' for every native soldier in the garrison. The ladies knew nothing whatever about any natives other than their own servants. Even ladies who indulged in missionary activities usually confined their evangelism to their domestics, while those few who took an earnest interest in 'the Hindoo way of life' wrote the mass of Indians off as quaint, heathenish and childish, in fairly equal proportions. But every station seems to have had a pet prince, or raja.

At Cawnpore, for example, there was the Nana Sahib who was very popular with the inhabitants of the station. He was the adopted son of a distinguished prince who had, at one time, ruled a great state; defeated by the British, he had settled in luxurious exile at Bithur, a few miles from Cawnpore. For thirty-three years the British had paid him a lavish pension. When he died in 1851, the British refused to transfer his pension to his 'son'. This did not seem to upset the Nana Sahib greatly. He entertained generously, and, whatever his religious beliefs, had no prejudices about serving beef and pork. His palace was full of European wares, deployed in such confusion that they were the cause of much innocent, and sometimes badly concealed, amusement. During the early period of his contact with Europeans, the same confusion reigned over his dinner table. A guest might be:

> sat down to a table twenty feet long (it had originally been the mess table of a cavalry regiment), which was covered with a damask table-cloth of European manufacture, but instead of a dinner-napkin, there was a bedroom towel. The soup . . . was served up in a trifle-dish which had formed part of a dessert service belonging to the 9th Lancers – at all events, the arms of that regiment were upon it; but the plate into which I ladled it with a broken teacup was of the old willow pattern. The pilao which followed the soup was served upon a huge plated dish, but the plate from which I ate was of the very commonest description. The knife was a bone-handled affair; the spoon and the fork were of silver, and of Calcutta make. The plated side-dishes, containing vegetables, were odd ones; one was round, the other oval. The pudding was brought in upon a soup-plate of blue and gold pattern, and the cheese was placed before me on a glass dish belonging to a dessert service. The cool claret I drank out of a richly-cut champagne glass, and the beer out of an American tumbler, of the very worst quality.

As time went on, the Nana Sahib became more sophisticated and his parties were well attended. The Nana was extremely charming, his manner courteous, his gifts munificent – and it would have been bad manners to refuse such elegant shawls and jewels. The Nana, of course, was assumed like most native princes to indulge in nameless orgies in the Indian-style part of his palace, in rooms decorated with pornographic pictures. It made him all the more attractive (though no one would have admitted it).

★ ★ ★

In the nineteenth century the British in India lifted their eyes up unto the hills – and went there to recover their strength. Before they had really established their rule in India, they had found themselves confined to enclaves on the coast; they went no further than the adjacent countryside in an attempt to gain some respite from the hot weather. But by the time of Victoria's accession, the British conquest of India had opened up the high hills, and the practice of going there was firmly established. To leave the sweltering plains produced, in many, a sense of ecstasy. 'The scene was grand, and the effect upon the mind almost overpowering; but soon this feeling of exultation subsided into an extreme exhilaration of the animal spirits, as involuntary as though we had swallowed a tolerable dose of laughing-gas, and recklessly bid defiance to the grovelling cares of the world below.' And the first weeks merely confirmed that here was paradise. 'You luxuriated in the cool air. Your appetite improved. The mutton had a flavour which you did not recollect in India. Strange, yet true, the beef was tender, and even the "unclean" pork was not too much for your robust digestion. You praised the vegetables, and fell into ecstasy at the sight of peaches, apples, strawberries, and raspberries, after years of plantains, guavas, and sweet limes. You, who could scarcely walk a mile in the low country . . . wandered for hours over hill and dale without being fatigued. With what strange sensations of pleasure you threw yourself upon the soft turf bank, and plucked the first daisy which you ever saw out of England! And how you enjoyed the untropical sensation of sitting over a fire in June! – that very day last year you were in a state of semi-existence, only "kept going" by the power of punkahs and quasi-nudity.'

Each of the great centres of Anglo-Indian life had its hill station, sometimes more than one. The English in Bombay, for example, had Poona and Mahableshwar. Until 1819 Poona had been the capital of the Maratha prince who became the adoptive father of Cawnpore's pet raja, the Nana Sahib. The hot-weather residence of the governor of Bombay was at Dapoorie, eight miles from Poona. Lady Falkland found it extremely pleasant, a simple place consisting of a number of bungalows in an extensive garden which, in the rains, became 'daily more beautiful. Trees and plants seemed to revive, creepers burst into blossom, running over large trees, and hanging in graceful festoons, or garlands, which are seen peeping through the thick foliage'. There were disadvantages. In the rains, at any rate, there was no respite from pests, and the garden of Eden did not lack its snakes. Lady Falkland, however, 'soon became accustomed to the sound of a snake coming to an untimely end, and have sometimes been awakened in the morning, by the servants killing one in the verandah'.

Dapoorie was all very well for the governor and his lady, but it was rather inconvenient for people staying at Poona, who were expected to make morning visits to pay their respects, and to attend dinners and balls. The distance that had to be covered required 'a considerable portion of fascination in a host and hostess to reconcile their guests to such an expedition on a wet night, or when the thermometer stands above 88°'. Still, few men in the hierarchy of Anglo-India had a greater 'portion of fascination' than a governor.

Even with the best will in the world, the roads could make very hard going for carriages. This meant that everyone might be late and the hostess might find herself wondering if anyone would come at all. At last, however, carriages would be heard. 'But out of them came people perfectly useless at balls – a middle-aged colonel, or a collector, who I knew made a point of never dancing. Then wheels approached again, and a troop of young hussars advanced. I began to think all womankind had been drowned. At last, some ladies appeared. I always knew, by the expression of the aide-de-camp's face, who was about to enter: he was all smiles when flounces, feathers, and fans were at hand; while his face lengthened at the sight of swords, spurs, and sabretaches.'

Safe arrival did not mean that the tribulations of the hostess (and her guests) were over. The ballroom might be invaded by blister-flies; if one of these insects were crushed against the skin a large and painful blister immediately developed. 'Some of these little tormenters climbed up into flounces, hid themselves in folds of net, visited the mysterious recesses of complicated trimmings; some crept up gentlemen's sleeves, others concealed themselves in a jungle of whisker, and there was something very attractive in a bald head, the owner of which, in removing the insect, was sure to blister his hand, or skull, or both. One heard little else all the evening but "Allow me, sir, to take off this blister-fly, that is disappearing into your neck-cloth", or "Permit me, ma'am, to remove this one from your arm"'. But the dancers were not to be discouraged. 'They polked and waltzed over countless myriads of insects that had been attracted by the white cloth on the floor, which was completely discoloured by their mangled bodies at the end of the evening.'

The main problem at Poona (and most other hill stations) was the difficulty of finding accommodation, 'for in addition to the three or four regiments always stationed in Poona, and the numerous visitants from Bombay; all the civilians and engineers, flock in with their families, from their respective districts, too happy to exchange their tents and jungle life for comfortable bungalows and a regular holiday-making in Poona. The best houses are frequently engaged from the previous year; but woe to the unwary man who has delayed providing himself with a shelter before the season begins!' A number of people had opened hotels, but all proved unsuccessful owing to 'the exorbitance of the charges, and the total disregard of comfort and cleanliness of the establishment'.

The Poona station, though larger than most because of the presence of so many soldiers, was very much like any other down in the plains. Everything, however, was really designed to suit the garrison – even the church, which the architect had designed in such a way that there were plenty of seats for the military but very few for the civilians. If the churchgoing civilian did not arrive early, there was very little chance of finding a seat, or even standing room in the aisle. 'This very economical arrangement', one visitor decided, nevertheless had 'its peculiar advantages, inasmuch as it greatly tends towards filling the Scotch church which is immediately opposite; and doubtless the engineer who superintended its construction had some such object in view'.

The presence of so many soldiers meant that each regiment vied with the others in giving balls and dinners. The expense of the entertainments, and of furnishing the mess with plate, usually fell heavily upon the junior officers. Most of them, in fact, laid the foundation of debts that followed them throughout their service. These 'accumulating rapidly from year to year, by the fearful interest charged upon borrowed money, reach at length to a height of inextricable involvement, which dooms the victim to a perpetual residence in India'. Most of the senior officers in the Company's regiments were married men who only used the mess on rare occasions. Other officers were almost permanently absent on other duties, on the Staff, perhaps, or as political agents. This left the young subalterns to carry the burden. It was nothing rare to find that the junior officers, 'thus shackled by heavy mess expenditure, have actually not received one rupee of their pay for several months! The small surplus remaining from the inevitable items of Mess Bill, Military Fund, Library, and Band, being totally absorbed in the extra charges for "guest nights", balls, and "contributions for new mess kit"'. Even the delights of a good amateur theatre and fancy dress balls could not prevent many of the young officers from seeking other employment which would release them from the costs of regimental life.

Madras, like Bombay, had its military hill station. At Bangalore, the air smelt 'of hay and flowers, instead of ditches, dust, fried oil, curry and onions, which are the *best* of the Madras smells'. Furthermore, the station had 'an English church, a Heathen pagoda, botanical garden, public ballrooms, Dissenting meeting-house, circulating library, English shops, and Parsee merchants, all within sight of each other'.

Bangalore was not quite a hill station. It was not really high enough up for that, and though the climate was very pleasant for someone coming up from the humid heat of Madras it had its dangers. Though the gardens of the bungalows were sometimes very beautiful, they were also damp, and a sharp attack of fever often resulted from a walk down the 'sweet, shady walks which all smelt of ague'.

At Bangalore, as at Poona, most of the British were military. The wives rode about 'in habits made according to the uniform of their husbands' regiment'. The more superior, senior ladies 'seem never to become Indianised . . . Some of them keep up schools for the English soldiers' children, girls especially – superintend them, watch over the soldiers' wives, try to keep and encourage them in good ways, and are quite a blessing to their poor countrywomen'.

From Bangalore it was possible to go up to a real hill station in the Nilgiri hills. In about 1850 a line of what were called 'transit coaches' was established between the two places. 'The carriages were what were known as "nibs" and were two wheeled and water proof with venetians and glass windows. They were drawn by bullocks which were changed every five miles . . . If not pressed for time this was a pleasant way of travelling, with a chance of some shooting *en route*. A servant could be carried on the covered seat by the driver, and there was room for a portmanteau, gun-case, etc. in the well of the conveyance.'

The station in the Nilgiri hills was Ootacamund, or Ooty, as it became affectionately known in the late 1840s. When Captain Burton visited it, he found it delightful, at least for a time. But many things began to annoy him, once he had recovered his usual jaundiced attitude to all things Indian. The architecture he found particularly repellent. 'The style bungalow – a modification of the cow-house – is preferred: few tenements have upper stories, whilst almost all are surrounded by a long low verandah, perfectly useless in such a climate, and only calculated to render the interior of the domiciles as dim and gloomy as can be conceived.' If the diminutive, scantily furnished rooms, 'with their fireplaces, curtained beds, and boarded floors, faintly remind you of Europe, the bare walls, putty-less windows and doors that admit draughts of air small yet cutting as lancets, forcibly impress you with the conviction that you have ventured into one of those uncomfortable localities – a cold place in a hot country'. In the rain, Burton found the country impassable, 'the cantonment dirty, every place wretched, everyone miserable'.

The ladies at Ooty were the usual Anglo-Indian assortment, from the elderly, delighting in scandal to the youthful, like the 'young lady who discourses of her papa the Colonel, and disdains to look at anything below the rank of a field-officer'. The men were no improvement – 'misanthropes and hermits who inhabit out-of-the-way abodes, civilians on the shelf, authors, linguists, oriental students, amateur divines who periodically convert their drawing-rooms into chapels of ease rather than go to church, sportsmen, worshippers of Bacchus in numbers . . . We have clergymen, priests, missionaries, tavern-keepers, school-masters and scholars with *précieux* and *précieuses ridicules* of all descriptions'.

Burton could not even find a good word for the dances, though a hill station was the only place in India where there were often more women than men. After the ladies had retired at the early hour of 3 a.m., worn out with their exertions, the men would settle down to a substantial hot meal, followed by singing and 'a little horseplay in different parts of the room', until finally, with 'very pallid complexions', they wound off 'along a common road, leading, as each conceives, directly to his own abode'.

There was sport to be had, and a pack of hounds. There was bison, though hunting it required 'a cool head and a steady hand'. It was usually shot 'with an ounce or two ounce iron or brass balls, and plugs made by the hill-people, who cut a bar of metal and file it down to the size required with the rudest tools and remarkable neatness'. The ibex was another favourite quarry, though it was 'addicted to scrambling down and rolling over tremendous precipices', which meant that the hunter either lost the beast or had to risk his neck to retrieve the carcase.

In the north, there were a number of 'sanatoria' in the foothills of the Himalayas. There was Mussoorie, for example, which quite inexplicably reminded Fanny Parkes, when she visited it in 1838, of 'the back of the Isle of Wight'. There was an excellent family hotel run by a Mr Webb, with a ballroom and five billiard tables.

The most important of the Himalayan hill resorts was Simla, which was to become the summer residence of the governor-general and, because of that, the Anglo-Indian Olympus – though it was also to be known by many less complimentary names. The heyday of Simla came after the Mutiny, but it had been known and liked since the area became part of British India after the Nepal war in 1815. The first house built by a European in Simla was erected in the 1820s, and the town had grown and continued to grow because as one visitor wrote in 1828, 'the temperature of Simla seems peculiarly adapted to the European constitution. We have reason to be thankful that we are here far elevated above the atmospheric strata that have hitherto been subjected to the cholera, a disease now raging in Calcutta'. When Emily Eden arrived in Simla ten years later, she could reflect that:

There we were, with the band playing the 'Puritani' and 'Masaniello', and eating salmon from Scotland, and sardines from the Mediterranean, and observing that St Cloup's potage à la Julienne was perhaps better than his other soups, and that some of the ladies' sleeves were too tight according to the overland fashions for March &c; and all this in the face of those high hills, some of which have remained untrodden since the creation, and we 105 Europeans being surrounded by at least 3,000 mountaineers, who, wrapped up in their hill blankets, looked on at what we call our polite amusements, and bowed to the ground, if a European came near them. I sometimes wonder they do not cut all our heads off and say nothing more about it.

But it was another hill people who were actually about to cut off English heads. While the Eden sisters were in Simla with their brother, the governor-general, British forces were on their way to put a long deposed ruler of Afghanistan back on his throne. At first, the British appeared to be successful, but, in the end, British troops were massacred, envoys murdered and their weakness revealed for all to see. At Simla, they heard only of the victories. The ladies who had refused to dance until their husbands returned from Afghanistan weakened, and gave in. After all, the triumph of British arms had to be celebrated.

In Emily Eden's time in Simla there was a remarkably beautiful young woman who became a focus for stares and criticism. The newcomer was only seventeen and had eloped with an army officer whose surname was James. Mrs James and her husband – 'a smart-looking man with bright waistcoats and bright teeth' – came up to Simla to stay with her mother, and everyone found her very attractive. Miss Eden considered her 'very pretty, and such a merry unaffected girl'. She even felt quite sorry for her, married to a man fifteen years her senior, with very little money, and a lifetime in India before her. Simla society would have been incredulous had they been able to look into the future of 'little Mrs James'. A few years later, she made a second elopement and left for Europe, there to embark on a career which was notoriously scandalous. Under the name of Lola Montez, she became, for a year, the virtual ruler of Bavaria, having entirely captivated the king. Her life ended in New York in 1861.

Simla began to find itself more than just another hill resort during the governor-generalship of Lord Dalhousie, who spent a great deal of time there despite the fact that in 1849 he remarked that the place was 'overrated in climate and everything else'. This sourness may have been induced by his going down, on his arrival, 'with an influenza – a genuine Piccadilly influenza'. He also found that there were too many festivities, 'balls here, balls there, balls to the Society, balls by the Society, amateur plays, concerts, fancy fairs, investitures of the Bath &c., &c.. I quite sigh for the quiet of Calcutta'. Nevertheless, he built a new road over the mountains and was able to claim that 'most of it has been done by free labour, which the native tributary states are bound to contribute, and its cost in actual outlay has thus been inconsiderable'.

Sir Charles Napier, when commander-in-chief, took a dislike to hill stations and the custom of going there for months on end. His orders restricting officers' leave were much resented in the army. Napier's point was that, if the British soldier had to remain in the plains, his officers should, too. In the usual Anglo-Indian manner, Napier was heavily attacked by anonymous authors and, in particularly, in a humourous periodical called the *Delhi Sketch Book*. The standard of the verse was not very high, but the feeling behind it was much to the point:

> And all leave to the hills
> Has been stopped, and one grills;
> In the plains, like a Shadrach in his furnace flame;
> While all the time he [Napier] swears
> That public affairs
> Prevent him from doing, *as he'd like to do*, the same!

Society in Simla revolved round the governor-general. As one visitor wrote: 'An officer aspiring to get a civil or military appointment, who desired to get to some place where, by currying favour with the great, he might create an influence for himself sufficient to secure that object, would select Simla.' The gentlemen, and their wives, adopted various methods of attracting attention. One lady was very good at sketching portraits, and she drew the governor-general – without his knowledge, of course – in every conceivable attitude, on horseback and on foot. These sketches were placed in a prominent position during a ball, and very soon the name of the artist was being passed about. 'The wife of another civilian, however, maliciously neutralised the effect these sketches probably would have had, by falsely saying, loud enough for his Lordship to hear, "Ah! she said she would do the trick with her pencil!" The consequence was, that when the lady's husband begged his Lordship would accept this collection of portraits, as well as a few sketches of the house inhabited by the Great Man, his Lordship – as delicately and gracefully as the circumstances would admit of – "declined them with many thanks"; just as though they had been so many unsuitable contributions to some popular periodical.'

Another amateur artist was more successful by appealing to a typical love of animals. She sketched in full colour a likeness of the commander-in-chief's favourite charger, and presented it to him. 'And the next *Gazette* made known that Captain C – was a Major of Brigade.'

By the time of the Mutiny, Simla was acquiring an enduring reputation for 'bright ladies and gay gentlemen'. There appear to have been some wild spirits around, some high living and high gambling and a great deal of not-so-harmless flirting. Yet at the same time such ladies as Mrs Colonel Mackenzie were visiting the Simla church to take drawings of the new stained glass window for the Bishop of Calcutta. The window had been causing trouble. There were some people who objected to it on the grounds that the natives would regard it as an object of worship, an idol, while others thought that the figure of the Redeemer with a lamb was not only irreverent but calculated to distract the congregation. The Bishop had even received a letter which talked of the inexpediency of having 'these figures in the midst of a heathen population'.

Still, Simla was pleasant even for Christian ladies. The Mall was crowded with people, and the women were wearing finer bonnets than Mrs Mackenzie had seen for many a day. The servants who carried the *jampan* – a kind of armchair supported on two sticks, which was the normal transport for ladies – wore livery. 'Most of them are in plaid tunics and trousers edged with red, looking like magnified little boys; but others are in long robes, generally black down to their feet, with deep red borders, and red caps; so that the first man having a wand in his hand, they look like a company of magicians.' No wheeled carriages were allowed at Simla, and the only alternative to the *jampan* was horseback. The favourite ride was round a hill called Jakko where, thoughtfully, a macadamised road was provided.

The time inevitably came when there must be a return to the plains. Even though this meant that the cold weather had arrived, it was still something of a wrench to leave Simla, 'poor, dear Simla', as Emily Eden called it when she turned back for her last view of it. Wives went back to their husbands and a more discreet existence, until the next time. Men went back to their lonely outposts and cuffed a servant or two, to let off steam. The average season at Simla was 'a very pleasant one . . . enlivened by several exciting incidents – to wit, a duel, a police affair, court martial, and an elopement'.

—— *ENTR'ACTE* ——

# THE DEVIL'S WIND

It was the Devil's Wind, your Honour, that blew us into madness.
Subadar Mansab Lal in answer to the question:
'Why did you mutiny?' Court Martial. Lucknow 1858

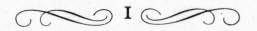

# AT THE EDGE OF THE ABYSS

I N Northern India in 1857, as the hot weather approached, people commented on its mildness. They were eating strawberries in Lucknow as late as the end of April, and even in Calcutta the punkah did not come into use until May. Everywhere, the routines of Anglo-Indian life ran smoothly. On Sunday the churches, pleasantly cool, were full of officers in summer uniforms, civilians in black coats and white trousers, ladies in light sprigged muslins. Life was comfortable, or as comfortable as it could be made. Delicacies from Europe were now easily obtainable, and so were the foods that made the British feel they were at Home – tinned Cambridge sausages, Cheddar cheese, Portuguese sardines. But these were costly, especially in the up-country stations, and the substantial Anglo-Indian breakfast was more likely to consist of devilled turkey, Irish stew, fresh fish, or a pigeon pie, with tea, beer, and iced claret.

Yet there were ripples in the great dark sea that surrounded the little islands of white life. For months there had been rumours of dissatisfaction in the Bengal army. Tales were told of secret meetings in the sepoy lines, where the terrible news that the British intended to turn all sepoys into Christians was discussed and discussed again. In the countryside, too, there was a strange unrest. It was said – by whom, nobody knew – that British rule was coming to an end, and that it would happen on the centenary of the battle of Plassey, which had begun it all on 24 June 1757. From village to village, they were passing the flat cakes of flour and water known as *chapatis*. A messenger would arrive, bearing them, saying that they had been brought to his own village and must be passed on. No one knew their meaning, no one dared disobey the summons to pass them on.

The news reached British officials. What could it mean? Some argued that it was a method of carrying away disease. In one part of the country, in fact, cholera broke out after the chapatis had circulated. One official believed that their message was the message of the fiery cross, but his superior, to whom he reported these fears, replied that it was probably a case of 'a dyer's vat having gone wrong and the dyer was trying to propitiate the gods'. When the Indians were questioned, they said the chapatis meant that something was coming but they did not know what it might be. Others replied that they believed it was by government order.

There was every reason for tension. Behind the bland face of Anglo-India lay a different reality – the great world of India, the India of the village, of the princely state, of the native army. As the British had conquered India and begun to impose their own kind of government, they had stamped on many toes. Princes had been dispossessed of their rights and pensions, landowners found their estates confiscated because they had no written titles to their land – in a country where such things were unknown. Many of these acts were, to some extent, justified, but to people who suffered the consequences there did not appear to be any justification but that of power. Because Indians had already been adjudged by the British as morally despicable, little attempt was made to mollify their feelings. The dispossessed, and those who felt that their turn might very well come next, felt deeply aggrieved; some were already conspiring against the British before the mutiny broke out. Chief among the conspirators were Ahmad Ullah, 'the Maulvi of Faizabad', adviser to the ex-king of Oudh who had been dethroned and whose state had been annexed in 1856; the Rani of Jhansi, whose state had been annexed in 1854; and the Nana Sahib, darling of the British at Cawnpore. But the real threat lay with the sepoys of the Company's army, whose loyalty, in spite of mutinies in the past, had never really been questioned. In 1806, sepoys had rebelled at Vellore, in Madras province, because they had been instructed to shave off their beards, wear a new type of head-dress, and give up caste marks. The men thought this was a deliberate attempt to turn them into Christians. In 1824, a sepoy regiment refused to move for action in Burma because it felt its caste endangered by the refusal to supply special transport for its cooking utensils, and caste usage compelled each man to have his own set. Guns opened fire on them on the parade ground where they had assembled, and next morning six of the ringleaders were hanged and hundreds more condemned to fourteen years' hard labour on the public roads. Five more were later executed and their bodies hung in chains as an example to their fellows. In 1852, another regiment had also refused to cross the sea to Burma. This time the men were merely marched away to another station. A number of smaller mutinies and near-mutinies had taken place. All resulted from fear of caste-pollution and the attempts of over-zealous officers and missionaries to convert the sepoys to Christianity.

It was not only princes, landowners and sepoys who felt them-selves threatened. Ordinary people, too, had suffered under the heavy hand of government. When great estates were sold up, peasants were uprooted as well. Taxes fell heavily on those least able to support their weight. A man could not travel without having to pay a toll to cross a river. Salt, so essential in a tropical country, was a government monopoly, its price inflated by tax. Justice, through the process of law, was too costly to seek. Even oblivion was expensive, for the government exacted its dues on opium and liquor. A tradi-tional society, conscious that something was in the air, turned to traditional magic to protect itself. There was a wide sale of charms against unstated evils. Magical symbols began to appear upon walls. Prophecies were heard throughout the land. The agents of the dispossessed moved freely around, spreading and embroidering rumours. Religious mendicants whispered of the horrors the British were planning.

Naturally, the agitators looked to the sepoy army as fertile ground. Each of the three presidencies into which British India was divided – Bengal, Madras and Bombay – had its own army. The Bengal army was not, in fact, recruited in Bengal, but farther west. Many of the sepoys had their homes in Oudh, an area which was already seething with discontent over the deposition of its king and annexation by the British. The Oudh sepoys had had many privileges in their own country – 'that great nursery of soldiers' as someone called it. The sepoys could, and often did, ask for and receive the British Resident's support against the native government. With annexation, such privileges had disappeared, and, with them, prestige. 'I used to be a great man when I went home', an Oudh cavalryman told Sir Henry Lawrence. 'The best of the village rose as I approached; now the lowest puff their pipes in my face.' Fear of the British and of their inexplicable actions had prepared the sepoys to believe anything, however wild. The old order was undoubtedly being destroyed, and it was by no means improbable that the white man intended to destroy the old religion as well. The situation was emotionally explosive, and it needed only the feeblest of sparks to set it off.

In January 1857 a new weapon was scheduled to be introduced into the Bengal army to replace the old musket affectionately known as 'Brown Bess'. Ironically enough, many senior officers in both the Company's and the queen's forces had resisted the introduction of the new rifle. Most of the men commanding stations were over sixty, set in the ways which many of them had learned under the Iron Duke years before. They were great believers in the virtue of 'cold steel', the bayonet and the sword, but they seem to have felt a similar nostalgia for that inefficient arm, the musket. Their attitude inspired one critic to parody that old Irish song whose first line runs 'Believe me, if all those endearing young charms':

> Believe me, if that most endearing old arm,
>   Which we miss with so fondly today,
> Which never did Afghan or Sikh any harm,
>   Was to shoot straight for once in a way,
> It should still be the weapon for Guardsmen and Line,
>   Let the windage increase as it will;
> And we'd think the performance sufficiently fine,
>   If one ball in five hundred should kill.

The new Enfield rifle had to be loaded with a greased cartridge, the end of which was bitten off before loading. Soon the rumour grew that the grease was made from beef fat or hog's lard, and that an attempt was being made deliberately to break the caste of the Hindus and to insult the religious prejudices of the Muslims. The cow is sacred to Hindus, and the pig is an unclean animal to Muslims. It is difficult for Westerners to understand the sepoys' response to such rumours, because there is nothing in the West so everyday yet so fundamentally sacred as the system of caste. The sepoy envisaged pollution so great that it amounted to a threat of damnation and an interruption of the divine order whose consequences would be terrifying beyond belief.

The greased cartridge rumour had its first effect at Berhampur in Bengal, on 26 February 1857, when the 19th Native Infantry refused to use the cartridge. There were no British troops there, so its officers marched the regiment to the military station of Barrackpore, near Calcutta, to be disbanded under the eyes of a British regiment hastily brought back from Burma. That a regiment of Europeans had to be brought from such a distance merely emphasised the thinness of the British presence in northern India. Most European troops from Bengal itself – and the command stretched from Calcutta to the Afghan frontier – had been moved into the Punjab when it was conquered and annexed eight years earlier, and which had been acquired complete with the troubled Afghan frontier. At Calcutta there was one infantry battalion, and another was stationed about four hundred miles away at Dinapur. One regiment was stationed at Agra, and one at Lucknow. Altogether, in an area as large as France and Germany combined, there were only four battalions and a few batteries of artillery totally manned by Europeans, and therefore reliable. The queen's forces had been considerably reduced because of the demand of the Crimean war. In the spring of 1857, there were no artillery or engineer units, and only four regiments of cavalry and twenty-two infantry battalions in the whole of India. Altogether, there were about 40,000 Europeans of the Company's and royal armies, and the immense total of 300,000 Indians, an overwhelming majority of almost eight to one.

As the hot weather approached, European troops were being moved to cooler stations in the foothills. Officers were going on leave. The commander-in-chief, General Anson – who had seen no fighting since the war against Napoleon over forty years before – had retired with his staff to the hill station of Simla, nearly a thousand miles away from Calcutta, the governor-general, and the civil government.

At Barrackpore, news of the imminent arrival of the 19th Native Infantry had its effect on the sepoys stationed there. On 29 March, a young sepoy fired the first shot in the great Mutiny. Convinced that the British would turn against all sepoys, he put on his uniform and, seizing his musket, walked down to the quarter-guard, calling on his comrades to follow him. At the guard, the sepoy ordered the bugler to sound the call for 'assembly'. The bugler would not, but the men on guard did nothing even when the sepoy fired at an English sergeant-major. The shot went wide.

The adjutant, Lieutenant Baugh, now appeared on the scene, having been alerted by a European colonel. He had loaded his pistols, buckled on his sword, mounted his horse, and ridden down to the guardroom where, as he arrived, another shot was fired. It missed Baugh but brought down his horse. The situation now developed into tragic farce. Baugh fired at the mutineer – and missed. He drew his sword, and he and the sergeant-major rushed at the sepoy. The sepoy seems to have been a much better swordsman than either of the Europeans, for he wounded them both. He might even have succeeded in killing them if another sepoy had not restrained him. But the guards now turned on the two Europeans striking them with the butts of their muskets. One even fired at close range – and missed.

News of what was going on finally reached the officer commanding the station, General Hearsey. He and his two sons had their horses saddled and then galloped to the guardroom. There they saw a crowd of sepoys, mostly unarmed, and a number of European officers milling around in great confusion. The mutineer raised his musket to fire – then turned it on himself instead. But he only succeeded in wounding himself slightly, and was taken prisoner by the guard, now loyally carrying out its duty. This first mutineer's name was Mangal Pandy, and soon all mutineers came to be known as 'pandies'.

## 2

# UP AMONG THE PANDIES

O N Saturday night, young Lieutenant Gough sat on his verandah in the harsh darkness of an Indian May. The city of Meerut, away from the military lines, bubbled with more noise than usual, but it was quiet on the lieutenant's verandah, except for the perpetual hum of insects which forms the background to night in India.

Lieutenant Gough thought back over a day which was the most disturbing he had ever spent. It had been dark and heavy, with low clouds, and a dry hot wind had blown across the parade ground. There had been some 4,000 men there, drawn up to form three sides of a hollow square. What a sight they had been – the shining brass helmets and leather breeches of the Bengal Artillery officers; the black horsehair plumes of the Dragoon Guards; the olive green of the 60th Native Rifles; the silver-grey of his own 3rd Cavalry; and, of course, the scarlet coats and white collars of the Native Infantry. To the casual eye, it might have been just another of the ceremonial parades which the commander loved to mount. But no eye at that parade had been casual. All had been wary, some angry, many a mirror of fear. The Indian troops carried their arms, but everyone knew that their ammunition pouches were empty – by order. The British troops had their rifles, the new Enfield rifles, loaded, and they pointed them at their Indian comrades.

On the fourth, open side of the square stood eighty-five sepoys. They were clad in their uniforms, but their feet were bare and they carried no weapons. Around them stood a guard of British soldiers, themselves wary and hard of face. A British officer read aloud from a paper, but the dry wind seemed to blow his words away like fallen leaves. An Indian officer, with no flicker of emotion, translated into Hindustani, and the words appeared to touch all the sepoys present. Then there was silence – and afterwards soldiers ripped the buttons from the sepoys' uniforms and the coats from their backs. Armourers with tools and shackles came forward and slowly began to fix fetters on the condemned men.

Among the condemned were many who had served the British government in harsh battles and strange places, and had never before wavered in their allegiance. As the fetters were placed upon them, they lifted up their hands and implored the general to have mercy on them, but seeing no hope there they turned to their comrades and reproached them for standing aside and allowing them to be disgraced. There was not a sepoy present who did not feel indignation rising in his throat. Many of them were in tears but what could they have done in the face of the loaded field guns and rifles, and the glittering sabres of the Dragoons? For a moment, it had seemed to Lieutenant Gough as if the sepoys were about to attack the British with their bare hands; but the prisoners were marched off and the tension eased.

Gough had gone down to the temporary jail and had been deeply shocked by the grief of the men, who had begged him to save them. Now, in the dark of the verandah, he wondered what would happen next. It was just over a fortnight since the eighty-five men had refused to use the new cartridges, and only a day since the court-martial – of native officers – had found them guilty of mutiny. Gough's reflections were shattered by a rustle in the darkness, as a figure approached silently, almost furtively. But it was no thief. A whisper identified it as a native officer of his own troop, who had come, he said, to discuss the troop's accounts. Gough found this puzzling. It was a Saturday night, a night for leisure, not for routine business. Then suddenly the true reasons for the visit came pouring out. The lieutenant-sahib must know that tomorrow, Sunday, the men would mutiny – all of them, even the cavalry, the sahib's own men. They would break open the jail and release their comrades. Murder was planned, murder and fire.

After the man had left, Gough went to the Mess and informed his colonel. His story was greeted with laughter and contempt, and he was told that he should be ashamed of listening to such an idle tale. But Gough was convinced, and he made another attempt – he went to the brigadier commanding the station. His reception was no better here. If no one else was worried, why should Lieutenant Gough concern himself?

The next day was 10 May, and all Gough could see when he went out on his verandah was a sea of flame on the horizon. Galloping down to the cavalry lines, he found 'a thousand sepoys dancing and leaping frantically about, calling and yelling to each other', and blazing away with their muskets in all directions. By nightfall, Meerut was a city of horror. British officers had been cut down by their own men, women had been violated – not by men, but by sticks of burning tow and thatch thrust far into their bodies.

Everywhere there was chaos and confusion. Senior officers seemed struck with paralysis. There were as many British as native troops in Meerut, and the British had artillery, yet nothing was organised. Some of the younger officers did what they could, but the mutineers broke open the jail and, unhindered, set off for Delhi, some forty miles away to the south-west.

No one pursued them. Next morning, the first of them reached Delhi. Some went to the palace of Bahadur Shah, titular king of Delhi and last sad remnant of the once powerful Mughal empire. They proclaimed him emperor of Hindustan. Others joined their fellows in the three native regiments stationed in Delhi and persuaded them to kill their officers and then hunt to death the Europeans in the city. A last message went out on the telegraph line: 'The sepoys have come in from Meerut and are burning everything. Mr Todd is dead and we hear several Europeans . . . We must shut up.' Delhi was in the hands of five thousand rebel soldiers; the English who had survived the massacre fled the city. The Indian Mutiny had begun.

In spite of all the warnings, the British were caught by surprise, which in most cases they compounded with ineptitude. For a time, British rule disappeared from large areas of northern India, and men and women were freely tortured and murdered. The story of the

Mutiny is one of many heroisms – some great, many small. But perhaps the most remarkable courage of all was shown by the women. Used to a life in which they were wholly pampered by their menfolk and by their servants, under stress the majority of them showed a toughness and determination no one would have suspected to exist behind the façade of the 'gently-nurtured' lady of Victorian convention. Nowhere was this courage shown by as many as inside the besieged Residency at Lucknow.

Until 1856, Lucknow had been the capital of the kingdom of Oudh. When Oudh was annexed, the king had been sent off to a comfortable exile in Calcutta, but he left behind hundreds of functionaries, tradesmen who had depended on the court for their livelihood, and pensioners who would have to wait for the British to investigate their claims. Many of these men and their families were starving. Furthermore, three-quarters of the state's forces had been disbanded. And lastly, there were new taxes and new laws which pressed heavily upon the people. A tax on opium raised the price to such a level that there were many suicides among addicts who could no longer afford the drug. The people of Oudh were ready for rebellion.

On 20 March 1857, Sir Henry Lawrence, well-tested in the service of the Company, was appointed to the charge of Oudh. The situation in Lucknow and the countryside was immediately clear to his unprejudiced eye – the materials of revolt lay everywhere. Lawrence's reports to the governor-general were precise and accurate, but there was to be no time to rectify the wrongs, no time for the British to do anything but fight for their lives.

By early April, the new cartridges were having repercussions in Oudh, and incidents had occurred among the sepoys. Lawrence did his best, by a mixture of firmness and conciliation. He was temporarily successful in reminding the sepoys of their loyalty, but the emotions that had been roused were not capable of being calmed by reason or crushed by inadequate strength. And the strength was inadequate. The number of European troops in Oudh was ridiculously small and widely scattered, and the men were outnumbered by nearly ten to one. Lawrence began preparations to meet the crisis he could foresee. He began to fortify the Residency.

Lucknow was an extravagant and magnificent city. William Howard Russell was astounded by it:

A vision of palaces . . . domes azure and golden, cupolas, col-onnades, long façades of fair perspective in pillar and column, terraced roofs – all rising up amid a calm still ocean of the brightest verdure. Look for miles and miles away, and still the ocean spreads, and the towers of the fairy-city gleam in its midst. Spires of gold glitter in the sun. Turrets and gilded spheres shine like constellations. There is nothing mean or squalid to be seen. There is a city more vast than Paris, as it seems, and more brilliant.

The Residency area, which included a large number of offices as well as the houses of officials, stood to the north of the city on a raised plateau backing on to the river Gumti. Further up the river was an old fort, in which there was a garrison. The houses and narrow streets of the city embraced the Residency area closely; militarily, it was almost indefensible.

News of the rising at Meerut arrived at Lucknow on 13 May. Five days later, after outbreaks of arson and in the face of disturbing rumours of more trouble to come, work began on fortifying the old fort, the Màchchi Bhawan, and preparations in the Residency were speeded up. By the end of May, the revolt had begun in earnest, but the European force was able to prevent a massacre. It even chased the mutineers into the countryside – which was also in revolt. By early June, British rule in Oudh no longer existed. 'Every outpost, I fear, has fallen', wrote Lawrence on 12 June, 'and we daily expect to be besieged by the confederated mutineers and their allies'. The British in Lucknow withdrew into the Residency.

On 9 June, Mrs Katherine Bartrum had arrived at the Residency from the tiny out-station of Gonda. Her husband, Captain Robert Bartrum, was the station surgeon. Katherine was twenty-three, a shy, dark-haired girl, daughter of a Bath silversmith. Happy in Gonda with her masterful husband and little son, Bobbie, who was fifteen months old, she resisted being sent off to Calcutta because she believed it was better to die with her husband than to leave him. Never 'very brave', she claimed, the news of the fresh outbreaks made her tremble. 'I could neither sleep, eat, or do anything', she wrote to her sister, 'but look to my husband for protection against foes which I fancied near at hand'. But she gained courage and no longer expected Bobbie, 'the merriest little fellow you ever saw', to be snatched from her arms and murdered before her very eyes.

Nevertheless, she and Robert slept with a loaded pistol and a sword under their pillows, and Katherine consoled herself with her husband's promise that, 'should things come to the worst, he would destroy me with his own hand rather than let me fall into the power of those brutal Sepoys'.

When the order came from Sir Henry Lawrence for women and children at the out-stations to go into Lucknow, Katherine still did not want to leave. Robert was adamant. If only for the sake of the baby, she must go to the safety of the Residency. 'God alone knows', she wrote later, 'how bitter was the struggle to feel that it was my duty to leave him'. Robert accompanied his wife and the wife of a civilian for the first sixteen miles of the eighty-mile journey to Lucknow. Then they parted, the two women and the child on the backs of elephants, to continue to Lucknow with an escort of sepoys, and the men back to their stations.

The two women were far from sure of the sepoys. 'Sometimes they made our elephant stand still whilst they lay upon the ground laughing and talking; but whenever I asked them for water for baby to drink, they would give it to me.' On one occasion Katherine saw the men of the escort loading their muskets. When she asked what they were going to do, they replied: 'Oh, there are so many bad people about, we are going to fight for you'. Finally, the party caught up with another, larger one. As the seven women, twelve children, and four officers moved on through a countryside which was full of marauders and burning buildings, they became even more doubtful of the loyalty of the sepoy escort. In the end, when they sighted Lucknow, they fled from the escort and arrived at the Residency exhausted, covered with dust, and full of anxiety as to 'the fate of those dearest to us, whom we had left behind'.

The Residency came as something of a shock to Katherine Bartrum. The house she was assigned to was 'a most uninviting looking place, so dirty, having neither a punkah to cool the air or a scrap of furniture to set if off'. She knew no one nearby, and never even met most of the few people she did know elsewhere in the Residency area. She was alone, 'left for the first time to take care of myself, separated from dear Robert, and ignorant of what had become of him'. As well as being separated from her loved one, Katherine was also – unprecedentedly – without servants and, above all, without the space and privacy she had always been accustomed to. 'On that first night we slept, fifteen in one room, packed closely together, so that each might feel the benefit of the punkah, which Mrs Boileau with her usual energy and forethought had managed to have put up during the day. We had to endure intense heat (for this was the hottest part of the year) mosquitoes and flies in swarms. How great a change after the comforts of our own homes!'

Robert escaped from Gonda when the sepoys mutinied, and his letter telling his wife of his escape was full of comfort: 'I trust that grace may be given us both to support this spirit of perfect dependence upon the Almighty, and that if we do not incur danger the effect may not pass from us; but that I may be a more fitting companion to you in the road that leads to life.' Katherine was to receive only one more letter from her husband.

'Each day brought in fresh fugitives from the out-stations, and fearful were the tales they told of the cruel scenes they had witnessed, and from which, through the mercy of God, they had escaped.' The place to which they had escaped was to provide its own cruel scenes as the weeks dragged on. Many of the children were already beginning to look sickly, through the effects of close confinement in the intense heat. Bobbie was still 'fat and bonnie', but Katherine Bartrum could not overcome her fears for him.

By 27 June, it was clear that the siege of the Residency had begun in earnest. It was now impossible to get food cooked, and Katherine had no means of doing it herself. However, the wife of an English soldier was found to bring hot water for breakfast and tea. Katherine found herself 'fully occupied in nursing, and washing our clothes, together with cups and saucers, and fanning away the flies, which have become a fearful nuisance'. So bad were they that sometimes, when food was placed on the table, they swarmed to cover it, black and loathsome.

[143]

Because the other occupants were too ill to keep the room clean, Katherine undertook the task. 'So long as God gives me health and strength I will do my best to add to the comfort of others, even if I afford them amusement by giving them occasion to call me the servant-of-all-work.' Her day was very simple. She was up as soon as it was light to wash and dress the children and tidy the room that was both bedroom and living room. After breakfast, which was never appetising, the rest of the day was occupied with such domestic chores as were necessary and possible. Time dragged so much that 'it was almost a blessing to have no servants, because it gave us so much occupation that we had less time to dwell upon our troubles and anxieties concerning those absent from us'. When the children at last fell asleep, 'we used to gather round a chair, which formed our tea-table, sitting on the bedside, and drinking our tea (not the strongest in the world) by the light of a candle which was stuck in a bottle, that being our only candlestick, and then we talked together of bygone days, of happy homes in England where our childhood had been spent'.

Soon the blows began to fall. On 29 June, Mrs Hale died – 'she was taken ill at three o'clock in the afternoon with cholera, and though everything was done for her by the medical men and those around which skill and kindness could suggest, it was all in vain; at 6 p.m. all pain left her, and we saw that she was rapidly sinking; the dews of death began to gather on her brow and she soon became unconscious'. It was the first time Katherine Bartrum had seen death. Mrs Hale left a little daughter. 'Poor little lamb, how unconscious was she of her sad loss: a motherless babe amongst strangers and her father far away.'

After an unsuccessful sortie against the mutineers, the garrison found itself immured in the Residency. Food was rationed, each person receiving 'attar, or flour, which we made into chupatties; rice; dall, or peas; salt and meat'. There were no proper cooking facilities, so all were cooked together, with ship's biscuits, in 'a saucepan with some water and made into a stew; but as the saucepan was of copper and could not be relined during the siege, the food when it turned out was often perfectly green – hunger alone could make it enjoyable'. The children suffered most. The heat was intense and there were no coolies to pull the punkah. When the besiegers attacked the Residency, all the lights had to be put out and the children lay and trembled in the darkness.

On 2 July, the garrison blew up the Machchi Bhawan fort. No one had warned the women that this was to happen, and they all jumped to the conclusion that the sepoys had penetrated into the Residency. The room 'was so thick in dust when we had lighted a candle we could scarcely see one another; the bricks and mortar had fallen from the ceiling and the poor little children were screaming with terror'. But all was well – though a stray shot killed Sir Henry Lawrence soon after.

So it went on. Katherine was standing by the door one morning watching a child play with a round shot when the little girl was struck in the head and killed instantly. The only news was of injury and death. There was smallpox to add to the dangers. One of the women in Katherine's house died of smallpox, leaving 'a little girl who looks as though she would not long survive her'. Another woman and her child were dying, too. 'I have been listening to her during the night; she frequently exclaims, "Lighten my darkness I beseech Thee, O Lord", and many such beautiful expressions'. The woman's mind was failing. 'She wanted to sit up, and asked me to bring her boxes and pack them up as she was going on a long journey and must have everything prepared. I did what she asked, sorted her things and put them back in the boxes. "Thank you", she said, "now I am quite ready: the doolie is here but the bearers have not come."' What a mournful scene it was, thought Katherine, 'that poor young thing and her child dying far away from all she loved'. The baby had been born ten days earlier, during the siege, and died two days after its mother.

By early August, there were only three adults left in Katherine's room, 'and we looked at each other, as much to say: "Who will be the next to go?"' But little Bobbie, who had almost died of cholera, recovered, and someone was even able to provide a little milk for him. There was nothing to be done but pray, cook what food there was, fan the flies away, and read a psalm for comfort in tribulation. 'How touchingly applicable were many of those beautiful psalms to our own case. Never before had been breathed forth with such earnestness those words, "O let the sorrowful sighing of the prisoners come before Thee: and preserve Thou those that are appointed to die."'

Katherine's hands were so painful with the unaccustomed work and the diet, that she had to have the doctor to lance the boils which covered them. The doctor brought Bobbie a little sugar, which he said he had stolen. He was in 'a sad state of anxiety', for his wife was in Cawnpore, from which there was no news. There was no news from Robert Bartrum, either. And of relief, no sign. 'Are we forgotten altogether by our friends in England, that reinforcements never appear?'

As time went on, Katherine became more and more worried about her child. Food was becoming even more scarce, and there was no wood for a fire. 'One of the soldiers broke down some railings for us; but it is a difficult matter to chop them up, since I have only my dinner knife to do it with, and this will be worn out should the siege last much longer.'

Rations were once again reduced. The weary days went by, days punctuated only with tragedy. Would it never end?

Then, on 23 September, 'such joyful news! A letter is come from Sir J. Outram, in which he says we will be relieved in a few days: everyone is wild with excitement and joy. Can it really be true? Is relief coming at last? And oh; more than all, will dear Robert come up? And shall we meet once more after these weary months of separation?'

The sound of firing was heard in the city beyond the Residency. Were the distant guns those of the relieving force? On 25 September the answer came, 'and at that moment the noise, confusion, and cheering were almost overwhelming'. The relieving force had broken into the Residency. Was Robert with it? 'I was not long left in suspense, for the first officer I spoke to told me he was come up with them, and that they had shared the same doolie on the previous night.' With her son in her arms, Katherine rushed out to find him, scanning every face along the way, but she was told that her husband was with the heavy artillery and would not be in until morning. 'I could not sleep that night for joy at the thought of seeing him so soon, and how thankful I was that our Heavenly Father had spared us to meet again.' Next day there was disappointment. A gentleman told her that he had shared the same tent as Robert the night before, and that he would be along soon. But still he did not come. 'So I gave baby his breakfast and sat at the door to watch for him.' But still he did not come.

Next afternoon, the doctor came on his usual visit, looking kind and sad. '"How strange it is my husband is not come in!" "Yes", he said, "it *is* strange!" and turned round and went out of the room. Then the thought struck me: Something has happened which they do not like to tell me! But this was agony too great almost to endure, to hear that he had been struck down at our very gates. Of this first hour of bitter woe I cannot speak . . . My poor little fatherless boy! who is to care for us now, baby?'

Robert had been killed on the threshold of the Residency. At first, Katherine could not understand why God had 'forgotten to be gracious', but she pulled herself together and thought of her son, hers and Robert's: 'Poor little fellow, how often had I said to him, "Papa is come: now baby will get quite well!" He could not understand why I was so sad, and would clasp his little arms around my neck and kiss away my tears. Now he was doubly dear to me: all I had left to make life endurable'. Robert 'had fought the good fight, he had finished his course'; she knew that he would 'rise again at the last day'. Now there was only the child to live for.

The relief was no relief. The force which had been strong enough to break in to the Residency was not strong enough to break out again. The ordeal was not yet over. Although the weather was becoming cooler, sickness and famine still haunted the Residency. It was difficult to keep clothes and body clean, as there was no soap; 'we have to use the dall, or pease, by grinding it between two stones and making it into flour, and this is a good substitute for soap; but we have so little of it, that it is a question sometimes whether we shall use it to wash with or to eat'. The renewed siege was not, however, to last so long. In the second week of November more troops arrived to hold the way clear long enough for the garrison to be evacuated. 'November 17 – Heard that we are to leave Lucknow tomorrow night, with just what we can carry. Well! I can only carry my baby, and my worldly effects can be put into a very small compass, since they consist merely of a few old clothes. My heart fails me at the thought of the terrible march, with no one to look after me or care for me but

God. I have lost my kind friend Dr Darby, who has been wounded; and they say he will not recover. He promised to take care of me on the journey to Calcutta, but now I am utterly friendless.' Even yet, the ordeal was not over.

Katherine and her child were placed in a doolie, a kind of palanquin, to cover the five miles to the British camp. The bearers had lost their way. 'It immediately occurred to me that they were taking me to the sepoys: I sprung out of the doolie, and ran with my child in my arms, screaming across the plain until I heard voices answering.' The voices belonged to British soldiers, and they helped her to the camp. 'I had been on my feet with my baby in my arms for upwards of three hours, walking through deep sand and wet grass, and my dress had become so coated with mud, that it was with difficulty I could get on.' At last, here were welcoming faces, milk for Bobbie, and a cup of tea for Katherine. When there was time for thought, even the kindliness and the safety seemed to intensify Katherine's sorrow, 'but the God of the widow and the fatherless will not forsake me'.

In the security of Calcutta, on the eve of sailing for home, Katherine Bartrum's tragedy played itself out. Bobbie had grown very delicate, and the doctors in Calcutta had assured her that only a sea voyage would restore him to health. Instead of rushing home by the overland route, therefore, they were making the four-month voyage by way of the Cape. As the time came to board the ship, Bobbie became weaker. On 11 February, they boarded the *Himalaya*. By then, the child was very ill, 'but I cannot spare him, and I do not think God will take away my little lamb when I have nothing else left'. Katherine was frightened. A friend who had also survived the ordeal at Lucknow kept watch with her. 'Look,' she said, 'how bright his eyes are growing'. But Katherine had turned her head away, 'for I *could* not see my child die'. On 12 February Katherine Bartrum sailed for England, alone.

Katherine Bartrum passed through the valley of the shadow. So, too, did Lieutenant Gough of Meerut, who won one of the new Victoria Crosses and died a general. But others, like Robert Bartrum and his son, did not, and their bones became part of the earth they had walked upon as kings.

[148]

# 3

# *BLOODY ASSIZE*

WHEN news of the outbreak at Meerut reached Calcutta there had been panic. The majority of the European inhabitants of the City of Palaces were non-officials – businessmen, and the like. They were known by the more worldly soldiers and civilians as 'ditchers', because most of them had rarely travelled outside Calcutta and seldom even went beyond the old defensive line known as the Maratha Ditch. They knew nothing about Indians, except those with whom they did business, who formed a growing middle class not very different from themselves. Safe, as they thought, in their great houses, they relied upon the government for their protection. But suddenly the government's power was in doubt. At Barrackpore, only a night's march from the centre of the city, men whom they had once looked upon as the trusted guardians of life and property had turned into potential despoilers and murderers. There was, too, a fear, 'dominant over all, that the vast and varied population of the Native suburbs and bazaars would rise against the white people, release the prisoners in the gaols, and gorge themselves with the plunder of the great commercial capital of India'. And to make it worse, the governor-general, Lord Canning, did not appear to grasp the extent of the danger. By 28 May, a correspondent of the newspaper *Friend of India* was recording that: 'Men went about with revolvers in their carriages, and trained their bearers to load quickly and fire low. The ships and steamers in the rivers have been crowded with families seeking refuge from the attack, which was nightly expected, and everywhere a sense of insecurity prevailed.'

The governor-general's appearance of calm reassured none. On 25 May he had given a ball at Government House to celebrate the queen's birthday, even though rumours had been rife in the bazaar that, on that day, attempts would be made – what kind of attempts no one quite knew – to convert all Hindus to Christianity. The celebratory *feu de joie* for the queen was not abandoned, but it was fired from muskets, not from the new rifles. Some Europeans, fearing that the gathering would be used as an opportunity to murder all the leading members of the community, stayed away. One young lady hired two English sailors to sit up in her house and protect her on the night of the ball, 'but they got tipsy, and frightened her more than the imaginary enemies'.

A few days later, the sound of fireworks set off at the marriage of a princess of Mysore brought all the menfolk out with their guns. 'I never came across such a set of old women', complained Lord Canning.

Canning refused offers from the Masonic Lodges, the trade associations, and the French and Armenian communities, to enlist in a volunteer corps. This convinced most people that the governor-general was incompetent, and there were calls for his instant dismissal. In October 1857, when it at last seemed that the British had taken a grip on the Mutiny by recapturing Delhi, Queen Victoria's loyal Calcutta subjects sent her a petition. This alleged that Lord Canning, by his moderation and his interference with the rights of British subjects, had been:

a principal cause of the great calamities which have desolated this land, has strengthened the hands of the enemy, weakened or destroyed the respect before entertained for the name of Englishman in the East, imperilled British rule, exposed the Capital of British India to massacre and pillage, excited the contempt of all parties, estranged from the Government of India a large and loyal body of Christians, and in every way proved himself unfit to be further continued in his high trust.

And all because Canning had turned his face against indiscriminate violence and sought to restrain British officers and civilians from indulging in a reign of terror.

[150]

But a reign of terror there certainly was. The distance between panic and bellicosity is only a sense of shame. The British in Calcutta and elsewhere, smarting with the realisation of their own fears, turned in hatred against all Indians. Something had to be done to erase suggestions of cowardice – which had been admirably summed up in an announcement in a Simla paper, after many of the menfolk had deserted the ladies and taken refuge in the ravines surrounding the town: 'The ladies of Simla will hold a meeting . . . for the purpose of consulting about the best measures to be taken for the protection of the gentlemen. The ladies beg to inform those who sleep in the *khuds* [ravines] that they sincerely compassionate their sufferings, and are now preparing pillows for them stuffed with the purest white feathers . . . Rest, warriors, rest.'

Demands for vengeance were strongly supported by people even further removed from danger than those who lived in Calcutta. In newspapers in England, opinion had switched from incredulity – surely a collection of damned niggers could hardly present a threat to the Empire? – to outrage. Stories of atrocities, of Englishwomen boiled alive in butter, of children barbecued on bayonets, filled the most staid of journals. A letter in *The Times*, obviously published with approval, declared: 'Not one stone in Delhi should be left standing upon another . . . Every sepoy should be a pauper, his house in flames, himself fleeing from man who hunts like a wolf.' Soon, however, *The Times* was editorialising in more ponderous terms: 'This blind and indiscriminate exasperation is resolving itself into the mere hatred of a dark skin.'

Europe accepted the solidarity of the white-skinned races. In Paris, the emperor Napoleon III immediately agreed that Britain's India-bound reinforcements should be permitted to use the overland route through France to Marseilles.

In England, it became a wet-afternoon amusement for country house parties to sit around a billiard table devising tortures for the leaders of the revolt. The palm was awarded to an ingenious gentleman who proposed that the chief villain 'should be forced, first, to swallow a tumbler of water in which all the blue papers in a seidlitz-powder box had been emptied and then a tumbler with the contents of all the white papers, in a state of solution'. In the better clubs, too, it was common to chuckle over the exquisite punishments devised by psychopaths like General Neill, who 'had forced high Brahmans to sweep up the blood of the Europeans murdered at Cawnpore, and then strung them in a row, without giving them the time requisite for the rites of purification'.

'Have you heard the news?' said a celebrated author to an acquaintance, as they stood together under the porch of the Athenaeum club. 'The sepoys have taken to inflicting the most exquisite cruelties upon the Sikhs, and the Sikhs in return swear that they will stamp the Company's arms in red-hot pice [copper coins] over the body of every Sepoy who comes in their way. These are the sort of tidings that nowadays fill every heart in England with exultation and thankfulness.'

After the suppression of the Mutiny, a young man just arrived in India discovered that there were two men who were accounted the most welcome new additions to society in Calcutta. 'One was a jolly comical-looking chap, an excellent officer and a capital man for a small dinner-party. The other was most refined and intelligent, with a remarkably courteous and winning address. It was said that these two had hung more people than any other man in India.' One of them, however, 'was blamed by many for excess of leniency'. This man, Mr Hume, had distinguished himself by keeping down the number of executions in his district to seven, and by granting the culprits a fair trial. 'These he treated with fatherly tenderness, for he invented a patent drop for their benefit; so that men prayed – first, that they might be tried by Mr Hume, and next that, if found guilty, they might be hanged by him.'

Mr Hume was something of an eccentric. Hanging – and humane hanging at that – was certainly too good for mutineers. It was more usual to blow them from guns. This method was, however, still thought to be humane. It also contained two elements of capital punishment; 'it was painless to the criminal and terrible to the beholder'. The ritual was certainly hideous. With great ceremony, the victim was escorted on to the parade ground while the band played some lively air. Above, in the sky, the vultures waited as the victim's back was ranged against the muzzle of the gun and the straps tightened. Then the band would fall silent and the only sound would be the faint crackle of the port-fire, ready to be placed at the touch hole. At last, the air seemed to split. A head would come dancing across the ground, and an obscene shower of blood and entrails would cover both gunners and observers. Once, at Barrackpore, two Englishwomen clad all in white and riding white Arab horses spurred their mounts at the moment of explosion, and then rode away covered in scarlet, their horses dark with blood.

The Mutiny was a war carried on with sometimes bestial ferocity on both sides. Crazy with fear, the sepoys murdered English women and children, and the British retaliated with lynchings and village-burnings which made no discrimination between the guilty and the innocent. By 20 June, J. W. Kaye – the historian of the Mutiny – records:

> Soldiers and civilians alike were holding Bloody Assize, or slaying natives without any assize at all, regardless of sex or age . . . Volunteer hanging parties went into the districts and amateur executioners were not wanting to the occasion. One gentleman boasted of the numbers he had finished off quite 'in an artistic manner', with mango trees for gibbets and elephants for drops, the victims of this wild justice being strung up, as though for pastime, in the form of figures of eight.

Violence and cruelty bred further violence and cruelty.

Even the smile disappeared from Anglo-Indian portraits. A Calcutta journal reported favourably on the 'portrait of Captain Hazlewood which may be seen in Thacker and Spink's Gallery. The friends of the gallant officer will at once recognise the likeness, and feel confident that no undue lenity on his part will be shown to the murderers of women and children, for he has a stern expression of countenance as if he had just given an order to hang them and their favourers'.

It was little wonder that, in a climate of hysteria richly adorned with stories of atrocities, the British soldiers who were pouring into Calcutta and Bombay should have regarded the entire population as the enemy. They were very annoyed when their officers refused to allow them to kill all the Indians they saw. At one stage, it became necessary to double the guard on Fort William to prevent the soldiers from setting off into the streets of Calcutta at night to polish off a few natives. The soldiers' ignorance of any language other than their own sometimes led to farcical tragedy, particularly when they *thought* they heard a word they knew. One soldier, his head full of the shocking tales which were current about the mutiny and massacre at Cawnpore, reported: 'I seed two Moors [Indians] talking in a cart. Presently I heard one of 'em say "Cawnpore". I knowed what that meant; so I fetched Tom Walker, and he heard 'em say "Cawnpore", and he knowed what that meant. So we polished 'em both off.'

Across the country was cut a swathe of burned villages and battered towns. The great city of Delhi suffered terribly after its recapture. 'All the city people found within the walls when our troops entered were bayoneted on the spot; and the number was considerable, as you may suppose when I tell you that in some houses forty or fifty persons were hiding.' The mutineers had purposely left vast quantities of liquor behind, and the British troops went berserk. 'The troops', wrote Saunders, the Commissioner of Delhi, 'were completely disorganised and demoralised by the immense amount of plunder that fell into their hands and the quantity of liquor which they managed to discover'. They spared neither people nor buildings. Troops occupied the mosques. The Red Fort was taken over and some of the most exquisite of its buildings were destroyed (apologists argued that, in any case, they were of 'little architectural interest'!). In a Bombay newspaper, one writer advocated the entire destruction of the city, and suggested that a vast pyramid should be raised from the ruins. Mutineers and their supporters would provide the labour, and when they died, as the writer believed they would (from overwork), their bodies could be thrown into a tube in the centre of the pyramid. When the work was finished and surmounted by an immense statue of Retribution, a plaque was to be appended, reading:

BENEATH THIS PYRAMID
LIE BURIED
A PALACE, ITS KING, ITS PRINCES
AND THE

MONSTERS OF THE BENGAL NATIVE ARMY THEY
INCITED TO MUTINY, TO MURDER, AND OTHER
CRIMES UNUTTERABLE.
STRANGER!
IF YOU WOULD KNOW WHERE
DELHI WAS,
BEHOLD ITS DEBRIS IN THE PYRAMID
YOU STAND ON
ANNO DOMINI MDCCCLVII

Fortunately, wiser counsels prevailed, and most of the destruction was limited to a number of buildings which intervened in the fire-path of the guns of the fort.

When the correspondent of *The Times* arrived in Delhi in May 1858, he found the Commissioner installed in a 'fine mansion with turrets and clock-towers, something like a French château of the last century'. On closer inspection, it showed signs of cannon-fire, but the interior was untouched by war: 'I found myself at once back in civilised life, amid luxuries long unknown . . . The comfort and luxury of the house itself were a positive gratification to the senses. Large lofty rooms – soft carpets, sofas, easy chairs, books, pictures, rest and repose, within. Outside, kuskus-tatties and punkah-wallahs. The family were at their first breakfast when we went in. I found there were two breakfasts, one at eight, the other at three o'clock.' For visitors, an evening's amusement consisted of driving into the city to see the 'emperor'. 'In a dingy, dark passage, leading from the open court or terrace in which we stood to a darker room beyond, there sat, crouched on his haunches, a diminutive, attenu-ated old man, dressed in an ordinary and rather dirty muslin tunic, his small lean feet bare, his head covered by a small, thin cambric skull-cap.' When Russell was there, the ex-king was sick; 'with bent body he seemed nearly prostate over a brass basin, into which he was retching violently'. Was this 'dim-wandering-eyed, dreamy old man, with feeble hanging nether-lip and toothless gums' – was he, indeed, wondered Russell, the one 'who had conceived that vast plan of restoring a great empire, who had fomented the most gigantic mutiny in the history of the world, and who, from the walls of his ancient

[155]

palace, had hurled defiance and shot ridicule upon the race that held every throne in India in the hollow of their palms?'

In an attempt to answer such questions, the British had put the king on trial a couple of months earlier. The trial had failed to clear the matter up. The 'emperor' was, of course, found guilty, but there was no question of executing him, for he had been guaranteed his life. But the trial gave a halo of martyrdom to the last of the Mughals.

By October 1858 the British had decided to send the ex-king and his immediate family into exile at Rangoon, in Burma. The party consisted of the ex-king himself and two of his wives, with two of his sons and a number of female relatives. With them went four women of the harem and five male and eleven female servants. In charge was Lieutenant Ommanney, who found the slow journey much to his liking, even though he had to get up at 1.30 a.m. in order to get the party organised for the road. This he found 'rather hard', especially as he did not manage to return to his tent for breakfast until 9.00 a.m. 'But', he assured the Commissioner of Delhi, 'I don't care a straw for any amount of work and am very jolly. I am an Honorary Member of the Lancer Mess, breakfast, dinner and tiffin, good stags at dinner twice a week, a pack of Hounds accompany the column on the march, and we have a run when we succeed in getting a jackal, there is a Hook[ah] Club and in short it is as comfortably and perfectly managed as any'.

As Ommanney with his escort of Lancers, their pack of hounds, and their royal charge, moved slowly across northern India, the obsequies of the Honourable East India Company were being pronounced. On 1 November 1858, at Calcutta, Madras, Bombay and a number of other places throughout India (including Delhi), a high-sounding proclamation bearing the name of Queen Victoria was read with suitable ceremony:

Whereas, for divers weighty reasons, we have resolved, by and with the advice and consent of the Lords Spiritual and Temporal, and Commons, in Parliament assembled, to take upon ourselves the government of the territories in India, heretofore administered in trust for us by the Honourable East India Company . . .

[156]

The sonorous words of the proclamation rolled on, and translations were made into no less than seventeen languages.

The proclamation contained something for everyone. For the princes, security of tenure; 'we desire no extension of our territorial possessions'. For the heathen, a certain condescension; 'firmly relying Ourselves on the truth of Christianity . . . We disclaim alike the right and desire to impose Our convictions'. And for all, the proposition that, with the aid of a beneficent God, a new and happy era was about to dawn; 'when, by the blessing of Providence, internal tranquillity shall be restored, it is Our earnest desire to stimulate the peaceful industry of India, to promote works of public utility and improvement, and to administer the government for the benefit of all Our subjects resident therein. In their prosperity will be Our strength, in their contentment Our security, and in their gratitude Our best reward . . .'.

The Devil's Wind had blown across the plains of northern India bringing with it destruction and death, not only of men, women and children, but of institutions and traditions, above all of trust between Briton and Indian. Now, the Queen's Peace was about to descend and nothing would ever be the same again.

—— *ACT TWO* ——

# *THE QUEEN'S PEACE OVER ALL*

On us the shame will fall,
If we lift our hand from a fettered land,
And the Queen's peace over all,
Dear boys,
The Queen's Peace over all!

Rudyard Kipling
*The Running of Shindand*

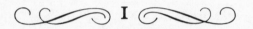 I

# MIRROR OF INDIGO

I N the new India, the largest body of Europeans apart from those
in the civil service and the army consisted of planters. Europeans
had never been greatly interested in Indian agriculture as a
whole, but the government held the opium monopoly, and indigo
cultivation offered scope to European enterprise. At the end of the
eighteenth century, planters had been invited to come to India from
the West Indies, and very soon a thriving industry was established,
mainly in and around Bengal.

The planters had soon proved themselves a tough and violent
crowd, beating up the peasants and not infrequently murdering
them, assembling armies of their own retainers and making war on
their rivals. Because their estates were so inaccessible from the main
centres of government, they had always been difficult to control.
Though some of the planters were, in fact, men of humanity and even
of taste, who built themselves great mansions in the prevailing
Classical form, all lived in a patriarchal style – usually in more senses
than one. There was often a sizeable Eurasian population on an
indigo estate. The planters kept in close contact with other Europeans of the non-official community, particularly in Calcutta, where
their interests dominated the English-language press. It was they
who sponsored the abuse of Lord Canning and demands for
vengeance on the mutineers, and they who constantly campaigned
against officialdom, especially in the shape of magistrates who
tried to interfere when the planters 'disciplined' their workers.
Planters had been active in the volunteer units raised at the time
of the Mutiny, and they took back to their estates afterwards

[161]

a racial animosity which seemed to surpass any they had felt before.

Very soon – encouraged, perhaps, by the disturbances of the Mutiny years – peasants began to refuse to cultivate indigo. The source of the trouble was the contract system. Few planters actually cultivated the indigo crop themselves. The usual method was to advance money to the peasant, who then grew the crop and sold it back to the planter when it was ripe. His buying price was often too low, and the peasant preferred to grow a more profitable crop, such as rice. Some peasants took the advance and then neglected the indigo, so the planter, even though no contract had been signed, would send his men to sow the land forcibly, while bullies with clubs and spears drove the peasant off his own holding. When a courageous magistrate took action – and it needed courage, for the planter was quite prepared to threaten the magistrate with violence, too – the whole planting community howled to the governor of the province, and its newspapers hurled abuse at the magistrate concerned.

Under attack, the government did what all governments do in such circumstances. They appointed a commission of enquiry. The missionaries, in particular, provided evidence of the planters' oppression and brutality. The planters, in turn, accused the missionaries of inciting the peasants to refuse to grow indigo. While the commission was in the course of its enquiry, the government passed a temporary law which made breach of contract a *criminal* offence. This, of course, resulted in even greater hardship for the peasants, as the planters took every advantage of the law. Contracts were forged without a moment's hesitation. 'It makes one's blood creep', wrote the viceroy, 'to think of what may have been done under cover of this gigantic system of fraud, bearing in mind the cases of blind men, lepers, bed-ridden men and children' who had been jailed for so-called violation of contract.

In the midst of a situation which one civilian thought might be the beginning of a full-scale agricultural uprising, a missionary placed a bomb on the fire. He had discovered a play written in Bengali, entitled *Nil Durpan* (the Mirror of Indigo), which criticised the whole business of indigo planting from the peasant's point of view. He mentioned it to J. P. Grant, the lieutenant-governor of Bengal.

[162]

As it had now been recognised that one of the reasons for British unpreparedness at the time of the Mutiny was lack of information on native opinion, Grant asked the Revd Dr Long to translate the play. When the translation had been made, copies were – without Grant's knowledge – distributed to a large number of officials. When the planters heard of it, they complained strongly to Grant. He refused to apologise, except for the fact of its unauthorised distribution under a government frank. The planters' response was to take out a libel action against the translator.

The trial was a travesty. The Revd Dr Long was given no chance of defence. The judge interpreted passages from the play in the most perverted manner. In the course of the dialogue, one character asked: 'Did not the magistrate say he will come here this day?' and another replied: 'No, sir. He has four days more to come. On Saturday they have a champagne-party and ladies' dance. Mrs Wood can never dance with anyone but our Sahib the magistrate. I saw that when I was a bearer. Mrs Wood is very kind'. This stimulated the judge to rousing condemnation. Would the jury believe, he demanded, 'that those women were in the habit of prostituting themselves in order to gain the decision of magistrates who were bound by oath to administer the law in strict impartiality? Would they believe that those magistrates were in the habit of violating the solemn obligation of their duty and conscience to gratify licentious desire?' This terrible slander, he argued, was aimed not only at the wives of planters; it was 'for the jury to consider whether it was not intended as a reproach on the whole middle class of the women of England'.

The judge's peroration was reported with great glee in the English papers. 'Would the reverend gentleman Dr Long point out how far he thought this *filthy* statement was calculated to bring about improvements in social morals. When he [the judge] read these *filthy* passages he blushed to think that a clergyman of the established Church of England could have lent himself to the propagation of so malicious and unfounded a slander. That statement would go forth to the mothers and daughters of the middle class in England to make them think that is the fate of their daughters here. Not a gentleman in any station but would tear the *filthy* production; but, above all, every civilian, soldier, and merchant, and he hoped every clergyman, would agree that it should never reach the firesides of England'. Poor Dr Long was sentenced to a month's imprisonment – in a very unpleasant cell – and a heavy fine. Pleased with themselves, the planters went home and bullied a few more peasants, an occupation they continued to enjoy throughout the good queen's reign.

Though indigo production declined as chemical substitutes took over, a flood of Englishmen arrived in India after 1860, many of whom became planters of new crops, tea and coffee. All had been influenced by the wave of anti-Indian feeling which had swept over Britain at the time of the Mutiny, and in the closed society of lonely plantations they maintained their racial hatreds undisturbed, moderately secure in the knowledge that justice would never catch up with them – or if it did, that it would be mild. For the murder of his coachman, one Englishman was fined thirty rupees, a couple of pounds at the then rate of exchange. Even as late as 1901, two English planters, 'in order to obtain a confession of theft from a native Syce or groom, tied him up to a tree and flogged him to such an extent that he died in the evening of the same day. They then carried off his body to a distance of two miles and buried it, in the hope of escaping discovery'. When the affair came to light, other planters subscribed £1,000 for their defence and they were sentenced to only three years' simple imprisonment.

As the price of indigo declined, so too did the great mansions. Life became a little less extravagant, a little less like a pretence of Home. Pleasures became more rustic, but they still had their appeal.

In the 1880s, and after, the first task of a young man who found himself in Calcutta en route for a plantation in such a place as Tirhut, for example, would be to partake of an official luncheon with the proprietors or their agents. He would then spend a day or two at the Great Eastern Hotel – a favourite resort of planters on leave – waiting for the order to join his 'concern'. The new assistant would be helped on his way by the railway, and at the station nearest his destination he would find awaiting him a bullock cart for his baggage, and a pony or horse for himself. These, and relays of fresh mounts, would have been arranged by the manager of the plantation. The mounts were never particularly good ones since the ordinary indigo planter, though the 'very soul of generosity', had more respect for his horse flesh than to bestow it on a stranger, especially on roads which had been repaired with 'two feet and a half of loose earth and large clods just before a long season of heavy rains' and were usually in a state that 'may be imagined but cannot be adequately described.' All in all, it was wise for the new arrival to treat his mounts with suspicion. He himself might not have experienced up-country roads before, but they probably had, 'and they knew a trick or two, and he must not be surprised at somewhat violent and exciting starts – full speed reckoning as the very lowest order of velocity, graduating from that upwards, to the sensation of being shot out of a rocket'. A really recalcitrant animal of the kind that sat down and firmly refused to move might be given the well-tried stimulus of having a fire of straw, sticks and dry grass lit under him. Generally speaking, however, the plantation hacks were not quite as bad as that. The alternative to a horse was a light cart made from an old indigo chest and four pieces of bamboo. It had the advantage of being practically indestructible as long as the wheels stayed on.

Arrived at the plantation, the assistant would spend a day or two becoming acquainted with the manager at his house, and would then move into his own bungalow, a simple but often pleasant place. The kitchen was, as usual, some little way off from the house. It was probably still the traditional kitchen of Anglo-India. 'It is not hare (hair) soup served up regularly until the cook's ambrosial locks are perforce seized and shorn by the stern order of the sahib, who – with all his love of game soup and pie, to say nothing of curry – holds, in this case, with the fastidious man in the backwoods restaurant, who preferred his flies and molasses in separate plates, and likes his "hair", if it must come to table, placed in a prominent place, say, on a separate dish of the largest size, and sent thereon, with best compliments, back to the chef in the cook-room.'

The assistant's bungalow was small, but quite large enough for a bachelor. The doors would rarely be an exact match, nor would they be opposite each other. This was rather an advantage than otherwise, as aligned doors exposed the assistant to any 'Aryan brother who has a complaint of a peculiarly noxious or distressing character, such as wanting to borrow money on personal security or anything of that sort'. The hopeful borrower, unless his efforts were foiled by erratic

architecture, 'simply reconnoitres until he finds a place in the garden
. . . from which he can distinctly see through the house, so that,
move which way the assistant will, the "grievancer's" eye is upon
him'. Nothing could escape that basilisk stare. 'It's no use, he
KNOWS you MUST look at him; he never stirs, he never speaks; he
sits there, mute, asking for nothing, seeking nothing. Oh, no!
Wishing for nothing. Only you will have to, and MUST, eventually,
LOOK AT HIM; and herein lies his triumph!' The moment the
'grievancer' succeeded in catching the assistant's eye, there flashed
upon his face, 'as from a lighthouse on the coast, suddenly such an
expression of abject misery and woe, want and injured innocence, as
no words but mute appeals can do justice to, dying away again as
suddenly the instant your eye is removed from him'. This kind of
harassment, of course, could wear down even the kindest-hearted of
mortals; 'and it has even been known to attract a boot-jack, half a
brick, or similar heavy bodies with great velocity to within an ace of
the "watcher's" head, accompanied with much low and violent
rumbling, as of bad language and ill-temper of a furiously aggressive
but suppressed kind'.

Such distractions apart, the assistant found little in the way of
entertainment on the plantation. There would be a visit from another
assistant, once a month, perhaps, or one from the manager who
might invite the assistant to return with him and spend the night at
his house, where 'if the manager is a family man, he may hear a few
tunes on the piano, and a few of the Old Country songs which will
remind him of those at Home'. Otherwise there was little until the
cold season came round and the assistant could take off for Calcutta
for a few days, 'where his numerous wants will inevitably lead him to
China Bazaar, there to be assailed by native brokers, hawkers,
and middlemen clinging to his gharry with cries of "tin-box",
"originette", "meershum pipe", "portmantoo", "esleepinsuit",
"ready med close", "photogripes taken" etc'.

The ordinary day meant rising at 5 a.m. and departing on a tour of
inspection after a light breakfast of a cup of tea, a slice of toast, and a
couple of eggs. Back home at 11 a.m., the young man would bathe,
write a few letters, have lunch, and do the office work. Finally, an
evening meal, a little recreation, and bed. It was a monotonous life,

although frequently enlivened by a run with the hounds. 'Hounds' was, perhaps, rather an ample word, as the dogs were usually of assorted breeds or no breed at all, 'from the squab little bow-legged, half-bred, cur doggie to the no-less half-bred, lanky, big jointed cross between a Rampore and a pariah dog, or a greyhound and a kangaroo dog'. There was no fox, only a jackal, which could be run best in the evening.

Such excitements were not for every day. In the normal course of events, the assistant spent much of his time in his bungalow, which could be made quite snug now that everything came from Home 'at such cheap rates'. A few choice and artistic oleographs on the walls – landscapes, perhaps, or some of Landseer's fashionable animals – might be offset by photographs of celebrated beauties. An assistant might keep birds, or fish. He could take up carpentry, or study 'the reading and writing of the language if inclined'. If evening still hung heavy on his hands, he might decide to exercise his talent for music. He could practise the violin to his heart's content, without fear of offending anyone. 'The native of India', in fact, was 'positively *fond* of discordant sounds; and he [the assistant] will probably, on slipping out into his verandah in the darkness of the stilly night, after performing every direst kind of excruciating discord on his instrument for the time being . . . find, as one assistant did, his chowdikar [watchman] behind the door, wrapped in profoundest ecstasies at the dulcet sounds he had been producing'.

Anyone who could play an instrument was appreciated at the festivities that the cold season brought. Racing, hunting, and hockey meets were held at the various plantations, and men rode more than a hundred miles to stay for a few days and enjoy the fun. Everybody who could attend, did. And what a sight it was, if only because of the hats. The Bengal planter was famous for the strange variety of his headgear. 'Some resemble copper boilers in shape, with broad brims, and innumerable air-holes; others have a peak in front, and an apron behind, just (as far as shape is concerned) as if a child's pinafore had been tied upon a dragoon's helmet to cover the back of the neck; others rise in the most outrageous manner – cauldron-fashion – as if the unfortunate individual's head had been introduced by mistake into a wooden washing-basin and had become fixed there.'

There was less variety in the names, for most of the planting families – and it was very much a family affair – were of Scottish origin. In fact, it was said that if anyone, at a Christmas week gathering, were to shout 'Mac!' from the verandah of the Tirhut Club, every face would simultaneously turn towards him.

Among the occasional events which lightened the planters' life were parades of the volunteer cavalry, the Bihar Light Horse to which many of them belonged. Their uniform consisted of 'blue blouse, breeches, and Blucher boots, white pugree and regulation helmet with silver spike and chain, black and brown belt, Martini-Henry carbine and light sword'. They formed a brave sight, and they were efficient, too. But even thirty years after the Mutiny, fear still lingered. The government would not build forts. There was nothing to give the slightest protection in case of trouble. 'Have we again lapsed into that false and deadly feeling of security and *laissez faire* which preceded the Mutiny and its horrors? . . . Are we to disregard all due precaution and to be in jeopardy even to the eleventh hour, because the sky is clear, and all seems tranquil around us? As the darkest night precedes the dawn, so also does the deepest calm forbode the storm. We are not pessimists – all we would urge is that we are a small handful of British folk in a foreign land, amongst the teeming populations of which, with friendship there is mixed up hate, with fairness fanaticism, and with justice intolerance.'

In the lonely up-country stations, even the queen's peace seemed fragile.

## 2

# THE MAKING OF A MEMSAHIB

WHILE he was on leave, George Browne went to a tennis party at a Wiltshire rectory, where he met a girl named Helen. He had intended to go on from England to Switzerland before returning to Bengal but, instead, he got engaged to be married. It was arranged that Helen would follow him out to India, and they would be married in Calcutta.

Helen knew nothing about India except what was in the history books and what George himself, rather confusingly, had told her. She was a vicar's daughter and, in daydreams, fancied herself 'seated under a bread-fruit tree in her Indian garden, dressed in white muslin, teaching a circle of little "blacks" to read the Scriptures'. But there was little time for daydreams when she had to prepare her trousseau and all the other things she would need in India. She received a great deal of advice from ladies experienced in the ways of India, including the recommendation to take as little as possible with her. 'It is impossible to keep good dresses in India, the climate is simply *ruination* to them . . . Besides, the *durzies*, the native dress-makers, will copy *anything*, and do it *wonderfully* well, at about a fifth the price one pays at home.' She was also advised to take as much as possible with her. 'I should say make a special point of having everything in reasonable abundance. The European shops ask frightful prices, the natives are always unsatisfactory.' She was warned, too, that India was at least two years behind Europe, as far as fashion was concerned, and that unless she wished to offend people she should take care that her dresses were not too up-to-date.

The trouble was, as she was to discover later, that the advice came from people who had spent their Indian years in widely separated places, some in the dry north-west, others in the moist south. But on one thing all were agreed – Helen must wear flannel next to the skin. It helped to avoid chills which, according to the general consensus, were in India almost inevitably followed by fevers, diarrhoea, dysentery, and even cholera. As far as stockings were concerned, she was told that the open pattern 'commonly worn at Home in summer' was to be avoided at all costs, as it greatly facilitated 'the attacks of mosquitoes when on the plains, and of fleas when on the hills'. Muslin dresses were to be preferred to silk, as the latter were 'unendurable in hot weather, and even if worn are speedily soiled by excessive perspiration'. It all sounded not only uncomfortable but unromantic. At least the journey outwards was no longer quite the ordeal it had been even in the first years after the overland route had been opened up. M. de Lesseps had done what every British engineer had said could not be done, and had constructed a canal across the isthmus of Suez. Through the canal to India went the vessels of the P & O. Passengers went ashore at Gibraltar and Naples, and visited Pompeii under the 'guidance of a black-browed Neapolitan, representing Messrs Cook'. Port Said, with its gambling houses and brothels, was passed by. The canal proved dull but full of surprising smells, and the steamer then penetrated into the Red Sea where, at the height of the hot season, even strong men had been known to die in their berths of apoplexy brought on by the temperature. The P & O line, of course, did everything possible to relieve the heat with punkahs and ices and salt-water baths.

Arriving at her destination, which happened to be Calcutta, Helen found things much the same as her predecessors had done at the beginning of the Victorian era. The carriages were a little more modern. There were telegraph wires in the streets. Clothes, though a little out of date, were by no means antiquated. The church, in which the marriage of this new addition to Anglo-Indian society was to be celebrated, was a little unexpected, with its white stucco pillars, its cane chairs, and its punkahs, motionless now because of the cold weather.

Helen's honeymoon was to last for only five days, and was spent in a dak bungalow. She and George travelled by train, that great transformer of life – or of travelling life, at any rate – in the world of Anglo-India. There were now thousands of miles of track, and the traveller could go from Bombay to Calcutta or many other places in a state of reasonable comfort. Only if he travelled first class, of course, as the newlyweds did. George had once ventured into the second class, which proved to be no more than a large van with benches backed by a single wooden bar. There, at a temperature of 80 °F, he had discovered that Indians did not make 'agreeable *compagnons de voyage* in close quarters. In the first place, they lubricate the body with oil, sometimes cocoanut, but often castor or margosa oil, the two latter kinds having a most foetid and, to a European, a most disgusting and nauseating smell'. They had other unseemly habits too, such as chewing betel, 'which causes a copious red expectoration, which is freely distributed on all sides, and dyes their teeth of every shade from crimson to jet black'. Worst of all was their habit of belching 'on all occasions, without the least attempt at restraint. Nothing is more surprising to an Englishman, accustomed to look on such an act as a gross breach of good manners; but the natives argue, that after a substantial meal, this is an appropriate method of venting their satisfaction – as it were by way of grace'. Fortunately, there was no chance of this kind of thing in the first class, which was deliberately made as expensive as possible simply to keep Indians out.

The dak bungalow had suffered no improvement through the decades. It remained as bare and inhospitable, and its menu varied not at all. Breakfast – *chota hazri*, or 'little breakfast' in Anglo-Indian jargon – consisted of 'tea in a chipped brown teapot, and big thick mugs to drink it out of, one edged with blue and the other with green, and buttered toast upon a plate which did not match anything'. Beyond the desert of breakfast, there lay tiffin, and then dinner by lamplight. 'The courses consisted of variations upon an original leg of mutton which occurred at one of their earlier repasts, served upon large cracked plates with metal reservoirs of hot water under them, and embellished by tinned peas of a suspicious pallor'. There was also, inevitably, a fowl, which tasted to Mrs Browne like one of those 'indestructible picture books' printed on cloth. Sensible and experienced travellers normally carried with them what they chose to call a *pot au feu*, or 'pepper pot'. Helen came across this piece of advice in a compendium called the *Anglo-Indian's Vade Mecum*, which had been among her wedding presents. 'First get a medium sized iron pot, lined with enamel', she was advised. 'It ought to have a lid fastened with a hinge, and fitting tightly when closed. To prevent a tendency to burst when the pot is at the boil, there should be a little valve on the top of the lid, free to rise to the pressure of steam from below. So much for the pot; next for its contents. The evening before starting on a journey, put in a fowl, one or two pounds of mutton chops, some potatoes and onions – in fact any meat and vegetables; add a due porportion of water, salt, pepper, and spices, and then allow all to boil slowly, or stew, for as long as is necessary. Now add a little Worcestershire or Harvey sauce, for piquancy, and the whole is ready. Take the pot with you, and on arriving at the halting station, heat it up again, and *set it on the table*. After dinner, let your servant kill and dress another fowl, add it, or some chops, steak, a hare, jungle fowl, or anything else of the same kind that may be obtainable, a few hard-boiled eggs, vegetables, salt and pepper, and boil again; next day repeat the process *da capo*, and your pepper pot will last the whole journey, giving a savoury meal whenever required.' Helen was determined that there should be no such terrifying stews, or fowls, in the new Browne household.

But first they had to have a household. Before his marriage, George had lived in a *chummery*, a house divided among a number of bachelors who shared the cost of both house and food. There was no place for a wife there. The Brownes might have chosen to live in an hotel, but though some of these were good they were also expensive. The cheaper kind were usually owned by natives and were normally 'lacking in order, quiet, cleanliness and comfort – drawbacks which, though of comparatively slight moment to the passing traveller, are sufficiently serious to the permanent resident.' The Brownes might have taken a house with another couple, but Helen really wanted a house of her own, with a garden and a tennis court, and, if at all possible, a cocoanut palm. She also desired a verandah, with pillars. 'Pillars', it must be remarked, 'seemed so common an architectural incident in Calcutta that she thought they must be cheap'. George was more interested in drains, in which Calcutta remained deficient.

An empty Anglo-Indian house always had a melancholy air. If the previous tenants had been gone for only three weeks or so, still the garden ran wild, the walls had cracked, and there was a smell of desolation and decay. Some houses might have a 'luxuriant tangle of beaumontia and bougainvilleas, and trailing columbine' as well as a cocoanut palm and most other kinds of palm as well, but it usually turned out that many sahibs had died there – three in the last family alone, and of cholera.

At last the Brownes would find a house in a locality where a number of Europeans had already survived several years' residence. There might be room for a tennis court, and even for a formal garden. There would be palms, and a high wall sprouting with shrubs. Despite the pink outside walls and the light green interior, Helen might find that the house had some peculiarities. The rafters curved downwards, perhaps, and the floor sloped in several directions. Irregular holes appeared at intervals over the wall for the accommodation of punkah-ropes, each tenant having fancied a different seat outside for his 'punkah-wallah'. The bathrooms were at the rear of the house, 'arranged on the simple principle of upsetting the bathtub on the floor and letting the water run out of a hole in the wall inside the partition'. One of the rooms, which had once been lived in by Indian women, had iron bars on the windows.

The task of furnishing a house in Calcutta could be gone about in one of several ways. The first, which was obviously only for the great, entailed going to a European cabinet-maker and ordering up the latest fashions of six months earlier. As well as being six months behind London, this cost six times as much as it would have done there. Alternatively, there were shops which stocked ready-made English furniture, also rather expensive. On the whole, young people setting up house usually relied on the auction or the bazaar, 'where all things are of honourable antiquity'. There they would purchase 'pathetic three-legged memorials of old Calcutta, springless oval-backed sofas that once upheld the ponderous dignity of the East India Company' and similar items of Anglo-Indian history. These, with a few pieces of basketwork furniture, were almost enough. But no respectable household could do without one or two *almirahs*, vast cupboards designed to receive 'all your personal property, from a dressing-gown to a box of sardines'. It was not possible to live decently and respectably in India without an *almirah*. A few plated forks and some bazaar china completed the domestic appointments. There was no need for decorative extravagance. No one respected an Anglo-Indian for it, and the monsoon and the servants soon tarnished its initial bloom. That kind of pretension was, in fact, frowned upon. The really acceptable index of wealth and status was 'the locality of your residence and the size of your compound'.

George brought two servants with him. The bearer, who had been with him for four years, looked after his clothes, rubbed him down every night before dinner, and kept his money for him. Anglo-Indians very rarely carried money. Even the collecting plate in church was filled with notes of hand which had to be presented at the donors' houses in the following week. George's other servant was the butler who, in spite of having been dismissed every day for a week (during a particularly trying hot-weather season), had continued to turn up behind his master's chair each morning. When George went home to England, he had told the butler that he never wanted to see his face again. But 'it was the first one I saw when the ship reached the P & O jetty. And there was a smile on it. What could I do? And that very night he shot me in the shirtfront with a soda-water bottle'.

The household needed many more servants than these. In the domestic hierarchy, after the bearer and the butler came the cook. Choosing a cook demanded great care. It was by no means unknown for a cook to use his toes as a toast-rack, or his master's socks as a sauce-strainer. Without actually giving a man a trial, it was very difficult to arrive at an estimate of his worth. The reference system still flourished, and the battered written certificates were as misleading as ever, having been bought in the bazaar or inherited from a relative. It was useless to try and follow up a reference, even a genuine one, since the master or mistress who had written it was usually either dead or departed for Home.

George's bearer helpfully relieved Helen of the problem of finding servants by collecting a full complement. Doubtless he was 'in honoured receipt of at least half their first month's wages for securing situations for them'. Among his finds was a scullion, whose function was to do everything he was told to do by the cook, the bearer, or the

butler. Scullions were, on the whole, rather dubious characters –
according, at least, to Mrs Flora Annie Steel, joint author of *The
Complete Indian Housekeeper and Cook*, which was to become Helen's
domestic encyclopaedia. 'In most houses', she said, 'the scullion is an
unknown quantity, a gruesome ghoul of spurious cleanliness, bearing, as his badge of office, a greasy swab of rag tied to a bit of
bamboo'. There were eight immutable laws of sculliondom:

1. Plates are plates, and include cups and saucers, teapots, side-
   dishes and milk jugs.
2. Spoons are spoons, and include knives, forks, toastracks, &c.
3. Water is water, so long as it is fluid.
4. Cloths are cloths, so long as they hold together. After that, they
   are used as swabs.
5. A floor is a floor, and nature made it as a table.
6. Variety is pleasing; therefore always intersperse your stone-
   ware plates with china teacups.
7. At the same time, union is strength; so pile everything
   together, use one water and one cloth, and do not move from
   your station till everything is dried and spread carefully in the
   dust.
8. Only one side of a plate is used by the *sahib logue* it is therefore
   purely unreasonable for them to cavil at the other side being
   dirty.

Perhaps the most important but least-considered servant was the
sweeper. He did much more than sweep the floors. Indeed, he was
the guardian of good health, for it was his task to empty the latrines
and see that they were clean. He was always of the lowest caste, or of
no caste at all, and was generally despised by the other servants. Less
important was the water-carrier who, if in full-time employment,
was responsible for bringing the water, seeing that it was boiled for
use in the kitchen, and filling up the water pots in the bathroom.
There was also a part-time servant who waged war on the family's
clothes. If there was no well in the compound, this washerman took
the bundle of clothes away for washing; he was not above washing
them in water which had already been used for the clothes of

smallpox or cholera victims. His laundry technique, though brutal, was ineffectual. 'Cold water, bad soap, and much beating on stones remove the dirt with less certainty than the buttons.' The only other indoor servant was Helen's maid, and the outdoor staff consisted of gardener and groom. The gardener's first duty was to produce flowers, and he managed this even when the household did not have a garden. It was said that a departing master once gave his gardener a reference which read: 'This [gardener] has been with me fifteen years, I have had no garden, I have never lacked flowers, and he has never had a conviction.' Like most legends of Anglo-India, this story was based on fact.

The new servants' references examined (and disbelieved), their wages established – and even the cost of this small establishment seemed very large to Helen – the staff were put to their duties. An Anglo-Indian household on the traditional pattern had been established, and the time soon came for its first dinner party. But, what to serve?

There was plenty of advice available. Older Calcutta residents still served the turkey and ham that had featured on Calcutta menus for longer than anyone could remember. At the dinner tables of others, no less out of date, saddle of mutton and boiled fowl were invariably preceded by 'almond soup', which could include practically any ingredients as long as blanched almonds and buffalo milk were among them. The more progressive hostess might serve what the author of Helen's encyclopaedia tartly described as 'a badly cooked dinner in the style of a third class French restaurant'. Helen's other cookery book, hopefully subtitled *A Treatise on Reformed Cookery for Anglo-Indian Brides*, unfortunately turned out to have been designed for brides in Madras. It was full of recipes for what Helen's little experience of marketing told her must be a strictly local cuisine. One suggested menu for a 'little home dinner' included a dish of *Podolongcai au jus*, which proved to be something called 'snake vegetable' in a brown gravy!

The Brownes' dinner party produced no crisis in the kitchen, and the cook did not have hysterics. The table looked pleasant, with flowers the gardener had produced (from some other garden). Protocol was carefully observed, and none of the ladies found herself preceded by her junior in the Anglo-Indian hierarchy. Fortunately, this presented no real problems, as a thoughtful government published everyone's post and pay and place in the order of precedence. At the end of the evening, according to custom, the gentlemen were sped on their way with cigars and whisky laid out on a table in the verandah.

All Anglo-Indian dinners were much the same, though hostesses higher up in the social scale would serve champagne, pâté de foie gras, and exotic puddings.

The next excitement after Helen's dinner party was a Viceregal Drawing Room. The first problem to be surmounted concerned the kind of conveyance they should use to get themselves to Government House. The Brownes' only carriage was a *tum-tum*, which was the local name for a dog-cart. They decided they would have to use a hired carriage, or *ticca*. 'The ticca is an uncompromisingly shuttered wooden box with a door in each side and a seat across each end. Its springs are primitive, its angle severe. When no man has hired the *ticca*, the driver slumbers along the roof and the syce [groom] by the wayside. When the ticca is in action, the driver sits on the top, loosely connected with a bundle of hay which forms the casual, infrequent *déjeuner* of the horses. The syce stands behind, and if the back shutters are open he is frequently malodorous. There may be some worldly distinction between the syce and the driver, but it is imperceptible to the foreign eye.' A *ticca* would certainly indicate the Brownes' proper place among the lower reaches of Anglo-Indian society when it rattled up with the broughams, the landaus, and the victorias to Government House.

The ladies wore trains, and there was a smell of camphor in the air which betrayed the fact that the dresses had recently been unpacked from their hot-weather boxes. Their Excellencies stood on a dais some little distance from the throne. Two stately officers of the Viceregal Bodyguard lined the approach, and ADCs moved swiftly around. On the viceregal right were the ladies of the Private Entrée. 'These ladies were the wives of gentlemen whose interests were the special care of Government. It was advisable, therefore, that their trains should not be stepped on, nor their tempers disarranged; and they had been received an hour earlier, with more circumstance, possibly to slower music, different portals being thrown open for the approach of their landaus – they all approached in landaus.' Helen's visiting card was passed from one ADC to another until it reached the Military Secretary, who read it out. Helen curtsied and passed on to join her husband who had been waiting outside the reception room. Everyone then retired to the ballroom, where they talked and bowed interminably until it was time to go home again in their broughams, landaus, victorias – and *ticcas*.

In the cold weather, Calcutta was almost pleasant, though some of the older men found it positively frigid and insisted on great fires. Most of the houses, unfortunately, did not have fireplaces. When the hot weather came round, the viceregal caravan moved off to the rarefied heights of Simla. Families who were due for leave departed for home on the steamers of the P & O, whose departures and passenger lists were chronicled in the newspapers. Everyone who could do so left for the hills. But some remained behind, and among these were the Brownes. Calcutta in the hot weather was like nothing Helen had ever known. The shops put up grass screens and employed coolies to keep the grass moist. The brain fever bird, so aptly named, kept up its incessant cry in the thickest parts of the trees – where no one could see it and shoot it. Cholera, a seasonal visitation, arrived at its appointed time. Life moved slowly. An early morning ride preceded a day's seclusion in bungalow or office, though time spent in the office was short since by noon no one was about and no one worked. From twelve until two it was best to lie down. Outside, 'the white sunlight lies upon the roads so palpable a heat that it might be peeled off: the bare, blinding walls, surcharged with heat, refuse to soak in more, and reject upon the air the fervour beating down upon them. In the dusty hollows of the roadside the pariah dogs lie sweltering in dry heat; beneath the trees sit the crows, their beaks agape; the buffaloes are wallowing in the shrunken mud-holes – but not a human being is abroad of his own will'. After the siesta came lunch, a little work, then a bathe and a breath of torrid air before dinner at eight and bed at half past ten.

The thermantidote (see page 106), that unique invention of Anglo-India, helped to make the temperature a little more bearable. One Mr Johnson had become a popular benefactor by inventing this automatic watering device which at least reduced the numbers of servants needed. As well as being more effective than a punkah, the thermantidote had two great advantages. It was more difficult for its operator to fall asleep, and, since the machine usually filled a doorway, when the operator did doze off, the perspiring householder was discouraged from bursting out upon the offender to 'slay him on the spot, since to do this you must go round deliberately by another door'. Many people still hired punkah pullers in the hot weather, though contemporary opinion claimed that their only advantage was to keep off mosquitoes at meal times.

One of the milder ailments of the hot weather was prickly heat, 'a sort of rash which breaks out on you, and, as its name infers, prickly in its nature; I can only compare it to lying in a state of nudity on a horse-hair sofa, rather worn, and with the prickles of horse-hair very much exposed, and with other horse-hair sofas all round, tucking you in. Sitting on thorns would be agreeable by comparison, the infliction in that case being local; now, not a square inch of your body but is tingling and smarting with shooting pains, till you begin to imagine that in your youth you *must* have swallowed a packet of needles, which now oppressed by heat are endeavouring to make their escape from your interior, where they find themselves smothered in this hot weather.' There was no cure and very little alleviation. Mrs Steel recommended sandalwood dust, but without much enthusiasm: however, she added consolingly, 'those who suffer most from prickly heat are, as a rule, free from more serious ailments'.

The only surcease came with the rains, though they had a habit of being late, whatever the new meteorological devices might say. The garden became a jungle, almost overnight, flowers which had died in May put out shoots, and the grass could actually be *seen* growing. Less happily, the furniture began to perspire, mats to rot, the roof to leak, and cockroaches to appear in hordes. Boots and shoes grew a green mould overnight, and snakes had to be slaughtered on the verandahs.

The weather became a little cooler, however, and Anglo-Indian society revived, gave dinners, and even enjoyed the air at the Eden Gardens. There was a bandstand, of course. There could have been no promenade without it. There were also 'tall palms and red poinsettias, a fine winding artificial lake with a beautiful arched artificial bridge, realistic artificial rocks cropping out of the grass, and a genuine Burmese pagoda of white chunam, specially constructed for the gardens, in the middle of it all. The pagoda runs up into a spire, or a lightning conductor or something of that nature; and on the top of this a frolicsome British tar once placed an empty soda-water bottle upside down . . . The native municipal commissioners regard this with some pride as a finial ornament; certainly nobody has ever taken it down.' After the promenade the carriages would roll away to the echoes of 'God save the Queen'.

When next the cold weather came round, George had leave and there was enough money to go to the hills – not to Simla, 'which is heaven's outer portal, full of knights and angels', but to a place more suited to their means and their status. Going to the hills demanded a great deal of preparation. A house had to be rented. All of them had romantic names like Moss Grange and Ivy Glen, or Eagles' Nest and Sunny Bank, but were silent as to their exact location. The best thing to do was to go and see for one's self. Helen's mentor, Mrs Steel, was firm on the question of location. She could not recommend a house on a ridge. 'Cholera (please do not start!) often dwells in the clouds . . . and may just rest on the ridge, to say nothing of its being enveloped in damp clouds, and at the mercy of the violence of the storm.' Mrs Steel also wrote feelingly about houses which had their back against the side of a hill, having had herself 'a providential escape from being buried alive in a landslip, by which, though life was saved, valuable property was lost'. Houses in valleys were too shut in and did not receive sufficient fresh air, and houses by the wayside lacked privacy.

Once a house had been chosen, whether by visit, recommendation, or chance, decisions had to be made on what to take. Hill houses were very sparsely furnished, and lamps, crockery and linen were the very least that had to be taken. As always, Helen found Mrs Steel invaluable. The following is a list showing the way in which the property of a family, consisting of a lady, three or four children, and an English nurse, might be packed and loaded:

[180]

1st camel load: Two large trunks and two smaller ones with clothing.

2nd camel load: One large trunk containing children's clothing, plate chest, three bags, and one bonnet box.

3rd camel load: Three boxes of books, one box containing folding chairs, light tin box with clothing.

4th camel load: Four cases of stores, four cane chairs, saddle-stand, mackintosh sheets.

5th camel load: One chest of drawers, two iron cots, tea table, pans for washing up.

6th camel load: Second chest of drawers, screen, lamps, lanterns, hanging wardrobes.

7th camel load: Two boxes containing house linen, two casks containing ornaments, ice-pads, door mats.

8th camel load: Three casks of crockery, another cask containing ornaments, filter, pardah [purdah] bamboos, tennis poles.

9th camel load: Hot case, milk safe, baby's tub and stand, sewing-machine, fender and irons, water cans, pitchers.

10th camel load: Three boxes containing saddlery, kitchen utensils, carpets.

11th camel load: Two boxes containing drawing room sundries, servants' coats, iron bath, cheval glass, plate basket.

Or the above articles could be loaded on four country carts, each with three or four bullocks for the up hill journey . . . A piano, where carts can be used, requires a cart to itself, and should be swung to avoid being injured by jolting. If the road is only a camel road, the piano must be carried by coolies, of whom fourteen or sixteen will be needed . . . When a march is made by stages, and one's own cows accompany, these latter should start, after being milked, the night before the family.

Since the Brownes were childless, they were able to take rather less than Mrs Steel had felt bound to include in her list. They travelled by train for part of the way, and were soon in Dehra Doon, 'where all the hedges drop pink rose-petals, and the bulbul [nightingale] sings love songs in Persian, and the sahib lives in a little white house in a garden which is almost home'.

[181]

As far as the little white house was concerned, Mrs Steel had prepared them for it. The house *was* dirty. But 'do not be alarmed', said Mrs Steel drily. 'It is English people's dirt, not entirely natives'.' The older inhabitants of the town – and there were some who had retired there, instead of going Home to the colds and draughts of an England which had forgotten them, as they had forgotten it – said that little had changed, except the prices for as long as they could remember. There were, of course, some new-fangled modes of travel. There was the jenny-rickshaw, for example, a kind of two-wheeled carriage (rather like a bath-chair with a hood) which was said to be the invention of an Englishman called Public-Spirited Smith. Some people gave the credit for inventing it to the Japanese, however, while others maintained that an American missionary named Goble had been responsible.

But to the Brownes, the pleasantest thing about Dehra Doon were the cool night winds and the real fire which burned in the grate.

Though, on that first splendid visit to the hills, there were no Browne children, Helen's baby arrived soon afterwards. A young mother had much the same problems in Imperial India as she had done in the days when the Company ruled. A few wealthy households had English nurses, but for the majority there was no choice. It was an Indian nurse and, if necessary, an Indian wet-nurse – or no nurse at all. Some mothers, including missionary ladies, were horrified at the thought of a native wet-nurse. Mrs Steel was very stern with them on this subject. 'It must surely rouse surprise and regret', she exclaimed, 'that even those who profess to love the souls of men and women should find the bodies in which these souls are housed more repulsive than those of a cow or donkey or a goat'. Medically, there could be no rational objection to an Indian wet-nurse. 'What remains, therefore, but race prejudice to account for the fatuity of fearing lest the milk of a native woman should contaminate an English child's character, when that of the beasts which perish is held to have no such power?'

Nevertheless, a careful eye still had to be kept on the nurse and other servants. The opium pill was still a nurse's answer for a restless child, and an uninterested mother – of whom there were quite a few – would soon see her child in the local cemetery. More careful mothers were still inclined to fret over the moral problems involved when a child was brought up surrounded by Indian servants. They believed that a child would accept the standards of the heathen as his own. 'Let India's champions say what they will – it is still less easy to keep the eager, all-observant little minds fearlessly upright and untainted in an atmosphere of petty thefts and lies, such as natives look upon as mere common sense and good policy.' They worried about other dangers, too. 'The staple foods of childhood have far less nutritive value in India than in England, and the constant moving comes harder every year upon their sensitive nervous systems, to say nothing of the difficulty of obtaining pure and suitable food at Indian rest-houses and railway stations.'

Helen Browne, like other young mothers, knew that she would have to take her children to England before they reached the age of seven – this being the age after which, it was generally agreed, the *mores* of India would inescapably handicap them 'in the race of life'. The choice was between husband and children. 'Early or late the cruel wrench must come – the crueller, the longer deferred. One after one England claims them, till the mother's heart and house are left unto her desolate.'

If at all possible, it was best for a mother to go Home with her child, to see him settled with those who were to look after him. Where there was no family in England, it might be necessary to employ one of the professionals who specialised in looking after the children of exiles, though this solution was by no means to be recommended. It was unlikely that a husband would be able to accompany his wife on such a trip, and on board ship her talk would be all of 'the busy husband she had left, the station life, the attached servants, the favourite horse, the garden, and the bungalow. Her husband would soon follow her, in a year, or two years, and they would return together; but they would return to a silent home – the children would be left behind'. Returned to India, Helen would continue life as if nothing had changed. 'Heartlessness? Frivolity? In a few cases, possibly, but in most the sheer pluck of the race that has a prejudice in favour of making the best of things as they are, and never whimpering over the inevitable.'

Helen Browne has become a memsahib, 'graduated, qualified,

sophisticated . . . She has lost her pretty colour – that always goes first, and has gained a shadowy ring under each eye – that always comes afterwards . . . Her world is the personal world of Anglo-India, and outside of it I believe she does not think at all. She is growing dull to India, too, which is about as sad a thing as any. She sees no more the supple savagery of the Pathan in the market-place, the bowed reverence of the Mussalman praying in the sunset, the early morning mists lifting among the domes and palms of the city. She has acquired for the Aryan inhabitant a certain strong irritation, and she believes him to be nasty in all his ways . . . She is a memsahib like any other!'

# 3

# *THE DAY'S WORK*

AFTER the mutiny, a new generation of administrators arrived in India. They were known to the old hands as 'competition wallahs' for the sound reason that, instead of having been nominated by some interested party among the directorate of the East India Company, they had sat a competitive examination. This did not bring family traditions of service in India to an end; sons still followed their fathers – if they could pass the examination. But it introduced a new type of mind to the service, better in some ways, perhaps, more adequately educated, and a little more inclined to see more than one side of a question. The 'competition wallahs', however, were no less sure of their purpose in India or of their right to be there.

The examination itself was fairly stiff. The candidate was offered a wide range of subjects – mathematics, English, Greek, Latin, European languages, science, and others – from which he could choose to sit as many as he liked. Many young men went to a crammer, since it was rare to have the kind of mind possessed by William Hunter, who sat the examination in 1861. 'Whenever I read up a subject I become so interested in it that I go into the minutest points rather as if I intended to write a book to stand a general examination. Never do I attack a subject without writing what would make a bulky pamphlet.'

A long and dusty hall in London's old Burlington House was the scene of the examination. Each of the 207 candidates had a little desk and chair upholstered in red leather. Around the depressing green walls hung stern portraits, which stared fixedly over the candidates' heads.

What kind of men were the young hopefuls? Some were the 'sons of clergymen who have staked a long and expensive education on the chance of success: younger sons of country gentlemen who have fallen into decay and just succeeded in giving their lads two or three years at Oxford, and then a 15-guinea-a-month cram with some private coach'. But there were also quite a few wealthy 'swells' who came up to town for the examination and stayed at such fashionable hotels as Morley's. Among them were men who had failed the previous year and were making a second and last attempt to succeed. The questions were altogether too hard for some of them, even at first sight. 'After eyeing their papers with a blank, dreary gaze, they slowly take out a cigar case, examine its contents, smell its Russian delicacy, extract a cigar, put on their hats and march out. "Cabby, drive to Morley's". And this is repeated twice daily; meanwhile they eat like prize fighters to support the waste of the body and of the mind'. Others would sit with the examination paper in front of them, 'looking suicidal for half an hour', then they too would disappear.

Young William Hunter, of course, did not leave until he had completed his papers to his satisfaction. He found the questions 'rational, well considered, and easily enough answered', as long as you had 'read extensively, and above all, thought carefully over what you have read'. Hunter himself had no intention of failing, for, as he wrote to his fiancée after he arrived in India, 'I aspire to a circle far above the circle of fashion. I mean the circle of Power'. Hunter was not a swell, but one of the new middle class on which India was soon to depend – and not only India, but the great expanding empire of the high Victorian age. When he set off for India, he left his fiancée a two-volume life of Edmund Burke and the gold chain of his watch, which he suggested she might use 'with a locket of my hair as a bracelet or a necklace'.

Hunter found Calcutta very pleasing, physically at least, but he was not much taken with the ways of Anglo-India. He did not approve of people who ate and drank too much and then blamed the effects on the climate. He also found that the social necessity of paying calls interrupted his work on learning languages. After putting in an appearance at Government House, he made the same comments as those who had gone before him, and those who were to go after, for there was very little change in the protocol of viceroys and their receptions. The mosquitoes were as energetic as ever, and the ladies as overwhelming. Hunter lamented to his future wife that, frequently, a woman 'takes away her husband's chance of greatness' by demanding, after her day of idleness, that he 'amuse her by conversation or backgammon all evening', instead of permitting him to study. Duly warned, his fiancée came out to India, where they were married and posted to an up-country station.

Hunter looked about him and saw an India that made him proud to be English. 'Here we Englishmen stand on the face of the broad earth, a scanty, pale-faced band in the midst of three hundred millions of unfriendly vassals. On their side is a congenial climate and all the advantages which home and birthplace can give; on our long years of exile, a burning sun which dries up the Saxon energies, home sickenings, thankless labour, disease and often-times death far from wife, child, friend or kinsman.' How had this all come about, he demanded rhetorically. 'How is it that these pale-cheeked exiles give security to a race of another hue, other tongues, other religions, which rulers of their own people have failed to give?' The answer was evident. 'There are unseen moral causes which I need not point out . . .'

Not all the competition wallahs married as early in their careers as Hunter, nor were they as articulate. As a man of ideas, an intellectual, Hunter was in a minority. But all went through the same procedures, and what they did with their experience was up to them. Most of them were first sent out to the great timeless countryside of India, the district. Changes might have taken place in the face and character of the cities during Victoria's reign; the appearance of Madras and Bombay might have been completely altered by great new buildings; and even Calcutta, least altered of all, might have acquired a few appurtenances of modern life. Under pressure from the Sanitary Commission, drains – of a kind – had been introduced, and the possession of a water closet became a symbol of rank and wealth. Tramways, electric light and telephones might have added luxury to life. But only in the cities. The countryside, except in a few places close to the railway lines, remained essentially the same as it had always been, and the competition wallah found himself at one with his predecessors – alone, ignorant, and responsible.

The principle of pushing its employees in at the deep end in the hope that they would soon learn to swim remained an integral part of Indian Civil Service policy. A young man was sent straight off into the district, given a few weeks to appreciate the difficulties, and then expected to deal with some of them. He would have to try cases which were apparently simple but, in fact, enmeshed in contradictions and dubious evidence. He would have to make a variety of inspections, of everything from ferries to police stations, and, most important of all, of the land records. With some such experience behind him – a year, perhaps, of decisions right and wrong – the civilian would move on to higher things, to similar responsibilities in a larger area with a greater need for action.

Work in the services was, however, becoming more specialised. Where there had been no fixed line between different types of appointment, one was soon to have to be drawn. Did the civilian wish to go into the political service? This might mean the North-west Frontier, or a native state. It could be interesting, boring, or even dangerous. It could also be a subject for satire.

> The Government of India keeps its Political Agents scattered over the native states in small jungle stations. It furnishes them with maharajas, nawabs, rajas, and chuprassies [orderlies] according to their rank, and it usually throws in a house, a gaol, a doctor, a volume of Aitchison's *Treaties*, an escort of native Cavalry, a Star of India, an assistant, the powers of a first-class magistrate, a flag-staff, six camels, three tents, and a salute of eleven or thirteen guns.

In some states the political agent, or Resident, might have nothing more to do than pay an occasional ceremonial visit to the prince. He might occupy himself by trying to persuade the ruler to build a school, or a hospital, and he might even succeed – especially if a visit of inspection by the viceroy or, at the very least, by a governor might result.

In the larger states, however, a political agent's life could be

[188]

hedged with real dangers. In the state of Baroda, the maharaja conspired to murder the Resident with, it was alleged, poison in a glass of fruit juice, and had to be deposed lest other princes were encouraged to follow his example.

For men who delighted in exotic display, there was nothing to beat a career as political agent. In the Rajputana, for example, one Resident found the 'whole feeling of the country . . . mediaeval. The Rajput noblesse caracoles along with sword and shield, the small people crowd around with rags and rusty arms . . . I am afraid we do not altogether improve the nobles by keeping them from fighting'.

Failing the political service, a man might choose between the judicial and administrative branches. A judge's work in India was very different from that at Home. There were no juries in cases involving Indians. The judge would have the advice of native assessors, men of standing in the community, but he was not obliged to accept it. As a job, it was difficult but not unrewarding, since promotion was comparatively quick in the judicial service. As time passed, the young civilian's life changed only in the degree of responsibility he bore. A description of life in the district in the 1860s could stand, with only minor changes, for the remainder of the queen's reign and beyond. 'Here is Tom in his thirty-first year, in charge of a population as numerous as that of England in the reign of Elizabeth. His Burghley is a joint magistrate of eight-and-twenty, and his Walsingham an assistant magistrate who took his degree at Christ Church within the last fifteen months. These, with two or three superintendents of police, and last, but by no means least, a judge, who in rank and amount of salary stands to Tom in the position which the Lord Chancellor holds to the Prime Minister, are the only English officials in a province one hundred and twenty miles by seventy.' Tom is all-powerful in his district, or very nearly so. Above him there is a senior official, and beyond, the secretariat and the governor, but they are a long way off.

Tom's day is full. In the hot weather, 'he rises at daybreak, and goes straight from his bed to the saddle. Then off he gallops across the fields bright with dew to visit the scene of the last dacoit robbery; or to see with his own eyes whether the crops of the zemindar [landlord] who is so unpunctual with his assessment have really

[189]

failed; or to watch with fond parental care the progress of his pet embankment.' After this, he might have a run with the hounds, as motley a collection as the indigo planters' packs. 'On their return, the whole party adjourn to the subscription swimming-bath, where they find their servants ready with clothes, razors, and brushes.' Afterwards, 'seated under a punkah on his verandah, he works through the contents of one despatch-box, or "bokkus", as the natives call it, after another; signing orders, and passing them on to the neighbouring collectors; dashing through drafts, to be filled up by his subordinates; writing reports, minutes, digests, letters of explanation, or remonstrance, of warning, of commendation'. Noon is the time for tiffin, then Tom goes down to the court house for a session of decisions on land and revenue. If there are few cases, time may permit a game or two of racquets before Tom sets out for a ride with his wife or billiards with the superintendent of police. By ten o'clock he has dined and gone to bed.

In the cold weather, like his predecessors before him, Tom travels around the further reaches of his district, enjoying the pleasures of camp life. After a morning of inspections, it is invigorating to bring down a bird or two for the pot, and pleasant, 'as you reach the rendezvous in the gloaming, rather tired and very dusty, to find your tents pitched, and your soup and curry within a few moments of perfection, and your servant with a bottle of lemonade . . . and the head man of the village ready with his report of a deadly affray that would have taken place if you had come in a day earlier'.

During the latter part of the nineteenth century, the practice of detaching military officers for civil duties declined, but did not cease. In the 1860s many young officers found themselves in charge of reorganising the police. One who did so ended up much wiser in the ways of persuading 'criminals' to confess. The police would fill the nose and ears of a suspect with cayenne pepper, or suspend him head downwards in a well. Women and children were merely hung up by their hair or their thumbs. Many of these practices, though not all, were swiftly stopped. Nor did bribery and extortion disappear when new men were appointed.

The usual serious crimes in an Indian district were murder and robbery. There was nothing straightforward about even a simple robbery. One young superintendent of police received a note from a senior British official complaining of a burglary and saying that his wife's jewels had been taken. When the superintendent arrived at the bungalow, the memsahib was in bed. Her servant, however, told him that the jewels were kept, with some silver spoons, in a box under the bed in which the master and mistress slept. She herself slept in the bathroom leading off the bedroom, in the company of two pet dogs. 'I thoroughly examined the premises, and set spies in the bazaar with curious results. In the first place, I found that the dogs had not barked, but passed a quiet night. It was true that the iron gauze outside the pantry window had been cut away, but no marks of violence or footsteps were visible outside, while in the bushes near, one of the police discovered a stout pair of scissors, freshly broken, the point of which fitted into the marks on both box and window. On searching the house of the chief goldsmith in the bazaar the jewels were found in his strongbox: I pointed out to him the serious position in which he was placed by this discovery, and he then stated that the jewels were sold to him by the lady's ayah, who, in her turn, on being threatened with the law, confessed that she had sold them by her lady's own orders. The result was an unpleasant one to communicate to the lady's husband.'

There could be danger for police officers as well as for Residents. Some of the areas were loosely administered and populated by tribesmen. While one police officer was peacefully engaged in playing his violin in his own tent, a bullet struck him, although the assault was apparently not intended as a criticism of his musical ability. His wound was in the thigh and bled badly, but his escort managed to get him to a dugout canoe and away from the scene of the attack. The wound soon healed – which the victim ascribed to 'the simple, abstinent life which I had led for so many weeks previous to the accident. No bread, no beer, no butter, no flesh save an occasional chicken, a dish of rice, and sometimes fish, with constant exercise in the open air was evidently an uninflammatory diet.' Recovered, he went off and did his best to kill himself in pursuit of the culprit. Yet he found many of the people he had to deal with 'the simplest, the most kindly folk'. They were 'truthful, and capable of strong attachments; having also a great appreciation of straight and even-handed justice. I found them ground down by ignorant, narrow-minded chiefs; harassed by litigious, lying Bengali usurers . . . They needed schools, they needed religious teaching, they needed simple, upright dealing, and protection for their lives, and their belongings. These needs I set myself to supply.'

Among the considerable difficulties which had to be overcome was the resistance of the more conservative elements among the tribal chiefs. One chief had even suborned the superintendent's subordinates and was able to read all his personal papers and reports. Carefully resealed, these were then returned to the police sergeant for delivery. The superintendent settled this matter by placing a large packet in the next postal bag, heavily and ostentatiously sealed, and marked 'urgent'. The bag was not given to the postal runner until a time which would make it impossible for him to reach the police post before sundown. It seemed likely that, when the package was taken to the chief, it would remain in his hut until the next morning. Journeying through the night, the superintendent himself arrived at the police post just before dawn. When the sergeant, who was himself a tribesman, was brought out and threatened with a loaded revolver, he admitted that the postbag was in the chief's possession. The small party, taking the sergeant with it, made its way to the village and surprised the chief with the letters open all about him. 'It was a strange scene, lit up by the first rays of the morning sun. The platform, with the astonished chief, surrounded by my five policemen with fixed bayonets, myself bare-legged, with pointed revolver, clad in country home-spun, all wet and dripping, muddy and torn, after our night's travel and swim across the river. Below us a surging crowd of muttering villagers, among whom some spears began to show.' But opposition failed to develop when it was made clear that the chief would unhesitatingly be shot if any attempt was made to prevent his arrest.

Back at the police station, the superintendent transformed himself into a magistrate and opened the trial. The defence was simple. It was not the chief who had opened the letters but his principal adviser. The chief's brother confirmed this. The adviser was immediately arrested and within quarter of an hour was on his way down river to jail. Then a deal was arranged. The police agreed to accept the

One of the means of transport between 'Stations'; a sort of Stage Coach.

*Above :* 'Our Station'. An up-country military and civil station, c.1840. *Below :* Entertainment at 'Our Station'. The band of a sepoy (i.e., Indian) regiment entertaining the adults while the children entertain themselves.

*Above :* The servants of a modest household, cook, butler, ayah (and her white charge). Behind the 'arras' the sweeper who cleaned out the latrines and with whom other servants would not mix. *Below :* One of the most vital of servants, the water-carrier.

The face of a reformer. Sir William Sleeman, known as the suppressor of the Thugs, gangs of religious bandits who roamed India in the early 19th century.

A Fantasy of Martyrdom. Entirely imagined view of Europeans in Cawnpore (Kanpur) during the Mutiny of 1857.

Until the discovery of artificial dyes at the end of the 19th century, the indigo planter could indeed be 'a farmer prince', living in good style, in a fine house on his estate.

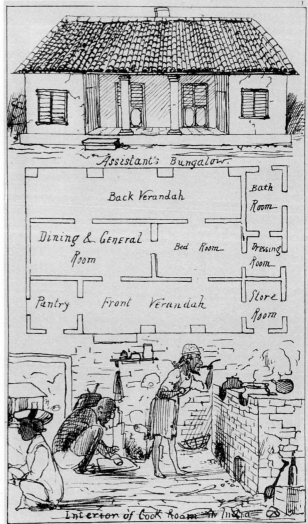

Assistant's Bungalow.

Back Verandah

Bath Room

Dining & General Room

Bed Room

Dressing Room

Pantry

Front Verandah

Store Room

Interior of Cook Room in India

An assistant on an indigo plantation lived a simple life, in a simple bungalow, with a somewhat primitive kitchen, though the latter differed only in scale from that of the 'farmer prince'.

'Anglo-Indians' were quick to resent interference in their lives by a member of the British Parliament, who, after a short cold-weather visit would suddenly become an expert on India. They laughed at him, but the laughter often concealed a genuine anxiety.

The British attempted to acclimatize their sports to India, and did so, at least in the hill-stations, with some success. Some concessions had to be made. The Ootacamund Hunt, here shown in 1896, had to settle for a jackal rather than a fox.

A house warming in Simla, 1923. The house is that of the Maharaja of Bharatpur and, of course, resembled an English rather than an Indian house. The lady in the front row with the threateningly large hat is the wife of the viceroy, Lord Reading.

*Above :* Viceregal Lodge, New Delhi. 1930. The late flowering of Imperial architecture designed, with some reluctance, as an Eurasian Versailles by Sir Edwin Lutyens. *Below :* At the end of Empire. The last viceroy and his wife with the new ruler of Pakistan, M.A. Jinnah and his sister, 1947.

adviser as scapegoat if, in return, the chief would resign his authority to his brother 'and seek the rest and repose he so much needed in a religious life'. At the jail, the adviser was told of the arrangement and invited to confess all, which, in return for a guarantee of protection, he did. So the chain of evidence was complete, to be held in reserve for any sign of trouble from the new chief. The superintendent himself had to pay a price for thus establishing authority, with 'a bad attack of fever and ague, brought on by the fatigue of the night march, the cold swim across the river, with the subsequent excitement, which prevented my drying wet clothes'. After twenty years' service, which included a full-scale military expedition against the tribesmen, the superintendent's rewards were ill-health, the honorary rank of lieutenant-colonel, and a pension of £190 a year. But he also had the consolation that, twenty-five years after his going, his name was still widely known in the wild hills – severely mangled by the tribal language – and his exploits had taken on the lineaments of myth.

The wild places and the lonely places were still the main centres of Anglo-Indian work. Elsewhere there was a vast spectrum of activity, from the world of the European businessmen to that of the engineers who built the railways. The immense extent of railway construction attracted time-expired soldiers to work as gang foremen and in the other middle layers of authority. The railways also became the cynosure of the Eurasian population, already entrenched in the posts and telegraphs.

At the head of all – and believed by some not to do any work at all – was what one satirist called 'the Great Ornamental'. The viceroy and governor-general was by no means just ornamental, however, and well the satirist knew it, for in going on to describe the viceroy's office (that 'censorium of the empire'), he was compelled to admit that 'every pigeon-hole contains a potential revolution; every office-box cradles the embryo of a war or dearth'. Some viceroys' pigeon-holes were fuller than others. More than one viceroy suffered physically from his period of service, however short that might be in comparison with the tour of duty expected from ordinary men. One viceroy even died in India at the hand of an assassin; his memory was enshrined in a number of memorial halls. The opening of one of these, at Allahabad, was distinguished by the presence of the then viceroy, Lord Lytton, and an enormous crowd – enormous, that is, for Anglo-India – gathered for the occasion. An amateur chorus 'of all the best and most cultivated gentlemen and lady singers of that part of India . . . accompanied by an admirably touched organ' sang an ode to Lord Mayo, the murdered viceroy, set to a tune from Rossini's *Moses in Egypt*:

> On thee, great Shade! We call –
> Unseen, though still at hand –
> To consecrate this Hall
> In Thine adopted land:
> Long may that honoured name
> Bestow its favouring fame,
>                     Mayo!

> While Jumna's water pours
> Her tribute to the sea,
> Still may these votive towers
> Proclaim our love for thee;
> Thy noble life laid low
> By treason's felon blow,
>                     Mayo!

> For thou wert of the few
> Who conquer Destiny;
> Brave, merciful and true,
> All that a chief should be.
> Hail to the mighty dead
> Whose life for us was sped,
>                     Mayo!

Usually viceroys achieved the memorial hall but not the assassin. Some of them, however, did inspire homicidal thoughts among members of the civil service and the army. Such a one was Lord Curzon who, though not by any temperament really a Victorian at all, was by an accident of history to preside over the obsequies of the queen's India. Curzon's day ran far into the night. He read state papers 'from 10 a.m. with the exception of an hour or two for meals, or a public function or a private drive, until 2 a.m. the following morning or sometimes later'. He protested strongly at the way his subordinates worked, for he found the bureaucratic methods of the government of India positively ludicrous. 'Your despatch of August the 5th arrived', he wrote to the secretary of state for India in London in 1899. 'It goes to the Foreign Department. Thereupon clerk No. 1 paraphrases and comments upon it over 41 folio pages of print of his own composition, dealing solely with the Khyber suggestions in it. Then comes clerk No. 2 with 21 more pages upon clerk No. 1. Then we get to the region of Assistant Secretaries, Deputy Secretaries, and Secretaries. All these gentlemen state their worthless views at equal length. Finally we get to the top of the scale, and we find the Viceroy and the Military Member, with a proper regard for their dignity, expanding themselves over a proportionate space of print. Then these papers wander about from Department to Department, and amid the various Members of Council. Each has his say, and the result is a sort of literary Bedlam. I am grappling with this vile system in my own Department, but it has seated itself like the Old Man of the Sea upon the shoulders of the Indian Government, and every man accepts, while deploring, the burden.'

Curzon enquired into everything and interfered in everything from the drains of Calcutta to the hushing up (by officials) of a case of rape in Rangoon. His inquisitions, his sarcastic style when giving a reprimand, alienated the services from him. But the machine went on. One day's work still followed the pattern of yesterday's work, and it seemed as if tomorrow's work would be much the same, too. Most of the men who operated the machine would have agreed with Curzon when he said at a banquet given in his honour in Bombay: 'If I thought it were all for nothing, and that you and I, Englishmen and Scotchmen and Irishmen in this country, were simply writing inscriptions on the sand to be washed out by the next tide; if I felt that we were not working here for the good of India in obedience to a higher law and a nobler aim, then I would see the link that holds India and England together severed without a sigh. But it is because I believe in the future of this country and the capacity of our own race to guide it to goals that it has never hitherto attained, that I keep courage and press forward.'

[195]

# 4

# PICNICS AND ADULTERY

A writer in the English satirical journal *Vanity Fair* once summed up the world of Anglo-India as 'duty and red tape, picnics and adultery'. There was a general impression that Anglo-Indian society was immoral. Most of the criticism was aimed at the women. In the Victorian ethos, men had their pleasures – but women 'fell'. One moralist went so far as to suggest that Anglo-Indian women were not only frivolous, but that they did their utmost 'to divert the energies of the men from work . . . to pleasure and frivolity likewise'.

Men scarcely needed to be diverted. In the wild and lonely places, the sahib had his Indian mistress or patronised the better class of courtesan from the nearest town. If his tastes were more specialised, he found no difficulty in satisfying them. The bazaars knew all about the sahib's weaknesses, and there was no shortage of pimps. In the army, homosexual liaisons were comparatively easy to arrange, although they often led to blackmail and, not infrequently, to dismissal from the service. The heterosexual requirements of the common soldier were reasonably and hygienically catered for, by registering prostitutes at the military stations. Unfortunately, Her Majesty heard of this. The practice was stopped, and the natural consequence was that there was an appreciable increase in venereal infection.

There was a steady business in pornographic books and pictures, which only the better-off could afford, and in the larger towns could be found one or two well-organised and furnished brothels offering a wide choice of European and Asian women. Calcutta had all the appurtenances of Europe, including a home for 'fallen' white women who had made their tragic journey down the scale from high-class establishments to the 'boarding houses' for visiting sailors. But the main reservoir of talent was, as always, among the amateurs. According to popular belief, most of the hardest-worked amateurs were to be found on the Olympus of Anglo-India, the viceregal hill-station of Simla.

Simla changed very considerably after 1860. When Lord Lawrence was appointed viceroy in 1864, his doctors made it a condition that he should spend the hot-weather months in the hills. The government in London agreed and, though other rulers of India had spent some time in Simla, it was because of Lawrence that it became irrevocably the summer seat of the Imperial government. 'No doubt such a change as I propose is a serious one and requires much consideration', he wrote to the secretary of state in London. 'I do not, however, think that a better arrangement is to be made. The work now is, probably, treble, possibly quadruple, what it was twenty years ago, and it is for the most part of a very difficult nature. Neither could your Governor-General and his Council really do it in the hot weather in Calcutta. At the best, as you say, they would work at half speed . . . This place of all hill stations seems to me the best for the Supreme Government.' Lawrence did not particularly enjoy Simla once he got there. He was not much of a man for gaiety. Lady Lawrence, too, found it 'one long round of large dinner parties, balls, and festivities of all kinds'. Even though she attempted to introduce some more rational entertainment in the form of 'Shakespeare readings, and tableaux', it all remained very trying.

The house Lawrence occupied was, for some reason, called 'Peterhoff'. Lord Lytton with his poetical turn of phrase, later described it as 'a sort of pigsty'. Lady Dufferin, the wife of another viceroy, found it too much like a cottage, very suitable for private life but not for official life, as the rooms were very small. 'Altogether', she wrote in her diary, 'it is the funniest place! At the back of the house you have about a yard to spare before you tumble down a precipice, and in front there is just room for one tennis court before you go over another.' The ADCs were billeted in various bungalows, equally precariously sited, and had to 'go through perilous adventures to come to dinner'. Earlier viceroys had put up with the disadvantages of the house because of the cost of building a new one, but Dufferin, feeling that imperial prestige (as well as the comfort of the queen's representative) was at stake, managed to persuade the home government that the expense was justified. Lady Dufferin, no doubt, had something to do with her husband's persuasiveness. When a ball was held at 'Peterhoff', the conservatory had to be converted into a sitting-room. The nights were cold, however, and the frequenters of the dark places behind the potted palms 'were unable to enjoy it as much as I had hoped'.

The new building was known, more appropriately, as Viceregal Lodge, and the Dufferins occupied it in July 1888. After 'Peterhoff' – in fact, by any standards – it was luxurious. There was even electric light, and Lady Dufferin found that 'the lighting up and putting out of the lamps is so simple that it is quite a pleasure to go round one's room touching a button here and there, and to experiment with various amounts of light'. The architectural style was reputed to be 'English Renaissance', but a later secretary of state described it as 'exactly like a Scotch hydro – the same sort of architecture, the same sort of equipment of tennis lawns and sticky courts, and so forth'. Lady Dufferin was as impressed by the 'offices' as she was by the lighting system. She also found the laundry of interest, and wondered how the washermen would like it. 'What they are accustomed to is to squat on the brink of a cold stream, and there to flog and batter our wretched garments against the hard stones until they think them clean. Now they will be condemned to warm water and soap, to mangles and ironing and drying rooms, and they will probably think it all very unnecessary, and will perhaps faint with the heat.'

With so much more space at their disposal, viceroys could now expand their social activities. Very soon after its first occupation, Viceregal Lodge became the scene of 'brilliant' entertainments. These owed much to the organising ability of the viceroy's military secretary, who, from 1881 until 1894, was Lord William Beresford. But the men who made or broke viceregal receptions and dances were undoubtedly the aides-de-camp.

An ADC had 'four distinct aspects or phases – (1) the full summer sunshine and bloom of scarlet and gold for Queen's birthdays and high ceremonials; (2) the dark frock-coats and belts in which to canter behind his Lord in; (3) the evening tail-coat, turned down with light blue and adorned with the Imperial arms on gold buttons; (4) and, finally, the quiet disguises of private life'.

In his first phase, the ADC was so gorgeous that 'the splendour of vice-Imperialism seems to beat upon him most fiercely'. Frock-coated and belted, he seemed to eager young ladies the key to the delights of Viceregal Lodge. 'He passes into church or elsewhere behind his Lord, like an aerolite from some distant universe, trailing cloudy visions of that young lady's Paradise of bright lights and music, champagne, mayonnaise and "just-one-more-turn", which is situated behind the flagstaff on the hill.' In his evening garb of 'tail-coat with gold buttons, velvet cuffs, and light blue silk lining', he might have a certain weakness for flirtations on the verandah. But off duty and in plain clothes the ADC was quite 'of the earth'. He had even been known to 'lay the long odds at whist, and to qualify, very nearly, for a co-respondentship'.

Behind the mask of brilliant entertainments and romantic ADCs lay the real face of government. In spite of its butterfly reputation, Simla did house the administration of the empire, and that administration was not carried out from the ballroom and the supper table. Throughout the season, the whole decision-making apparatus of India was concentrated on this ridge of the Himalayas, cut off from the plains by fifty-eight miles of indifferent road. From the end of this road, at Kalka, a railway had been constructed in the 1880s to Ambala in the Punjab. The journey from Simla to Kalka was made in a carriage, a special one for people of importance, a hired tonga for everybody else. The tonga, a two-wheeled vehicle pulled by one horse, covered the journey in stages. If there were no landslips or other delays, the route could be covered in eight hours. On more than one occasion, the government of India was totally cut off from the India it governed when the road was blocked by fallen rocks and the telegraph lines brought down by torrential rain.

It was, all things considered, an odd place for the government to roost for nearly seven months of the year. In fact, Simla was very odd altogether. It straggled across several spurs of mountain about 7,000 feet above sea level. None of its roads was really wide enough for a carriage, so only the viceroy, the commander-in-chief, and the lieutenant-governor of the Punjab were allowed to use one. Most other people used the rickshaw or the horse. The architecture of the town was terrible. Lady Curzon, on her first visit, decided that 'the Public Works and other buildings have made it monstrous. All the public buildings are crosses between chalets and readymade iron houses, and their fluted roofs cover the hillsides'. There was some-thing essentially un-Indian yet not-quite-British about it all, even though the Anglo-Indians had tried their best to cut the real India out of Simla and replace it with something that was more like Home. It had finished up a rather exotic Home. The scattered houses trembled on hilltops and clung precariously over deep valleys. They were usually one-storeyed bungalows built of wood and surrounded with flowers. Everywhere the roofs were covered with the ugliest building material ever invented – corrugated iron. The larger buildings ranged in style from railway Gothic of the most overpowering kind to publican's Tudor, and the army headquarters had been accurately described as looking as though 'a number of trams had been piled untidily on top of each other and bolted together with flying steel rods'. The whole town gave the impression of having been trans-ported from Surrey in a badly packed parcel and accidentally dropped in Tibet.

The new arrival first saw Simla from the Mall. The tonga office was there, crowded with the jaded faces of those who were just arriving from the hot and weary plains, and with the fresh, glowing faces of people about to leave Simla and return to duty. Just below the Mall was the famous Peliti's Grand Hotel where the comfortable sitting room invited the visitor 'to read and dream in the great chairs, and the well-ordered café is of never-failing interest, for here, in the groups of laughing, faultlessly dressed English men and women he finds the true Anglo-Indian'. Among them would be found most of the characters enshrined in Rudyard Kipling's *Plain Tales from the Hills* – which was not altogether approved of when it was published. People who were not staying in their own houses would live in one of the hotels, or, if they were unattached men, at the Club, a fine establishment with accommodation for about seventy members and all the fittings requisite for a club. There was a dining room, with

portraits of the late commander-in-chief and other worthies, a band
to supply music on Saturdays (which were guest nights), and a pretty
cottage-like annexe officially known as The Chalet, but generally
known as The Hen-House, in which members could entertain ladies.

Not everyone in Simla was a visitor. There were a number of
people who had made it their permanent home when they retired
from one of the services. Allan Octavian Hume was one resident who
had been in the civil service; he had ended his official career as
secretary of a government department. In Simla he lived in a house
called Rothney Castle, on which he had lavished a great deal of
money in the hopes, it was rumoured, that he might sell the house to
the government of India as a residence for the viceroy, in place of the
miserable 'Peterhoff'. He had added enormous reception rooms
suitable for large dinner parties and balls, a superb conservatory, and
an immense entrance hall festooned with a valuable collection of
animal horns. He had brought out a European gardener to see to the
grounds, and the results were so magnificent that many people were
prepared to venture the difficult approach road in order to admire
them. At one time, Hume had collected birds. 'Possessed of ample
private means, he had in his employ an army of collectors, some of
them Europeans working on liberal salaries even beyond the limits
of India Proper, while many private collectors, falling under the
influence of Mr Hume's genius, gave him strenuous assistance in
all parts of the Indian Empire.' But then Mr Hume discovered
Theosophy. As one of the tenets of this new belief opposed the taking
of life, Mr Hume sent off telegrams to the collectors instructing them
to shoot no more birds. The collection, now very large, was offered to
the British Museum, from which it was ultimately transferred to the
Natural History Museum in London's South Kensington.

It was, perhaps, fitting that Theosophy should find powerful
adherents in Simla. The town at least lay on the way to those
mysterious Himalayan fastnesses, so vaguely defined, which housed
the *mahatmas* who had revealed much arcane knowledge to the
founder of the movement, Helena Petrovna Blavatsky. For some
reason, very strong efforts were made to attract adherents in Simla,
especially from among the ranks of high government officials. It was,
in fact, rumoured that Madame Blavatsky was a Russian agent and

that she had been kept under constant surveillance by the police since she arrived in India. Allan Octavian Hume was indifferent to these slanders, and Madame became a frequent guest at Rothney Castle. There she would receive communications from her 'guide', Kut Humi, in the form of letters written on palm leaves. One such letter, which floated down from the ceiling at nine o'clock on a July evening in 1879, was handed, by Madame herself, to a sceptic. 'I read it. Addressed to Madame, the purport of it was that she need not trouble herself with attempts to make proselytes of the incredulous. Enough that those who believed and practised should gain the higher plains of knowledge and power. What mattered it to them that the rest of human kind wallowed in ignorance. The adepts could smile at them in contempt from their superior height! The text of the letter might indeed have been that to preach to the ignorant would be to "cast pearls before swine". Reading through the letter it struck me that Kut Humi must have had considerable intercourse with America, as more than one of the phrases appeared to savour of the Yankee dialect.'

Madame Blavatsky could produce more than palm-leaf airmail. At the dinner table, with a carefully selected body of believers and potential believers, she could be prevailed upon to give an example of the power 'which the true Theosophist acquires by asceticism, faith and self-denial'. First she would protest, 'like a young lady asked for a song: "It is very trying to me; it exhausts much; no, no, I cannot, I cannot"; but further pressed, at last exclaimed, "well then, I must, but it is hard, it is hard! Mrs Hume (turning to her hostess) what is there that you would find?"

'*Mrs Hume* – "Yes. A year or more ago I lost a brooch. Find that and it will be indeed wonderful".

'*Madame* – "It is hard but IT SHALL BE DONE!! Kitmatgar [butler]! Bring me one lantern!" The lantern brought Madame rose, led the way through the opened doors leading to the garden; there halting, she pointed to a bush and commanded, "Dig there!!" A spade produced, earth was removed and lo! there was the brooch. The guests wonderstruck and, some of them at least, convinced, returned to the table where a succinct account of the miracle was drawn up and signed by all present.'

On another occasion, Madame, finding that there were not enough cups at a picnic, discovered by her incredible powers of divination that another cup of exactly the same design had been buried under a bush.

These activities caused a considerable stir in certain sections of Simla society, a stir which even survived a number of exposures of Madame's conjuring tricks. Mr Hume himself had the best of both worlds by describing her as the most marvellous liar he had ever met, but excusing her on the grounds that her lies and her tricks were designed with the honest object of converting people to 'a higher faith'.

Eventually Madame Blavatsky disappeared from Simla and Mr Hume took up another hobby. This time it was more far-reaching. He founded the Indian National Congress, the organisation which was later to become the instrument of India's fight for freedom from the British.

Most Anglo-Indians regarded Hume's foundation of the Indian National Congress as just another of the eccentricities with which Simla abounded. Some of these were forgivable; others were not. It was virtually impossible, for example, to accept the propriety of Mr Charles de Russett becoming a *sadhu*, a holy man, especially as he had been educated in the best Christian tradition at Bishop Cotton's School in Simla itself. It was no good advertisement for the excellent establishment – intended for the education of children whose parents could not afford to send them to school in England – for one of its alumni to be seen about Jakko Hill, surrounded by monkeys, and clad only in a piece of yellow cloth. After spending a couple of years' novitiate with another *sadhu*, de Russett had wandered around Simla for a time wearing a leopard-skin headdress, but he soon retired into seclusion where, according to one man who met him in the 1890s, 'no doubt he commands the highest respect from the natives, and lives idle, happy, and contented, without any anxiety about the morrow!'

An eccentric of another kind was to be given a measure of immortality in the works of Rudyard Kipling. This was a dealer in curiosities who had arrived in Simla in 1871, after having apparently been an adviser to the raja of Dholpur. He called himself Jacob, though everyone doubted that this was his real name, and the doubts were fed by several conflicting stories which were circulated about his origins. His little shop was described by the novelist, Marion Crawford, in 1879: 'At first glance it appeared as if the walls and ceiling were lined with gold and precious stones; and in reality it was almost the truth. The apartment was small – for India at least – and every available space, nook and cranny, were filled with gold and jewelled ornaments, shining weapons, or uncouth but resplendent idols.' There were ghost daggers from Tibet, prayer wheels, gilt Buddhas rapt and serene, portable altars of fine red lacquer glistening with gold and pieces of coloured glass. There were Persian water jugs of elegant design, and incense burners heavily inlaid with turquoise and lapis lazuli. Great banners showing the terrible faces of the Buddhist hells hung from the walls or cluttered the floors in rolls. Jewellery, raw turquoises from Tibet, rubies and zircons from Burma, finely veined jade from China, all awaited the sahibs and memsahibs, the native princes, and the rich merchants of the bazaar. But Mr Jacob seemed to give the impression that he did not care about selling his stock, especially to fools who would not appreciate its rarities. His prices were high, and needed the support of a good sales technique. Jacob received potential customers in a room where 'lamps of the octagonal Oriental shape hung from the ceiling, and fed by aromatic oils, shed their soothing light on all around. The floor was covered with a dark, rich pile, and low divans were heaped with cushions of deep-tinted silk and gold. On the floor in a corner . . . lay open two or three superbly illuminated Arabic manuscripts, and from a chafing dish of silver near by a thin thread of snow-white smoke sent up its faint perfume through the still air'.

Without much difficulty, Kipling converted this mysterious dealer into Lurgan Sahib, the trainer of secret agents in *Kim*. Jacob was believed in Simla to be either a Russian spy – they were very popular in late Victorian India – or a British secret agent. Certainly, he was a remarkable linguist, an adept conjurer and, it was generally agreed, a hypnotist of a high order. Simla felt very much duller when he left, after having been ruined by the costs of a case he had successfully brought against the ruler of Hyderabad in 1891, for breach of an agreement whereby Jacob was to purchase 'the Imperial

Diamond' for the prince for over 4,500,000 rupees (about £300,000 at the then rate of exchange).

Madame Blavatsky and her black (or grey) magic, the European *sadhu* practising yoga and other heathen arts, and the strange activities of Mr Jacob in his house of wonders – all these were supplemented, in native eyes, by the mysterious rites the sahibs carried out in their *jadoogur*, or magic house. In English – the Freemasons' Lodge.

Freemasonry was very solidly established in Anglo-India. There was a lodge in practically every station of consequence, and everywhere it was thought by the Indians to be a house of magic. In western India, it was often known as the *shaitankhana*, the house of the devil. In south India, the Tamil name meant 'cut-head temple', because it was believed that part of the rite of initiation included the cutting off and restoring of the initiate's head! In Simla there had been a lodge since 1838, and towards the end of the century there were four. The only magic practised in public was the annual ball the Masons gave to the viceroy, which was one of the most brilliant functions of the Simla season. Lady Dufferin noted in her diary for 10 September 1888 that it was 'very pretty entertainment'. When the viceregal party arrived at the Town Hall, they 'were met at the door by a number of gentlemen in aprons, sashes, white cloaks, and black cloaks, red tunics, stars, crosses, medallions, orders and emblems of all sorts and kinds. Some of them carried long silver sticks with a dove on the top of each, and these marched before us, and we went in procession down the room between lines formed by the rest of the brethren'. The party stayed until twelve, 'and then marched away in procession, the Masons singing a song and sending us off with three cheers'.

Yet Simla was a worldly rather than an un-worldly place. Even the church had a distinctly secular aura. Sunday, of course, was a day of demonstration at which obeisance was paid to the god who watched over Anglo-India. But the service was more of a ritual than anything else. The viceroy would appear in his carriage, to join the ladies in their great hats and their menfolk inside Christ Church for a short sermon by the archdeacon.

The archdeacon of Simla was supposed to occupy an eminence in the church hierarchy above even bishops of the plains. Transported to the plains, he himself remained a mere archdeacon (usually the archdeacon of Calcutta), but the viceregal atmosphere of Simla lent him a special air of authority. He was believed by some to be the guardian of public morality. 'A word, a kiss, some matrimonial charm dissolved – these electric disturbances of society must be averted. The Archdeacon is the lightning conductor; where he is, the leaven of naughtiness passes to the ground, and society is not shocked.' He was assumed to be a man of the world, and his relations with the ladies of Simla were regarded as 'more than avuncular, and less than cousinly; they are tender without being romantic, and confiding without being burdensome. He has the private entrée at . . . breakfast; he sees loose and flowing robes that are only for esoteric disciples; he has the private entrée at five o'clock tea and hears plans for the evening campaign openly discussed. He is quite behind the scenes. He hears the earliest whispers of engagements and flirtations. He can give a stone to the Press Commissioner in the gossip handicap, and win in a canter. You cannot tell him anything he does not know already.' But even Archdeacon Baly, the original of this portrait, could hardly have known as much about the intrigues of Anglo-India as Horace Goad.

Horace Goad had the reputation of being the smartest police officer in north-west India. From 1877 until his retirement in 1895, there was little that did not reach his ears about what went on in Simla. No secret was safe from the servants in an Anglo-Indian household. When a clandestine meeting took place behind Jakko Hill, the rickshaw pullers only looked as if they were asleep. There was constant espionage, not necessarily with any hope of gain, but often merely for the sake of gossip. On the whole, it was innocent enough, although the native princes filled Simla with their agents during the season and kept the British under constant surveillance, hoping to discover some special knowledge which might later be used to their advantage. In due time, Horace Goad heard most of the scandal. He spoke a number of dialects with great fluency and, as Kipling said when he modelled a character on him, was supposed to have 'the gift of invisibility and executive control over many Devils'. Goad was also capable of disguising himself so well that he was thought to have occult powers. Indeed, native children were often silenced by the threat of being handed over to him. He committed suicide in Ambala in 1896, and no one was at all surprised that a government office in Simla should burn down the same evening. It was assumed to be Goad's funeral pyre, and ever afterwards it was insisted in the bazaar that his spirit had been seen in the flames.

What was there for Goad Sahib to know about Simla? Were the women really promiscuous? The divorce courts supply some evidence, but only in cases where people more intimately concerned than Horace Goad lighted on the truth. Newspapers in both India and Britain were full of criticisms of Simla. It was such a luxurious place that it was sometimes called 'the Capua of India'. Articles frequently appeared under such headlines as 'Revels on Olympus', but the detail was always rather thin and there was more innuendo than fact. One defender of Anglo-Indian virtue claimed that newspaper correspondents, forced to follow the Imperial government up to its summer residence, found themselves short of copy and had to fill up space somehow. Government business, he suggested, was conducted with such discretion that there was seldom any hard news. 'Hence there is little for the newspaper correspondents to write about except the gaieties of the place; and so the balls and picnics, the croquet and badminton parties, the flirtations and rumoured engagements, are given an importance which they do not actually possess.' Besides, he argued, 'wherever youth and beauty meet, there will, no doubt, be a certain amount of flirtation, even though the youth may be rather shaky from long years of hard work in the hot plains of India . . . and though the beauty be often pallid and passé; but anything beyond that hardly exists at Simla at all, and has the scantiest opportunity for developing itself'. Furthermore, 'the young officers and civilians who go up to Simla for their leave are usually far-seeing young men who have an eye to good appointments, and, whatever their real character may be, are not likely to spoil their chances of success by attracting attention to themselves as very gay Lotharios'. But this kind of defence, however comprehensive, was never really accepted. Undeniably, though the majority of women in Simla were as chaste as any heroine of Victorian verse, quite a number were not.

[207]

There were many temptations of the kind which breed quickly in boredom. Though there was plenty to do in Simla as well as dance and picnic, though there were 'good works' in the charitable societies which proliferated as a kind of surrogate for Victorian India's guilts, and art exhibitions full of amateur renderings of 'Sunset over Jakko Hill', yet society was so luxurious and cosseted that charity and art could fill only a small part of the time. The rest was thick with pitfalls. Among the very worst were 'amateur theatricals and military men on leave'. When both came together at the Dramatic Club there was plenty of material for scandal. Too much scandal, and the military man on leave might find himself back with his regiment in the plains, while the lady's husband would arrive up at Simla for a few days to enquire into the truth of a deliberately indiscreet letter he had received from a well-wisher. Many husbands found nothing more than gossip and were able to return to the cholera and the heat with doubts at least temporarily assuaged. Their optimism might not, however, match that of a distinguished fellow civil servant, who celebrated his return to the plains in the following terms:

> Farewell to Peliti, whose menus delicious,
>   Have helped our digestion the long season through,
> Farewell to the scandals so false and malicious,
>   And all the more piquant, for not being true,.
> Au revoir to the ladies, farewell to them never,
>   Who are most of them pretty, and all of them good,
> Whose saintly example and gentle endeavour
>   Would surely reform me, if anything could.

Nor might they gain much comfort from Lord Curzon's Olympian *fiat*, that Simla was no longer to be 'a holiday resort of an Epicurean Viceroy and a pampered government'. It was hardly the viceroy or the government of India that worried them.

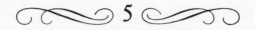

# THE 'DAMNED-NIGGER PARTY'

A T the time of the indigo disturbances in the early 1860s, the division between the administrators and the non-official community was precise. Few of the civil servants sided with the planters and their friends, and the majority were vocally on the side of the peasant. For nearly twenty years afterwards, the tradition that the civil service was there to protect Indians remained. But as time passed and the older men were replaced by the competition wallahs, the tradition began to include a proviso – i.e. for 'Indian' should be read 'peasant'. By the 1880s, officials and non-officials alike were united in their dislike of 'educated' Indians. The dislike was soon to turn to hatred.

Did the British fear that westernised Indians might insist on taking advantage of the promises in the queen's proclamation, to the effect that no discrimination would be exercised against Indians in recruitment for the civil service? Did they think Indians might, perhaps, come to dominate the service? Certainly, everything was done to make it difficult for Indians to compete with Englishmen. Wilfred Scawen Blunt, a contemporary and not always well-informed critic, thought such attitudes were a matter of breeding. 'A young fellow, say the son of an Ulster farmer', he wrote, 'is pitchforked by a successful examination into high authority in Bengal. He has no traditions or breeding for the social position he is called to occupy, and is far more likely to hobnob with the commercial English of his district than to adapt himself to the ceremonial of politeness so necessary in Oriental intercourse'. Blunt was, perhaps, though a radical, also something of a snob.

It was certainly true, however, that a different type of Englishman was now to be found in many branches of the administration. This was the case, not so much in the civil service, which still attracted men of some quality and education, but in the newer branches such as the police. Having originally been filled by army officers, posts in the police were afterwards taken over by the kind of men portrayed by Trollope – 'the amiable detrimental, the younger son, or the sporting public schoolboy, too lazy or too stupid for the Army, but prepared to go anywhere or do anything which did not involve prolonged drudgery'.

In time, even the civilians began to join an alliance of sentiment, which, for the first time, united what had once been the two warring nations of Anglo-India. Together they formed what an ex-viceroy, Lord Northbrook, described in 1883 as the 'damned nigger party'.

The characteristic of a party member was an arrogant attitude to the natives. This was particularly displayed on the railways. Indians had found this new mode of travel much to their liking and the result was that, for the first time, English men and women found themselves in really close contact with a large number of Indians. Every critic of Anglo-India was able to bring back at least one tale about the arrogant, and sometimes brutal, behaviour of the English on trains. Most of these tales were true. Blunt himself recorded what had happened when he was being seen off at a station by some distinguished Indians, including a local princeling who had been honoured with the Order of the Star of India. An English traveller took exception to the Indians crowding the platform near his compartment and threatened them with a stick. When Blunt intervened, the traveller responded 'with indignation at my venturing to call him to account. It was his affair, not mine. Who was I that I should interpose myself between an Englishman and his natural right?' The railway officials refused to do anything, and it was only under pressure that the police finally made some protest to the Englishman, a respectable-looking, middle-aged doctor. On this occasion, formal complaints were lodged and, with the interference of the viceroy, an apology was finally extracted from the doctor, though it was not a very gracious one. However, as the viceroy's secretary put it: 'The mere fact of a European addressing a formal apology to a native gentleman is worth something.' Most victims received no apology, nor any reply to their complaints, even in the not unusual event of their having been beaten, and thrown out of compartments for which they had purchased tickets, when some European chose to join the train at a wayside station.

In hotels, native guests, whatever their rank or standing, were not permitted. This was usually a matter of business rather than of race prejudice on the part of the proprietors. They knew very well that English guests would either insist on any Indian in the hotel being removed, or would leave themselves. There might even have been violence. Was it not still possible to find notices displayed in public places, saying 'Gentlemen are earnestly requested not to strike the servants'?

The attitude to 'educated' natives was salted with an extra dislike. The Anglo-Indian image of the 'good' Indian was usually the image of a child, wayward, sometimes immoral, but in need only of a little fatherly correction to keep him on the right path. In response to this treatment, he was expected to be loyal and not to question the master's rights or decisions. The educated Indian, however, *did* question. To the European, this was not only intolerable, but manifestly against the law of nature. It took no heed of that 'cherished conviction which was shared by every Englishman in India, from the highest to the lowest, by the planter's assistant in his lowly bungalow and by the editor in the full light of the Presidency town – from those to the Chief Commissioner in charge of an important province and to the Viceroy on his throne – the conviction in every man that he belongs to a race whom God has destined to govern and subdue'. That being so, 'However well-educated and clever a native may be, and however brave he may have proven himself, I believe that no rank which we can bestow upon him would cause him to be considered as an equal by the British officer'.

The trouble, from the Anglo-Indian's point of view, was that too many people in Britain were having liberal feelings about India. Members of Parliament travelled out to the country and took home ideas for reform. Of course, as every Anglo-Indian knew, they never understood anything about the real India – 'Mr Cox, the member of Parliament – perhaps you may remember him'. 'A little red-haired fellow, was he? who wrote a book about India on the back of his

two-monthly return ticket?' Unfortunately, they were still inclined
to be influential at Home. There was very little that the Anglo-Indian
could do about this kind of tourist except laugh at him. The
travelling MP usually arrived with a letter of introduction from the
last place he had visited. 'He will immediately proceed to make
himself quite at home in your bungalow with the easy manners of the
Briton abroad.' Announcing his plans, 'he will ask you to take him,
as a preliminary canter, to the gaol and lunatic asylum; and he will
make interesting suggestions to the civil surgeon as to the manage-
ment of these institutions, comparing them unfavourably with those
he has visited in other stations'. In the evening, when he 'ought to be
bathing', he will write an article for some well-known journal like the
*Nineteenth Century* with the title 'Is India worth keeping?'.

This type of criticism formed a kind of private joke amongst
Anglo-Indians, laughter among friends. But the serious side of the
itinerant MP was not to be ignored. 'Mosquitoes are troublesome and
cholera is disconcerting, but they are bearable beside the man who
invariably knows the answers to his own questions before he asks
them.' It was really too bad that 'this ridiculous old Shrovetide cock,
whose ignorance and information leave two broad streaks of laughter
in his wake, is turned loose upon the reading public! Upon my word,
I believe the reading public would do better to go and sit at the feet of
Baboo Sillabub Thunder Gosht, B.A.' – from whom he probably got
all his misinformation in the first place.

It was in the latter part of the nineteenth century that the inoffen-
sive word 'babu' began to take on an offensive connotation. Originally a term of respect, it had come to mean a native clerk who wrote
English. But with the expansion of English education after the
Mutiny it was applied to practically any educated Indian and, in
particular, to the Bengali. 'The pliable, plastic, receptive Baboo of
Bengal eagerly avails himself of this system of English education
partly from a servile wish to please the *Sahib logue*, and partly from a
desire to obtain a Government appointment.' What made a babu?
'When I was at Lhasa the Dalai Lama told me that a virtuous
cow-hippopotamus by metempsychosis might, under unfavourable
circumstances, become an undergraduate of Calcutta University,
and that, when patent-leather shoes and English supervened, the

thing was a Baboo.' The babu was something to be laughed at, especially for his comic English. His misuse of the language of Shakespeare was a proof of the foolishness of his pretence to equal, or come anywhere near, a real Englishman. His references to 'Simpson and Delilah' and 'Mr Monty Cristo' were typical of the breed, and how well Mr Anstey had crystallised the babu in the character who, confronted with the decision whether to accept a duel or receive a kicking, wept 'to find himself between a deep sea and the devil of a kicking' then 'accepted the challenge, feeling like Imperial Caesar, when he found himself compelled to climb up a rubicon after having burnt his boots'.

All the laughter was not quite loud enough to drown the fear. State education seemed to be producing a kind of Frankenstein monster. Government schools merely inspired young Indians to try for better scholarships to better schools and then to better universities. All would expect government jobs. Would they be satisfied when they got them? 'What are you to do with this great clever class, forced up under a foreign system, without discipline, without contentment, and without a god?' It seemed all too possible that the time might soon come when the babus might 'wax fat with new religions, music, painting, Comédie Anglaise, scientific discoveries; they may kick with those highly developed legs of theirs, until we shall have to think that they are something more than a joke, more than a mere *lusus naturae*, more than a caricature moulded . . . in a moment of wanton playfulness'. What was now laughable, 'the patent-leather shoes, the silk umbrellas, the ten thousand horse-power English words and phrases, and the loose shadows of English thought', could turn to sedition, with another Mutiny, perhaps, as the consequence. Anglo-India felt that it was best not to give the babus a loophole through which they might penetrate into the structure of power. In any case, it was argued, they were totally unrepresentative of the real India, the India of the peasants. Babus, 'whom we have educated to write semi-seditious articles in the native Press', represented 'nothing but the social anomaly of their own position'.

The general attitude of dislike, reinforced by the prejudices of Englishwomen – who were the most vocal in their abuse of 'those horrid natives' – had by 1880 produced a sullen mood among

[213]

Anglo-Indians. Within three years a new viceroy, Lord Ripon, had succeeded in changing this into one of violence and hysteria. The issue was a comparatively minor one, a matter of criminal jurisdiction. Should Indian magistrates be permitted to try Europeans? In the principal cities, they had the right to do so, but everyone believed that if an Indian magistrate tried to act harshly against a European the attempt would soon be squashed. In the countryside, however, there were few Europeans and the pressure of Anglo-Indian opinion could hardly be expected to carry as much weight as in the cities. Because of this, Indian magistrates in the countryside had not been given the power to try Europeans. This was a clear case of racial distinction, and it was underlined by the fact that, when an Indian magistrate who had had overall powers in a city moved to a post in the countryside, he lost them. Lord Ripon, a Liberal, was offended by the situation. He had already antagonised Anglo-India by introducing reforms into local government so as to expand Indian participation. Now he decided to correct the legal anomaly. The result was the Ilbert Bill, named after the Law Member of the viceroy's council, Sir Courtenay Ilbert. The viceroy did not anticipate opposition to the bill, since most of the local safeguards enjoyed by Europeans remained intact. The principle of *habeas corpus* was left unchanged; anyone charged with a capital offence was to be sent for trial to a High Court; and the right of appeal to a High Court against *any* conviction was confirmed. No one warned the viceroy that there might be trouble. Officials who were consulted on the matter, with one exception, considered the bill as no more than an administrative measure and foresaw no difficulties. As officials, they themselves were, of course, unlikely to be faced with criminal prosecution, but it was surprising, in view of their new close contact with the non-official community, that they gave no hint of the possibility of an impassioned reaction from that source. A day or two after the bill was announced in February 1883, however, the Calcutta correspondent of the London *Times* reported that the government had 'suddenly sprung a mine on the European community'.

Anglo-Indians, who had not been consulted over what they chose to regard as a matter of great importance to their lives, believed that there was a government conspiracy to raise up the Indian at the expense of the European. It was merely an error that not even members of the Calcutta bar had been consulted but Anglo-Indians did not care. The viceroy had already shown himself a traitor to British interests in India, and the Ilbert Bill was the last straw. The first to react were members of the bar, who met to organise opposition. An arrangement was arrived at with the influential newspaper, *The Englishman*. British businessmen who had interests in the countryside, in tea gardens and indigo plantations, immediately contributed support and money for a campaign against the bill. Letters were sent to Europeans resident outside Calcutta, and there was an immediate response from the planters who, more than anyone else, feared the coming of Indian magistrates who might try to put a stop to them 'beating their own niggers'. At meetings of planters, it was made quite clear that the first Indian magistrate who presumed to try a European would be summarily dealt with.

Support came in not only from planters, merchants and lawyers, but also from many officials who were disturbed at the liberal trend of Ripon's policies. The lieutenant-governor of Bengal openly opposed the bill. The Chief Justice and ten British judges of the Calcutta court supported the agitation. Elsewhere there were suggestions for amendments. *The Englishman* printed inflammatory comments and, when a certain amount of natural irritation was shown by the native-owned press, declared: 'We are on the eve of a crisis which will try the power of the British Government in a way in which it has not been tried since the Mutiny of 1857'. It was surprising that Indians showed little more than irritation in the face of so much abuse, the general tenor of which was summed up in the opening lines of a letter signed 'Britannicus', which appeared at the height of the agitation. 'The only people who have any right to India are the British', it said. 'The SO-CALLED Indians have no right whatever'.

At a large protest meeting held in Calcutta Town Hall, angry speeches were made denouncing the bill. A leading lawyer warned his fellow-countrymen to beware of 'the wily natives who creep in where you cannot walk, because you cannot walk unless you walk upright'. The wily natives, he said, had the ear of the viceroy and had poisoned it with lies. He called upon his audience to swear by all that was sacred to them not to surrender their rights.

[215]

A Eurasian and Anglo-Indian Association was formed that night to fight the bill, and a memorial was sent to the viceroy. 'Natives of India', it maintained, were not 'the peers or equals of Englishmen', and the trial of an Englishman by someone who was not his peer was, without doubt, 'a trespass on the principle which . . . [was] the foundation of English constitutional law'.

The meeting was almost hysterical in its denunciation of the bill, but the deep feelings expressed were not totally irrational. Genuine fear did exist, and not only among those activated by spite and bloody-mindedness. Apparently progressive people – and there were some – also found the bill repugnant. Mrs Annette Beveridge, who had gone out to India at the invitation of Indians, to help Indian women, wrote in a letter to *The Englishman* that the bill would sub-ject 'civilised women [she meant Englishwomen] to the jurisdiction of men who have done little or nothing to redeem the women of their own races, and whose social ideas are still on the outer verge of civilisation'. Her concern was not 'pride of race . . . it is the pride of womanhood'. The general impression was created that if women were brought before an Indian magistrate in the countryside, they would find themselves either in jail or in the magistrate's harem. 'Would you', wrote the editor of the *Friend of India*, in the hope of arousing sympathy in Britain, 'would you like to live in a country where at any moment your wife would be liable to be sentenced on a false charge, the magistrate being a copper-coloured Pagan?' The watchword became 'protect innocent womanhood', and a 'ladies' petition' was organised and sent to the viceroy in an attempt to appeal to his sense of English chivalry!

The opposition did not confine itself to memoranda and mem-orials. It organised itself for positive action. All the English press, with one exception, supported this agitation, and carried attacks not only on the viceroy but upon Indians in general. *The Englishman* was the most virulent of all, and was delighted to print such scurrilous material as the following advertisement:

WANTED Sweepers, Punkah Coolies, and Bhisties [water carriers] for the residents of Saidpur. None but educated Bengali Baboos who have passed the [university] Entrance Examination need apply. Ex-Deputy Magistrates (Bengal) preferred.

By the summer of 1883 opposition had spread. The English press was appealing to members of the volunteer forces to resign, and there was strong feeling among army officers. Three attempted rapes of Englishwomen by Indians were immediately associated with the bill, and European opinion was roused almost to madness. A Calcutta magistrate sentenced a washerman, whom he alleged had insulted his (the magistrate's) mistress, to six months' hard labour, and publicly boasted of his harshness. The suggestion was even made at a public meeting, and received seriously, that, as the government in London appeared indifferent to Anglo-Indian interests, India should secede from Britain. Unfortunately, the people of Britain were indifferent, too, though *The Times* was strongly on the side of the European community in India. The Anglo-Indian Association had employed an agent named Atkins to try to rouse the British working classes but he did not have much success. He was received by the secretary of state, however, and wrote to India to say – quite without foundation – that the government disclaimed all responsibility for the bill. This only inspired the Anglo-Indian community to continue in agitation.

Throughout the hot weather, Ripon had been in the hills. When he returned to Calcutta in December 1883 he was booed in the streets. There was even a conspiracy to overpower the guards at Government House, kidnap the viceroy, and place him forcibly on board a ship for England. *The Englishman* welcomed Ripon's return by describing him as 'the Mammon of unrighteousness whose temple has been set up on the banks of the Hughli'. The viceroy's advisers were now strongly opposed to the bill. There were reports from the criminal intelligence department that many planters were planning to come to Calcutta for a monster demonstration and that there might be violence. As there were only seventy European police in Calcutta and to use Indian police would inflame the situation, there seemed no alternative to calling the army out. But to use European troops against Europeans would be unthinkable. Under such a combination of pressures, Ripon gave in. Negotiations were opened with leaders of the Anglo-Indian community, and what was called a 'compromise' was arrived at. It was, in fact, nothing of the sort. The Anglo-Indians, a tiny minority in the mass of India, had defeated the viceroy. It was hardly an accident that in the last days of 1883, when the Europeans were celebrating their victory, the Indians of Calcutta were convening their first National Conference.

Ripon went home, and a viceroy with a proper sense of the fitness of the status quo arrived to replace him.

The 'damned-nigger party' did not dissolve itself after this success. It retained its membership and gained more adherents as the nineteenth century drew to a close. The Europeans' contempt for the educated Indian, with his English-style organisations asking for English-style political reforms, set other Indians to searching for more positive forms of action. Appealing mainly to the religion of the masses, they tried with some success to incite them against the British. Violence, and the assassination of British officials, were the not infrequent result. On such occasions, the Anglo-Indian press became its old self again and advocated the most indiscriminate 'justice', on traditional Mutiny principles. Even without the stimulus of terrorism, justice remained partial. Indians did not even have the right of self-defence. On one occasion, when British soldiers attacked and wounded a village boy and were themselves threatened with retaliation by the villagers, the local European magistrate acquitted the soldiers, sentenced the villagers to long terms of imprisonment, and had the wounded boy whipped.

But Anglo-Indians did not really fear Indians. What the Anglo-Indian was frightened of was that a liberal-minded government in London might try to force the government of India to bring in reforms which would allow Indians to hold positions of authority. Reform, not revolution, menaced Anglo-India. When Indians were cheeky, they could be slapped down. When they were violent, they could be shot. Until the end of the queen's reign, Anglo-Indians always comforted themselves with the thought that, as long as the government did not weaken, they were safe, for:

> Whatever happens, we have got
> The Maxim gun, which they have not.

—— *ACT THREE* ——

# *WAITING FOR THE LAST TRUMP*

We are just hanging on, hoping that the last trump will sound time.
Edward Thompson
*A Farewell to India* 1934

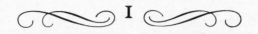

# EVERYTHING AS BEFORE,
# ONLY DIFFERENT

I N October 1919, a young man, still young though matured
beyond his years by his experiences in the War to End War,
arrived in India. He had not come to work, to rule, to police,
doctor, or convert Indians to Christianity. Nor had he come to buy
and sell or grow tea. He had no official position but did have a social
one, of the kind that could open as many doors as he wished. His
family, though not the immediate one of parents and siblings, had
long had a connection with India and still had, but 'James Furness'
had no particular personal interest in the Indian empire. The attraction, he admitted, was the contrast between the exotic image of India
and the humdrum horrors of the late war. He was to stay in India,
and die there nearly forty years later, but in 1919 he was merely
looking.

What 'James Furness' saw was not quite what he had expected,
though his expectations were innocent of real knowledge. The
seamless garment of what should have been the King's Peace was
fraying at the edges. In fact, it had been doing so for some time. In the
first years of the century, the Indian nationalist movement, dominated by mainly moderate nationalists asking for no more than a
steady – and dignified – evolution towards self-rule, was taken over
by virulently anti-British extremists. Secret societies advocating and
practising terrorism and assassination proliferated. British officials,
and in one unfortunate case the wife and daughter of a well-known
British lawyer known to be sympathetic to nationalist aims, were
murdered. In Bengal the violence culminated in 1908 in the arrest
and trial of a number of terrorists. An informer was shot inside a jail,

the public prosecutor was assassinated in Calcutta and a deputy superintendent of police murdered on the steps of the High Court.

The reaction to the wave of terror among the British took various forms, but all layers of society felt a certain *déjà vu*. Was there going to be another Mutiny? The British press in India, which was generally the mouthpiece of the non-official community, emphasised the parallels, such as they were, and suggested that the sort of vengeance meted out to the mutineers some fifty years before would not be out of place. 'The wholesale arrest of the acknowledged terrorists in a city or a district', trumpeted *The Pioneer* of Allahabad on 5 May 1908, 'coupled with an intimation that at any repetitions of the offence, ten of them would be shot for every [British] life sacrificed, would soon put down the practice [of throwing bombs]'.

Threats had little, if any, effect on the new generation of patriotic youth. Even London was not immune from terrorist violence. In 1909, Sir Curzon Wyllie, an official at the India Office, was assassinated by a Punjabi at the Imperial Institute, in South Kensington. Five months later, an unsuccessful attempt was made on the lives of Lord Minto, the then Viceroy, and his wife in the western Indian textile city of Ahmedabad. Successful attempts on the lives of senior British officials took place in widely separated parts of the country. In 1912, Lord Minto's successor as Viceroy was severely wounded in a bomb explosion as he was about to make a state entry into Delhi, the new capital of British India.

The war that broke out in Europe in August 1914 surprisingly brought a truce to nationalist agitation against the British. In fact, there was an outburst of enthusiasm for the war that, in the light of subsequent events, seems almost incomprehensible. But many nationalists thought helping the British would result in a victory which might bring its own rewards. Recruits flocked to the army – more than 1¼ million volunteered – and there were quite spontaneous contributions by Indians to such things as war bonds. The British reduced the garrison of white troops in India to 15,000 men, and many British administrators going off to fight handed over their jobs to Indian subordinates. In this way, two of the nationalist demands – a reduction in the 'army of occupation' and more higher posts for Indians – were unintentionally granted. But like everyone else, Indians believed the war would soon be over. When it dragged on, popular enthusiasm declined.

By the time 'James Furness' arrived in India, the old violence had not only returned, but generated a myth of such political consequence to the future of India that it is still impossible to question it without provoking accusations of pro-Imperialist revisionism. The source of the myth was the massacre of more than three hundred and the wounding of over a thousand people in the Punjab town of Amritsar on 13 April 1919. What I am convinced was an act of fear and panic by Brigadier-General Reginald Dyer, the officer commanding the troops, was taken by most Indians as a deliberate act of racialist policy. This belief was unfortunately confirmed by General Dyer himself, who in an attempt to cover up his shortcomings, claimed that his intention had been all along 'to create a sufficient moral effect from a military point of view throughout the Punjab'. He maintained, loudly, that he had saved the Empire, and there were many to agree with him, though the Government of India removed him from his command and a judicial enquiry censured him for his actions. Despite, or even because of this, a large subscription was collected for him in England and in India, and many politicians considered him a hero, though they did not include Winston Churchill, who described Dyer's actions as 'quite un-English frightfulness'.

Most of the British men and women 'James Furness' met supported Dyer. James did not know what to think. 'After all', he wrote in his journal, 'Indians *were* killing Englishmen and beating harmless lady missionaries almost to death'. And what were the British there for, if not to maintain law and order? But some were already beginning to have doubts about just how long the British would be staying in India.

A sinister omen was the reaction of Indians to the visit, in the cold weather of 1921, of the King-Emperor's son, Edward, Prince of Wales. Normally, most Indians had great respect for royalty, and enjoyed the display attendant upon their movements. But the Prince landed at Bombay to a *hartal*, a sort of general strike called by the Indian National Congress, now dominated by a very different sort of nationalist, Mahatma Gandhi. The Prince and his entourage moved

[223]

through empty streets, to a silence more significant than shouting. The Prince found British morale generally low: 'They one and all say the same thing,' he later reported to the Secretary of State for India, 'that they won't let their sons come out here to earn a living in the Indian Army or the Indian Civil Service etc., and that nor now would they recommend these services to any good fellow. India is no longer a place for a white man to live.'

And yet very little had changed.

The structure of British society in India remained unshaken: 'a separate caste, with several sub-castes, strictly preserving the usual characteristics of endogamy, commensality, and mutual control by members.' The rule book of the caste was still *The Warrant of Precedence*, a document which set people in their place, and not only at the dinner table. At the top of the pile remained the 'heaven-born' members of the Indian Civil Service, next, members of other administrative services. Then came the soldiers. Below them, and very much below them, came the *box-wallahs*, a derisive term for those in trade and commerce. This sub-caste further divided itself into two, an upper of those engaged in commerce and spent their time in offices, and a lower of those who actually traded and worked in stores. Below that again was a range of Untouchables including Domiciled Europeans, those of pure British blood born in India to parents who had chosen to make India their home, and Eurasians, who were really beyond any pale.

*The Warrant of Precedence* was still absolutely necessary when arranging the seating at a big dinner, and woe be to anyone who placed a member of the Indian Civil Service of twelve years' standing in an inferior position to an Assistant Director of Dairy Farms! At least there had been some loosening in the etiquette of dress. Before 1914, it had been unthinkable for a man to dine out privately except in formal attire, tail coat, stiff starched-front shirt, white waistcoat, stiff collar and white tie. Now a short coat was permitted and even a white one at that.

Women's clothes were in for revolutionary changes, too, though India remained slow to adopt the latest fashions from Europe. Long white gloves were no longer thought necessary at an ordinary dinner, but were still needed for official dining. The pompous protocol of

Government House remained virtually unchanged. The Prince of Wales was reported to have said that he had not understood the meaning of royalty until he stayed at the residence of the Governor of Bombay! Even when genuine royalty was not present, guests would be formed into a circle around which the governor and his wife paraded with an aide-de-camp, in order to be introduced to their host and hostess. The ladies would perform a half-curtsy and the men bow their heads. After this ritual – it was no more than that, as most of the guests would be well-known to the governor – His Excellency and his wife would lead the way into the dining-room.

The first to be affected by technological change – the continuing revolution of the twentieth century – were the cities and large towns. The telephone and electric light (and the electric tram, though the British *never* travelled in them) had reached India in the last decade of the nineteenth century. The use of electric power expanded, and that greatest of boons, the electrically-powered ceiling fan, displaced the omnipresent punkah. Attitudes remained unaffected by such valuable inventions except perhaps by a growing envy as the richer businessman increased the luxury of his living. The civil servant did not mix with businessmen. Not even in their clubs.

'In any town in India,' wrote George Orwell, remembering his experiences in the Imperial Police, 'the European Club is the spiritual citadel, the real seat of British power, the Nirvana for which native officials and millionaires pine in vain.' There is nothing particularly reprehensible in exiles constructing simulacra of 'Home' as the British did in their hill-stations, or preferring to relax in the company of one's fellow countrymen. It certainly removed the British from the rest of India if only for a few weeks or hours, as today those same clubs remove rich Indians from the presence of their less-fortunate compatriots.

For the British, the criterion for membership of a particular club was simply that of occupation. In Calcutta, the Bengal Club was mainly commercial, and an army officer would not be eligible for election as a member, just as someone eligible for the Bengal Club would not be for the United Service. Such divisions and many others existed throughout India. The members of private clubs do, however, have the right to decide on the eligibility of their fellow members as do such places even in the most democratic of Western societies. After all, exclusivity is a club's *raison d'être*. Unfortunately, superimposed upon the hierarchical preoccupations of the British in India – if not an altogether harmless snobbery, it was at least confined to the British themselves – was the question of racial exclusivity and discrimination. If there was one thing most members of clubs were agreed upon, it was the general undesirability of admitting Indians.

'James Furness' noted the fuss made over the suggestion that Indians might be elected members of the club of which he was as a visiting Englishman of the right social class, a temporary member. 'I came in one evening to find the members seething with what I took to be anger. It took me some time to get at the cause. I thought, at first, something really terrible had happened. But the club never did elect an Indian.' Other clubs adapted to the changes that were taking place because of the slow but steady Indianisation of the civil and military services. But most of these were in up-country stations away from the principal cities. One of the main objections to Indian membership was that if Indians joined, they would not bring their wives but hang around English ladies, for whom, it was well-known, Indians held lascivious yearnings. 'James Furness' thought such ideas very funny, but he was an exception. The stereotype of Indian sexuality and its implied threat to the purity of English womanhood was of considerable antiquity.

The object of this male solicitude was beginning to enjoy some of the superficial effects of women's liberation. Gone were the multi-layered underclothes and the long heavy skirts down to the ankles, to be replaced by slacks and jodhpurs, even shorts, much to the disapproval of the older British and also of many Indian servants, some of whom seemed to have looked upon the memsahib as a surrogate for the Great White Queen, Victoria. Only one item of clothing retained its hold upon both sexes: a continuing fear of the sun prolonged the life of the topee, one of the ugliest hats ever invented.

Life in the big towns and cities could now be made comfortable, even in the hot weather. The businessman still rose early, as his East India Company predecessor had done, and breakfasted with such pomp as he wished and could afford. He would now drive to his office in a motor-car, a form of transport which had even reached into the countryside, though there were very few suitable roads outside the urban areas. The businessman would keep himself reasonably fit by playing tennis and, if he cared to, by riding and playing polo. He was, of course, a member of several clubs and would spend his Sunday at them, playing golf, drinking innumerable pink gins, and eating curry for lunch. The afternoon was spent in rest, and the early evening would probably include a visit to a cinema, to be followed by a buffet supper.

The memsahib's life was very much as it had always been: morning consultations with the cook and other servants, perhaps a little flower-arranging followed by boredom. Eleven in the morning was the time for coffee – and gossip. The husband would come home for lunch. After the inevitable siesta, perhaps a game of tennis at the Club would be followed by drinks until time came to go home for dinner. After dinner a party or dance would end the day. Servants, naturally, did everything, or almost everything, and knew everything, or almost everything. It was virtually impossible for a man or woman to have an affair without it being known to the house servants and passed on to the house servants of their friends. This constant espionage extended to government offices, and the secrets of the government of India were often the talk of the bazaar.

The outlying districts were slow to receive the boons of modern civilisation, some never receiving them at all. The Model 'T' Ford car did manage to chug its way into the most improbable places, and the motor cycle was not unknown, though it was not considered a very dignified form of transport. Life 'up-country' changed very little. The mail-order catalogue remained one of the most important tools of living and the issues of the Army and Navy Stores are in themselves a short cultural history of the British in India. In the absence of refrigerators, ice could still be a problem, especially if there was no ice factory nearby. Then the best place to go was the nearest railway station, as ice was regularly carried by mail trains to be delivered at stations on their routes. Perishable goods were also sent this way, packed in ice.

Links with Home were sustained by English magazines and newspapers, though there were a number of very good English-

[227]

language newspapers in India. Their influence on the opinions of the British far exceeded their print order, as copies were passed from hand to hand. *Blackwoods Magazine*, which specialised in historical pieces and fiction about the empire, and *The Tatler*, a compendium of British society news and gossip, were among the most popular magazines from Home, though the *Illustrated London News* was among the top ten.

Letters and periodicals from Britain began to arrive with astounding speed after the opening of an airmail route to India in 1929. By 1935, Imperial Airways was carrying passengers as well as mail between India and Britain, making it possible to go Home for even the shortest of leaves. News, both from other parts of India and from the outside world, could soon be heard from the transmitters of the newly-established All-India Radio. The barriers of distance and the remoteness of exile were slowly being eroded.

Pastimes had changed very little; tennis and golf, bridge and poker, swimming and polo, still held sway. Juvenal's cry of *mens sana in corpore sano* continued to echo in the halls of public schools and down the corridors of empire. Physical fitness was a fetish. Plenty of exercise and a 'jolly good sweat' did no one much harm, but it was indulged in with an almost religious mania. The word *macho* had not been invented, but its meaning would have been understood.

The status of all sports took a very second place to *shikar*, shooting and hunting. The military in the second half of the eighteenth century first discovered the delights of shooting birds and animals as the garrisons spread out into the Indian countryside. In the 1920s, there was still an enormous amount of game waiting to be shot. A party of eight guns could easily claim a 'bag' of over a thousand birds, a mere trifle to the results of a viceregal or princely shoot. But many like 'James Furness' had had enough of shooting during the war to sicken them with the casual carnage of a shoot. Many who still shot, either for sport or more often for the pot, found the stalk more exciting than the kill. By the mid-1930s, tiger-hunting as a sport had declined, as had the tiger population, to the edge of being an endangered species.

One of the pleasures, to many the principal pleasure, of shooting was the necessary camping that went with it. The quality and luxury

[228]

of the camp of course varied with the official position of the campers. The viceregal camp was, naturally, the most impressive. It would consist of hundreds of tents of varying sizes and magnificence. One of Calcutta's finest caterers would handle the commissariat and even supply the servants to serve the excellent food and drink provided. Another Calcutta emporium supplied furniture, *not* camp furniture but house furniture, by the trainload. Motor cars would shuttle from the railway station to the camp. The shoot, of course, would be a big one, with elephants and hundreds of beaters. In the evening there would be a dance, with a band from Calcutta and the guests in full evening dress.

Of course, camping was not confined to shooting expeditions. The District Officer still went into camp in the cold weather as he toured the area for which he was responsible. Those who worked in the Public Works Department would often spend most of their time in camp, visiting irrigation projects or engineering construction sites: four or five weeks on tour followed by a week or ten days back at base for a rest. Many enjoyed going on tour for it brought them not only into contact with the land and its inhabitants, but also extra pay in the form of a travelling allowance.

Modes of travel as well as standards of luxury varied considerably. Camels would be used in the desert areas of Sind and Rajasthan, elephants practically anywhere, and one's own feet plus perhaps a hundred porters to carry the baggage in the hills and mountainous regions of the north. The camper need have no worries about the camp itself. As it had always been, everything was done for him. After dinner at one site, all the kitchen equipment, leaving only sufficient for the following morning's breakfast, would be packed up, as would the office furniture and files. These were transported to the next camp site, which might be ten or twelve miles away, during the night. After breakfast, the rest of the gear was packed, and by the time the officer reached his destination, everything had been set up as before.

The tents were of various shapes, but usually had the floor covered with a cotton carpet over straw. If the weather was cold, a stove made the tent very comfortable. The daily routine began with the officer leaving after breakfast to inspect whatever there was to inspect, return for lunch and a drink at one, and, after a short rest, receive local dignitaries and persons wishing to make petitions at a table set up outside the tent. Tea would consist principally of hot buttered toast with perhaps Gentleman's Relish, a tangy anchovy paste. Dinner might feature a pea-hen or a hare, shot by the diner before tea. Next day, the routine began again.

Other things remained essentially unchanged, among them inter-communal violence. One of the most dangerous times in the cities and large towns was that of the Muslim festival of Muharram, which in the Shi'ite Muslim community commemorates the martyrdom of Hasan and Husain, the grandsons of the prophet Muhammed. Representations of the tombs of the two martyrs are constructed out of gilded and painted paper, and borne through the streets with a great deal of shouting, wailing and drumming. These paper tombs are known as *tazias*. The route taken by the procession carrying the tazias was rigidly defined by the local superintendent of police, and detachments of police would accompany each tazia in order to protect them from attacks by Hindus 'who do their best to arrange some minor feast-day of their own to clash' with the festival.

Such clashes were commonplace, especially in towns where there was some rough parity between Muslims and Hindus. 'You could hear the sound of drums and shouting from the city in the civil lines [the "cantonment" where the British lived] and one of the police officers told me that trouble was expected' as 'all day deputations of Hindu gentlemen' had been besieging 'the Deputy Commissioner with assurances that they would be murdered ere next dawning by the Muhammadans.'

The crowd with tazias collected on a small plain outside the town before setting off in procession down the principal street. It was by now dark, and the light of torches made a little sea of fire. Very soon, the procession was within the town, and shouts of 'Ya Hasan! Ya Husain!' could be distinctly heard even though 'the brass bands were playing their loudest and at every corner where space allowed, Muhammedan preachers were telling the lamentable story of the death of the Martyrs. In the Hindu quarters, the shutters of all the shops were up and cross-barred.' As the first tazia, an extravagant and gaudy thing nearly twelve feet high, carried by about twenty men, approached a side alley, a brickbat 'crashed through its talc and tinsel sides'.

'The procession came to a ragged stop, and some of the men in it began to batter at the shutters of a house from which they thought the attack had been made.' This was the moment of truth. 'There seemed to me to be a silence, though how long it lasted, I have no idea. But then all Hell was let loose. The *tazias* swayed on their poles as if in a high wind.' There were shouts that the Hindus were dishonouring the tazias. The police escorts tried to maintain some sort of order by flailing indiscriminately with their bamboo staves. 'Tazia after tazia, some burning, others torn to pieces, hurried past us and the mob with them, howling, shrieking, and striking at the house doors in their flight.'

The town was now almost out of control. Houses had been set on fire and shops looted. The dead lay where they had fallen, the wounded tried to get away to safety. It was time to call in the troops.

Such violence between the majority Hindu community and the Muslims was a presage of the Partition of 1947, which divided the old Indian empire into the predominately Hindu India and the predominantly Muslim Pakistan. But though the idea of a separate state for Muslims had been put forward in 1933, no one considered it a possibility, especially the new type nationalists of the Indian National Congress, led by the new type of nationalist leader, Mahatma Gandhi. His idea of agitation was to offer non-violent passive resistance, though such demonstrations not infrequently ended violently, provocative acts being committed by criminal elements in order to create opportunities for looting. But many such political demonstrations would end after the arrest of the leaders, an easy task as most of them courted arrest rather than trying to avoid it. The rest of the crowd was usually dispersed with a few blows from the staves of the regular police.

In the 1930s not many of the British in India took Gandhi seriously, though some in high places did. Much more serious, though it affected only a minority of the British, was the revival of terrorism and assassination in Bengal. The new terrorists raised funds by attacking post offices and other government sources of cash. Terrorist activity reappeared also in the Punjab. In 1929 a bomb was thrown in the legislative assembly in New Delhi, and in the same year an unsuccessful attempt was made to wreck the viceroy's train. Other terrorist acts did result in a number of murders of British officials.

Amidst terrorism and political disturbances, self-government came to India, at least in a truncated form in 1937, and a number of British officials had the experience of serving under elected ministers in the provincial governments whom they had once sent to jail. Some began to think that there might be a term to British rule in India. No one seems to have thought of complete independence for India, but self-rule did imply the more or less rapid Indianisation of the administration.

In the hot weather of 1939, 'James Furness' went up into the hills. By this time he was no longer quite so naive about India as he had been on his first arrival nearly twenty years before. He had travelled a great deal and had learned as he put it 'enough to know how much there was still to learn'. At the time he was an adviser to the ruler of one of the smaller, and more progressive, of princely states. He did not mix much with fellow countrymen, and had not been in a hill-station for many years.

He did not find the general ambience of Simla much different from when he had last been there. Neither would someone of, say, fifty years before, except superficially. The cut of clothes was different, particularly of the ladies, but the motor car was still forbidden, except for the viceroy and the governor of the Punjab. Flirtations, amateur theatricals, walks and rides up Jakko hill, Simla might have been lost in a time-capsule, a Shangri-la where no one grew old but, at intervals, changed their bodies.

Dinners at Viceregal Lodge followed the same semi-regal protocol: full evening dress, curtsy and bow – and the order of precedence. At one such function, 'James Furness' felt a shiver run down his spine, though it was a warm night. He had no idea he was witnessing the last glittering season of a great empire, that unseen above the feast the hand was already posed to write upon the wall: *God hath numbered thy kingdom and finished it; Thou art weighed in the balance and found wanting; Thy kingdom is divided between the Medes and Persians.*

# 2

# *THE WRITING ON THE WALL*

W HEN 'M' left England, the 'phony war' still reigned in Europe. When he arrived in India, there was still no war at all in Asia. There was a *state* of war, as the viceroy had declared war on Germany in September 1939, without consulting any of the Indian political parties, as was his constitutional right. Indians, who only two years before had received a large measure of self-government in the provinces of British India, not unnaturally resented this. Attempts at negotiation failed, and in November all the provincial governments controlled by the Congress Party resigned. Those controlled by the Muslim League, the principal Islamic party, did not, emphasising the split in existing Indian nationalism which was to lead ultimately to the partition of the Indian Empire.

'M' had joined the army as a private soldier and was now a signalman by trade. Family and school background had not prepared him for the lowly status of the BOR, the British Other Ranker, in the hierarchical society of the British in India.

With the rest of his draft, 'M' was subjected to a lecture on the perils of service in India. In earlier years he would have been given a booklet of advice: Wear a pith helmet at all times during daylight or the rays of the sun would send one mad; Do not drink water anywhere outside the military station, or illness and maybe death from a variety of scary diseases, including typhoid, would result; Never go to brothels, or risk a certain dose of the clap. To combat the insidious sun, he was issued with a helmet, known as a Bombay Bowler, which looked rather like an enormous, and gangrenous, boil.

Fortunately, it would not be long before the myth of solar death would be dashed forever; the war, when it came, was fought in a cotton or felt bush hat.

The situation of BORs did not seem to have changed since the stories of Kipling's *Soldiers Three*. The military cantonment was always separate from the civil station, and the BOR doubly separated by his lowly social standing. Officers would mix with British civilians. BORs could not. Low-caste servants, vendors of food and services, and Eurasians were their contact with the world outside the barracks, though mixing with the latter was discouraged, for both army regulations and racial prejudice were against the BOR marrying Eurasian girls whom they might meet at the Railway Institute dances.

Every effort was, in fact, made to discourage the satisfaction of the BOR's heterosexual needs. Frequent medical checks, known colloquially as 'short-arm' inspections, ensured that anyone who had managed to satisfy a need and caught some venereal infection was treated, shouted at, and fined by having his pay stopped. The red-light districts of the large towns and cities were strictly off-limits, and the sighting of a white face in such areas was easily observed by the civilian police, and its owner easily caught. No wonder the poor soldier turned to homosexual relations and masturbation. It reminded 'M' of a somewhat demented, English public school.

All the BOR needed, except sexual satisfaction, was available inside the military cantonment. As far as possible, it was a self-contained world with its own bazaar and everything else strictly out of bounds. Parades were numerous; in fact, one paraded for all possible duties and activities, from meals to drawing stores, from 'short-arm' and other apparently pointless medical inspections, to organised games. There was no privacy, yet all these parades and inspections took up very little of the day. The rest was a sea of boredom – shared by about fifty others. It was said, with absolute justice, that a British soldier in India spent most of his time sleeping – because there was nothing else to do.

Of course, even the lowliest of the imperial race was attended by servants, known impartially as wallahs (men), preceded by what task they performed, as in char-wallah, tea-man. There appeared to be a wallah for every conceivable task or service, and not a few, to a newcomer, difficult to conceive. One that appealed to 'M' almost immediately after his arrival at a military station in western India, was the 'flying dhobi'. Dhobi means a washerman. An ordinary washerman took the soldiers' laundry once a week, but if something was required in a hurry, a *flying* dhobi would pick up the items in the morning, returning them in the late afternoon, brightly laundered and starched.

Such starching, or rather, *over*-starching, shirts and shorts with knife-edge creases and the seams thick with starch, could result in one of the most unpleasant of India's minor afflictions – dhobi itch. This was a hot-weather horror which somehow seemed to exceed the many other horrors of that worst of seasons. Tiny pimples would appear, usually in the groin or the armpits first, and then spread. The itching was maddening, and some, driven to the limits, would scratch their skin to ribbons. Camomile lotion soothed but did not cure. The army doctors did not seem to care.

The rainy season would add an enormous range of insect life to harass the soldier – and officers and civilians too, for they were quite indiscriminate. Snakes would appear in the most unlikely places, and the whine of the mosquito was heard in the land. When 'M' arrived, quinine was still the only specific against mosquito-borne malaria. DDT and mepacrin were still over the horizon. The stink beetle, as its name implies, stank noxiously when squashed. The little white jute fly could cause skin damage to the hand that brushed it off. And there were many more.

It was no wonder there was a tradition of hot-weather murders and suicides. The ghosts of Mulvaney, Ortheris and Learoyd seemed to walk the battlements of the military station, and there was a desperate feeling that life was aping literature with a vengeance. In fact, there was far too much Kipling around for comfort.

Sport played a similar quasi-religious role in the life of the ordinary soldier as it did in that of the officer and the civilian. It was at least an antidote to the corrosive boredom of barrack life. A more formal, though no less superficial religious activity was that of the mandatory Sunday church-parade. The parade was sometimes accompanied by the regimental band, and often the troops carried arms – a precaution

[235]

against being caught unprepared by another mutiny. The memories of those terrible days more than eighty years before were very much alive, especially so after the 'Quit India' campaign of Mahatma Gandhi burst into violence.

The Japanese were already moving into northern Burma, with 'M' in front of them, when in August 1942, after Gandhi's call for the British to 'Quit India!', he and almost the entire leadership of Congress were arrested. The arrests were followed by strikes and civil disturbance, much of it fomented by criminals and those anxious to whip up violent feelings between the Hindu and Muslim communities. A wave of sabotage and criminally-inspired violence spread across the country. By the middle of September, 250 railway stations had been destroyed or seriously damaged, and more than 500 post offices attacked. A large section of the railway system was put out of action, and communications so disrupted that the army on the northeast frontier with Burma, facing what was believed to be an imminent Japanese strike against India, was deprived of its main channel of supply. Police-stations and government buildings were set on fire, and Indian members of the civil administration were threatened with death if they did not assist the rebels. A number of those who refused were assassinated. British troops were called upon to restore order, aircraft were used against mobs.

Though the rebellion was over by the end of the year, some of the writing on the wall was becoming legible to many of the British establishment in India.

The expanding war with Japan not only brought many thousands of conscripts from all social classes, civilians in uniform, a species quite unknown in India, causing severe problems of social etiquette, it changed 'M's' status. No longer confined to the moveable ghetto of the BOR, he could take his 'rightful' place in the order, not only of precedence, but of social acceptability. This new freedom was as full of revelation as the restriction of the earlier experience.

'M' was surprised – after all, he was still very young and a little priggish – at the dullness of the city British. It took him some time to realise that those with the most minimal of intellectual interests were suspect. It was not that men of culture did not exist, but they always appeared to be at some place remote from 'M's' present one. 'I remember a chappie, used to play Bach on his gramophone, very rum. Don't know what became of him.' If one section of British India seemed to be living Kipling, another one was, almost, imitating P. G. Wodehouse. An air-conditioned Wodehouse, because that most valuable of technological advances now soothed the offices of the British businessman, and the homes of the richer ones, as well as movie-houses in the larger cities.

The Englishwoman in India may have been liberated in dress but not particularly in mind. Most of them had not attended a university and their interests were limited. The sort of society they lived in and its rather strict but undemanding expectations was against them being much more than appendages of their menfolk. In the cities they lived as English a life as they could, creating a middle-class suburbia as far as was possible. In many respects, they were indistinguishable from their social equals back Home. The War, however, did bring changes in the memsahib's life. The younger women joined the auxiliary forces and took over from the men in military offices. The older women discovered an interest in the welfare of those rather strange, socially-mixed conscript soldiers. Long-held barriers were, if not beaten down, at least breeched and once sacrosanct bastions were invaded by, in Anglo-Indian terms, some very odd people, the King's Commission being distributed more indiscriminately than ever before. Many English women found their horizons widened. There even developed a different attitude towards Eurasians when it was discovered that, given the opportunity, the majority proved their not inconsiderable worth.

The wives of members of the Indian Civil Service seemed to 'M' to be of a different calibre. Their husbands were frequently posted to small stations in the countryside and, more often than not, the women took an active part in their husbands' work. Their lives were often hard, uncomfortable, and fraught with loneliness. Up until World War II, children were still sent Home at the age of five, and the mother had to make a choice between going to England with her child, or staying with her husband in India until the next time came to take leave. In wartime, leave was suspended and some found their children unrecognisable and themselves unrecognised when they saw them again.

[237]

The British in India were not a particularly religious lot. The businessman would go to church as part of the social round rather than anything else. The church-parade of the army was more a demonstration by the rulers, of secular power; a symbolic act rather than one of worship. The professional Christian, the missionary, was always on the outer limits of Anglo-India. The missionaries belonged to and were sponsored by a wide variety of missionary societies: the Church Missionary Society, the Society for the Propagation of the Gospel, American Baptists, Methodists, Roman Catholics, a bewildering number, who would often stake out whole areas of operation which the members of other organisations were expected to leave alone. The converted were, to a large extent, still 'curry and rice' Christians, who could be attracted away from one sect to another by the simplest of material enticements. The converted came mostly from the lower orders of Hindu and Muslim society, and usually attended separate places of worship to their British co-religionists. The principal effect of the missionary effort was upon education and medical work. The legacy left by the medical and educational missionaries to the new countries that succeeded the British Raj, was arguably the most consequential, and probably the most altruistic, at least in material terms.

The end of the war with Japan brought with it the realisation that the days of the Raj were definitely numbered. A socialist government was elected in Britain with an overwhelming majority, in order, basically, to produce reforms *in Britain*, reforms that would remove some of the most pernicious of inequalities. The British Labour Party was also committed to self-government, if no more than that, for India, and it was generally accepted that it would not renege on its often repeated promises to Indian nationalists. No one in India – or even in Britain – dreamed that the end of the Raj would come in so short a time as two years, but neither could anyone pretend that the writing on the wall was obscure, even if the exact time of its fulfilment was vague.

The probability that the Raj was approaching its end came as something of a shock to 'M'. And there was good reason. After all, wars are by their very nature affairs of the immediate moment, at least for the ordinary soldier. For him, the future lies in a sort of hazy nostalgia, a time when it would be possible to reinstate the fondly-remembered pasts, to bring the lost things back again, to feel less at risk in a less risky world. Realising that he was witnessing an event he was unlikely to witness again – the decline and fall of a great empire – 'M' decided to see as much of it as he could. It was to be an interesting, instructive and even frightening experience.

In his travels, 'M' was assailed by a multitude of images, the majority of which he did not understand at the time. Among the British, the thing that, perhaps, impressed 'M' the most was their reaction to the certainty that the Raj was to be partitioned into two countries. Many considered that the justification of Britain's role lay in the fact that it had brought some sort of unity to an organically divided country, and that to break that unity was an attempt to destroy history. They were horrified at the prospect of partition, and at the time, it seemed to 'M' that they had reason on their side. Especially so, as communal violence between Muslims and Hindus and Sikhs began to spread across the country. It was as if the seams were coming apart, and there was not much the maker of the garment could do about it.

'M' met men who were watching their life-work unravelling around them, and felt their pain and sorrow. Others, more stoic, made their preparations to go Home – and never return as anything but a tourist in a not quite foreign land. Among Indians there was a curious mixture of regret and anger. As one Indian said to 'M', with some bitterness: 'It was simply a matter of "divide and rule", we divided and you ruled. Now we are dividing again, and you British are doing nothing about it.' But there was nothing the British *could* do. They no longer had the power or the political will.

In certain places, 'M' found fear, and felt it himself. While visiting Calcutta during what came to be known as the 'Great Calcutta Killing' of 1946, the airport bus squelched over dead bodies left lying in the road. He witnessed a murder outside his hotel after which the murderer, catching sight of 'M', raised his hand in the Hindu gesture of peace, before disappearing into an alley from which the sounds of a mob and the screams of its victims could be distinctly heard. There was a surprising feeling of security among the British, despite the carnage. If there was panic it was felt by the Eurasians who were perhaps the least prepared for what was about to happen.

Those Eurasians 'M' talked with seemed incapable of believing that the British would actually leave India to be ruled by Indians. They had been proud to be British, but now they were faced with a problem of identity, and one that could not be sidestepped. The Railway Communities in which most Eurasians lived – the majority of them were employed in the railway system – were rife with rumour and fear of the future. Deserted by the British, who had created their community, and to a large extent despised them for their mixed race, what could they expect from Indians, whom they had considered inferior to themselves?

One thing 'M' found himself quite capable of understanding was the attraction of India, felt by so many who had served or were serving the Raj. Some described that attraction evocatively, others were less articulate but no less sincere. Some of it was the smell of the place. Not, of course, the smell of the cities which was mainly the stink of excrement, both human and animal, inefficient drainage, and later, gasolene fumes, but the somehow innocent odours of the countryside. The smell of wet dust and vegetation in the rainy season; the perfume of wood smoke and sun-dried earth in the cold weather; the 'cow-dust' time of the painter of Indian miniatures, when the cattle are brought back from the grazing in the twilight. The twilight sudden, over so quickly, and the velvet-dark sky so full of stars that it was possible to read a book by their light. The incredible dawn in the northern hills, when out of the dark emerged a dome of the richest sapphire and from it vast shadows, followed by bright light, rolling in dense dazzling waves through the valleys. The sun, a vast eye, the snow, white on the tips of the distant peaks and the shadows no longer soft-edged, but sharp.

The smells, too, of the bazaar, the sometimes overwhelming perfume of flowers from the stall of the garland-maker, the spicy tang of curry from that of the vegetable-seller. At night, the harsh glare of pressure lamps – and the noise, a love song from a Hindi movie slicing the air, the silence that is never silence, for when the human is quiet, other orders, insects, birds, the wilder animals, take over.

Returning from a visit to a princely state – their days were probably numbered, too, though this particular ruler did not think so – the train 'M' was travelling in back to New Delhi passed another train. The official end of the Raj was only a few days away, and Muslims were already fleeing from what would be the new state of India to the new state of Pakistan, and Hindus and Sikhs from what would be Pakistan to India. The massacre of the innocents had already begun. The train, which was still moving, seemed to 'M' to be full of corpses. The Raj was coming to an end in a sea of blood, not the blood of the 'imperialist oppressors', but that of their subjects, ordinary innocent people: Muslims, Hindus, Sikhs, men, women and children, who, though they had not fought for their country's freedom, were paying for it with their lives. It *was* time for the British to go.

Once, in what must have been a moment of despair, the next to last viceroy, Lord Wavell, had thought it might be necessary for the British to withdraw from India in armed convoys, retreating across the country to the ports where, protected by warships, they would embark and sail away from an angry land. The land was certainly angry as the final days of the Raj came to an end, but the anger was not directed against the British. On the contrary, the friendship and goodwill displayed by Indians of all sorts and conditions was almost embarrassing. British soldiers and administrators were invited to stay on, at least for a time, during the transition from British rule to the successor states. The British businessman saw no reason to leave; after all, business is business, whatever the colour of government. So, for a while, there was a continuity, if only a personal one.

At midnight on 14 August 1947, the Raj came to an end in a suitably Eurasian manner. In the chamber of the Constituent Assembly in New Delhi, the chimes of an English clock rang out, punctuated by the mournful wail of a conch shell. The last trump had finally sounded, and it was time for almost all the British to go Home.

[241]

*—— EPILOGUE ——*

## *AFTER THE SUN SET*

Far-called our navies melt away;
   On dune and headland sinks the fire;
Lo, all our pomp of yesterday
   Is one with Nineveh and Tyre.

Rudyard Kipling
*Recessional* 1897

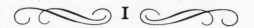

# THE PHANTOM LIMB

A N amputee is said to occasionally feel sensations in the part
that is no longer there. How much did the British feel in the
phantom limb that had once been the Indian Empire? Those
whose careers had been interrupted, no doubt felt irritation if no
more, at having to find new employment; those who took their
pensions, probably a conditional nostalgia when they discovered that
Britain was not quite the land of their dreams. The majority of the
British people felt nothing. The terrible events that followed the
transfer of power in August 1947 – at least 12 million people forced to
leave their homes in what was probably the greatest cross-migration
in history: Muslims to Pakistan, Hindus and Sikhs to India, and
more than half a million dead – was something taking place in a
remote part of the world for which the British no longer had
responsibility. When the events left the headlines of the newspapers,
they also left the consciousness of those who read them.

Throughout the history of the Raj, few Britons were interested in
what was going on in India. In 1833, Macaulay alleged that among
members of the British parliament 'a broken head in Cold Bath
Fields produces a greater sensation . . . than three pitched battles in
India'. The educational missionary and novelist, Edward Thompson, recorded that the quickest method of emptying an Oxford
lecture-room in the 1930s was to mention the word India. After 1947,
as if in response to a continuing indifference, an almost total silence
reigned about the Raj. When the present author began his series of
what have been labelled 'revisionist' studies of British rule in India
more than a decade after its end, the audience was small, though,

another decade later, there was sufficient interest for a commercial TV company to commission a low-budget series on the history of the Raj. Shortly afterwards the BBC produced in conjunction with the American media corporation Time/Life, a costly, glossy, and historically flabby series on *The British Empire*, which aroused some controversy and negative criticism, from both anti-imperialists and those who had survived its fall.

Survivors of the Raj were, however, given the chance to reminisce about their experiences in India in a BBC radio series playfully entitled *Plain Tales from the Raj*, which, though of lasting documentary value, lacked didactic structure, ending up mainly as entertainment of the 'aren't some people peculiar' variety.

But the Raj was near its apotheosis, and in living colour. After a movie on *Gandhi*, which gave what might generously be described as a comic-strip view of the Raj, and received the accolade of the American Academy of Motion Picture Arts and Sciences, came a TV version of the novels of the late Paul Scott under the series title *The Jewel in the Crown*, conjuring up the Raj in its death-throes, and portraying its ruling class as a collection of eccentrics, vicious bullies, psychotics and drunks. This was followed by a movie version of E. M. Forster's grossly overvalued novel, *A Passage to India*, and a docudrama on Lord Mountbatten's role as the last viceroy. The 'Raj-mania' that some publicists discerned early in the 1980s existed, primarily, in the minds of mediacrats, manufacturers, and the Indian Tourist Board, and reached, one hopes, its apogee in the neo-Raj clothes and accessories of an American designer, displayed in a pseudo-Indian environment created inside a fashionable New York department store in 1986.

Forty years after the end of the Raj, it can still arouse controversy, misunderstanding of its nature, and ideological bias. But there have been changes in attitude, albeit puzzling ones. The author's first books were frequently condemned – and praised – for their quite non-existent left-wing bias. His method was once described – by Paul Scott – as never to impose 'his own views upon the subject . . . but to present the facts, clear away the clutter of other historians, and let the reader make up his own mind'. That method has not been changed, yet a book published in 1986 (after a silence of more than eight years on the subject) which attempted to 'demythologise' part of the history of British India, was attacked by both right-wing and left-wing critics as a *defence* of the Raj! The phantom limb still aches from time to time.

On a more general level, the ache represents a nostalgia, not for the Raj in particular, but for the British Empire, for the loss of world power that was the inevitable consequence of de-colonisation. That nostalgia resulted in the neo-Imperial responses of the Suez catastrophe of 1956, and the victorious Falklands War of 1982, and the wide, though by no means total, approval of them by the British people. Even left-wing critics of the Falklands expedition seemed to feel a flow of the old adrenalin as, not for the first time, a costly foreign war diverted attention from the social, economic and political crises at Home.

Four decades are, perhaps, still not long enough for the British to look back and take an impartial view of the Raj. But it is enough for an interim assessment of those who made and sustained it. The preceding pages contain enough facts for the reader to make his own evaluation. However, there remains one more set of facts to assist him in his task, facts that reveal something of the *cost* of the Raj in terms of human suffering to the British, who lived and worked in a strange, and often dangerous, land.

# 2

# *COUNTING THE COST*

1863 is a date of some consequence in the history of the British in India. It is the year in which was published the report of a Royal Commission which had been appointed to examine the sanitary state of the Army in India.

This report makes nauseating but instructive reading. It is diffuse, wordy and unpleasant. It reveals a state of affairs in India about which little was known in England then and to which little importance has been attached by historians of the Empire. It gives the background to British rule, meaning to the myth of the hero, 'dying young'. Its mortality tables are the loss side of the balance sheet of Empire. The place, if one so chooses, to count the cost.

Throughout India there lie scattered the cemeteries of the British. Pathetic, not because they are neglected, the real necropolis of the Empire being still in use at New Delhi, but because of the tender ages recorded so often on the decaying stone.

Examples abound in Anglo-Indian literature of the atmosphere of the charnel house. Private Mulvaney (in Kipling's *The Daughter of the Regiment*), before describing a cholera-camp, put it with simple honesty.

Whin the childher wasn't bornin', they was dying; for av our childher die like sheep in these days, they died like flies thin.

Or for something from the real world, an entry in a diary: 'Poor Mrs Ducat died yesterday morning and was buried, her death I have no doubt hastened by the loss of three of her children in the last ten months.' (Oct. 28, 1826. Lady West, *Journal and Letters 1823–8*.)

Anglo-Indian society was inevitably made up of the young. Those who could, on growing older, retired to England. The British lived in a caravanserai – a stopping place on a journey from where many went no further. Mrs Lushington in her book, *Narrative of a Journey from Calcutta to Europe*, published in 1827, sums up the tragedy for those at home.

Among the Europeans in India there are scarcely any old persons as almost everybody is a temporary resident. Here, if you search the well-tenanted burying grounds of the large cities, you will discover few besides the graves of the youthful, who have been cut off by some violent disease amid the buoyancy of health, or the tombs of those of middle age arrested by death when just about to reap the fruit of long toil and privation by retiring to their native land. It is this which renders our Indian cemeteries so peculiarly melancholy: for though we bow to the decree which summons away the aged and the infirm, yet, humanly speaking, and in our blindness we are apt to pronounce the death of the young to be premature, and a fit subject of aggravated regret.

The routine heroism of every Englishman in India was the heroism of exile. Of being cut off from the crisp beauties of England's fields and streams. The exile of the earlier Empire-builder was not just the temporary nostalgia for the momentarily inaccessible, for that is something we carry with us always on our travels. The tragedy lies in the immanence of death, the fatal permanence of exile, the early grave, and the often unfulfilled longing for 'home'. There is always an undertone of fatalistic melancholy in the outbursts of Anglo-Indian literature. Comrades dead 'before their prime'. Obscure deaths far from the flood-lighting of battle. The very insecurity of life that is reflected in so much of the 'heroic' actions of the Victorian Hero. The arrogance of the short life, but a dynamic one. Always the necessity of getting things done before the country forced breath from the body. Throughout the early days of British rule in India there is always the sense of a race against time.

Disease was the true enemy of the British in India. It was responsible for much of the madness in high places, for the megalomania that passed for heroism. The Victorian pantheon-builders constructed their heroes with sword in hand, glorified the results of feeble judgment into canons of statesmanship, and ignored the true heroism because it was commonplace. The very elements of day-to-day living were more terrible than the Sikhs. The open drain, surface drainage, the pullulating bazaar, and the invisible bacilli – all more deadly than the Afghan passes or the ridge at Delhi. But there is no romance in drains, no glamour in the cholera camp. The literature of heroism is a selective documentation. Blood is stronger than carbolic.

To know something of an act we must at least have some idea of the motive behind it. We cannot by losing a dimension hope to increase reality. The Victorian hero must stand within his landscape. In that landscape there are no triumphal arches, no irrelevant, concealing pomp. The hero stands in a cesspool, surrounded by crosses. A description, perhaps, of exaggerated and unpoetic licence, but if ever men walked 'hand in hand with Death', it was the lot of the British in India until the immunological work of Ross and Haffkine. But to the nineteenth-century composer on Imperial themes, the portrait of the Hero is always placed against a stylised background like the paintings of eighteenth-century generals in which, surrounded by vignettes of battle, there is no way of knowing if there are lice in their wigs.

Anglo-Indian melancholy has a touch of the melancholy of the Bastille, as if the writ of habeas corpus no longer applies. But it is a *conscious* melancholy in which it is difficult to separate passion from contrivance. It became an attitude, another of the imperial gestures, but this time with meaning. For of all the scenes in the pageant of Empire, those of the hero dying of cholera, the comrades lying dead in obscure cemeteries, have a sickening reality. Although such things are muted in the works of the hero-builders, they are always threateningly present, like agents of the Eumenides, unresolved and inchoate. In the poetry of Empire, however, they have shape and reality if only to draw a tear.

Still as I cheer I can't expel the sorrow from my mind,
I cannot drown the memory of those we leave behind.
I wave my cap to India, fast sinking in the blue
But the shadows of my comrades seem to wave me their adieu.

Goodbye, my friends: although the bullet did not lay you low,
A thought, a tear upon your graves, at least your brothers owe;
Ye died for England, though ye died not 'mid the cannon's
    boom,
Nor any 'mention in despatches' glorified your tomb.
(*For England Ho!*: 'Aliph Cheem' *Lays of Ind.*, London, 1866.)

Poets, particularly bad ones, have a habit of speaking from the
heart, with the emotions of things transmuted by fear, delight, or
even resignation as so often with the laureates of Anglo-India. But
there is here a sound statistical background. The mortality tables
leave us with unsettlingly accurate facts on the toll of lives in
India.

The average death-rate from the commencement of records in
1770 until 1856 was 69 per 1,000. The *Report* gives average figures for
three periods.

1770–1779: 55 per 1,000
1800–1829: 85 per 1,000
1830–1856: 58 per 1,000

It shows there to be little advance in prophylactic and therapeutic
medicine in over eighty years. This belief is reinforced by the
statement that deaths in Calcutta in 1856 were the same percentage as
they were in 1772.

In the analysis of causes of death the highest percentage is for those
of 'zymotic' origin, i.e., diseases caused by multiplication of germs
introduced from without. These are given separately for the period
1830–1845 as 58 per 1,000.

The figures given in the *Report* are, by its terms of reference, only
concerned with officers and men of the European force maintained in
India. The mortality rates of officers are, of course, lower than for
the soldier. Better living conditions and, possibly, moral attitudes
account for this. The average for officers is given as 38 per 1,000 and
as low as 16 per 1,000 in 1861.

Briefly, in the summary of evidence, is given another side to the
conquest of India. The expenditure against dubious returns. The

[251]

cost, amongst the lower strata, of the great palaces of Calcutta and the arrogant wealth of the 'Nabob' at home. Disease was no particular respecter of persons, but the chances of the ranks of the European troops for survival were pitifully small.

Of the troops brought to Bombay in 1662, a force of 500 men, only 93 survived in 1664.

In 1759 only five survived out of a body of 250 Europeans landed in India in 1753.

Out of 1,064 men who arrived at Moulmein in 1842 only 93 returned to England in 1859.

The figures are implacable and their continual reiteration almost drains meaning from them. Their reality can, perhaps, be grasped more readily when put in another form.

*The equivalent of one company of every regiment was sacrificed every twenty months.*

Or, even more startlingly, as:

*The European army in India disappeared in about thirteen and a half years.*

To give perspective to these numbers it is necessary to know something of the figures for the European population in India. The following are from the Census of 1861. Naturally, earlier in the history of the British in India, the numbers were smaller, particularly those of women.

| | |
|---|---|
| Civilians | 22,556 |
| Soldiers (including officers) | 84,083 |
| Women | 19,306 |

The life expectation of European soldiers in India was tragically short even when compared with the comparatively short one for England. At the age of twenty, the *Report* shows it to be:

| | |
|---|---|
| India | 17.7 years |
| England | 39.5 years |

No better index can be found for any danger to life than the premiums on life assurance demanded by the insurance companies.

[252]

The comparison is instructive. The premium per £100 at the age of thirty for England was £2 14s.; for India, £4.

From these figures emerges certain information which puts rather a different colour on some of the more common facts of war in India. The sword is used less often than one might have thought, for the tables show that twenty times as many soldiers died from disease than died on active service.

Even one of the highly publicised examples of British courage in India, the Siege of Delhi in 1857, is a somewhat different affair from what Victorian historians would have us believe. More perished on the Ridge from the ubiquitous bacilli than from shot or sword!

The *Report* again translates the nightmare of the Mutiny into the cold horror of statistics:

Out of the men sent to India prior to and including the Mutiny, 9,467 died. *But only 586 men were actually killed in action.* The rest succumbed to disease and the effects of a tropic sun.

And the cost of death in hard cash? £588,000 per annum, no small sum in the currency of the time.

Why was the record so terrible? Florence Nightingale had the answer. Asked by the Royal Commission to comment on the evidence given to that body, Miss Nightingale supplied a lengthy series of observations, the gravamen of which she summed up as: Drains and dram-drinking. The first she put with her rather sharp humour as: When asked about Drains the Army in India was like the London woman who replied, 'No, thank God, we have none of them foul, stinking things here!'

The barracks, bungalows, and towns of India were without drains. Water-supplies in pipes were non-existent. The station reports on their drinking water are hair-raising. Filtration was virtually unknown.

Bombay it is true, has a better water supply; but it has no drainage. Calcutta is being drained but it has no water supply. Two of the seats of Government have thus each one half of a sanitary improvement, which halves ought never to be separated. Madras has neither.

The Indian towns were even worse than the cantonments of the British. The country around the Bazaars is described in the *Report* as 'one immense privy'.

At Agra it is proof of *respectability* to have cess-pools. The inhabitants (152,000) generally resort to fields.

The life of the European soldier fitted into the pattern of the nightmare. Stuffed into old and inadequate barracks, watching his comrades die. At Prome (in Burma) in 1853 there were five or six burials daily out of a European force of a little more than a thousand men. Such figures were almost commonplace. The European soldier was engulfed in the boredom of a soldier's day in the tropics. Miss Nightingale gives his routine as:

bed till daybreak,
drill for an hour,
breakfast, served to him by native servants,
bed,
dinner, served to him by native servants,
bed,
tea, served to him by native servants,
drink,
tea – and *da capo*

There can be little surprise that they turned to drink. They were no different from their officers or civilians in their actions and hope for forgetfulness. Furthermore, drinking was actually encouraged by the authorities for vast quantities were sold in the canteens. And though the sale of spirits to soldiers was strictly forbidden in the Bazaars, everyone could get as much as he wanted.

For, as might be expected, it is practically impossible to encourage and restrict an evil at the same time. Government sells the licence to sell drink in the bazaar, and orders the men not to profit by it. The present law is like lighting a fire and charging it not to burn anything.

[254]

Under pressure, of course, the Government denied any such intention and even agreed that spirit-selling should be abolished. But Miss Nightingale was not to be placated by fine phrases.

The only plea on the other side is a very old one, which has been used to justify other vices besides dram-drinking, viz. that 'if we do not give spirits in the canteen, which we all believe to be bad for health and discipline, the men will get worse spirits in the bazaar'. Thus the men are killed by liver-disease on canteen spirits to save them from being killed by liver-disease on bazaar spirits, Government in either case benefiting pecuniarily, as is supposed, by the transaction. May there not be some middle course whereby men may be killed by neither bazaar nor canteen spirits?

Miss Nightingale in her 'Observations' put her finger on many tender spots – and probed. The Government at home reacted by omitting her contribution from the abridged public version of the *Report* and dispersed the type of the full edition. Miss Nightingale responded by printing her 'Observations' separately and sending a copy to everyone of note in England and to every medical man in India.

The battle for Indian sanitary improvements had begun. Powerful allies appeared. Sir John Lawrence before leaving for India as Viceroy in 1863, went to see her. He had met her previously in 1861. Slowly the Englishman's home in India ceased to be his castle and became his water-closet. The background of heroism unobtrusively trickled away down the smooth bore of the Imperial cloacae. A revolution took place in living. It was a slow one, however. Improvements were made, but they took time and money. Malaria and cholera had to wait to be conquered.

The last mortality table of all is dated 15 August 1947. But this time it was the Indian Empire itself that was dead.

[255]

# 3

# *RESIDUES OF EMPIRE*

i. *Lays of Ind: The Literature of 'Anglo-India'*

There are nine and sixty ways of constructing tribal lays,
And – every – single – one – of – them – is right
Rudyard Kipling:
*In the Neolithic Age*

THE men – and women – who lived and worked in British India produced a variety of literary works in a variety of genres: history, memoirs, travel, fiction, and above all, poetry, that particular favourite of the 'Anglo-Indian' muse. Some of these works are of a lasting interest, most of justly forgotten mediocrity. Of the former, Robert Orme, in his still highly readable *History of the Military Transactions of the British Nation in Indostan* (of which the first volume was published in 1763), wrote of the period of Clive. One of Thackeray's characters (Clive Newcome) called it 'the best book in the world'. A number of the East India Company's servants produced historical works. Sir John Malcolm's *Political History of India* appeared in 1826, and he wrote other works of value. Mountstuart Elphinstone's *History of India* was published in 1841. James Grant Duff wrote his useful but virtually unreadable *History of the Mahrattas* in 1826. Malcolm's work was partly a justification of British rule. 'The great empire which England has established in the East', he wrote at the beginning of one of his books, 'will be the theme of

[256]

wonder to succeeding ages'. Elphinstone accepted the fact that India had once had some institutions of value, but was now in need of what the West – and specifically Britain – had to offer. Grant Duff was really writing a justification of the British campaign against the Marathas.

Thomas Babington Macaulay on his return from India, where he had been Law Member of the Governor-General's Council, wrote essays on Clive and Hastings (1840–1) which were highly critical and were designed, at least in part, to show how much the British administration had improved since the eighteenth century. The historians all had some axe to grind. J. D. Cunningham, whose *History of the Sikhs* was published in 1849 just after the annexation of the Punjab, was concerned with convincing the British that they must continue with their 'civilising' mission in India. 'The well-being of India's industrious millions', he said, 'is now linked with the foremost nation of the West, and the representatives of Judean faith and Roman polity will long wage a war of principles with the speculative Brahman, the authoritative Mulla, and the hardy believing Sikh!' J. W. Kaye, who became the chronicler of British administrators in India, wrote his *History of the War in Afghanistan* (1851) to remind the British that expansion for the sake of expansion could often lead to disaster.

Soldiers, civilians, and their wives, wrote of their travels to and in India. From their works it is possible to gain a fairly clear picture of the life of the British. James Forbes, who was in India between 1765 and 1784, disclosed in his *Oriental Memoirs* (1813) that he was driven by loneliness 'to investigate the manners and customs of the inhabitants, to study natural history, and to delineate the principal places and picturesque scenery'.

Later, it is possible to relate the reaction of the writers to their type of employment. Soldiers such as Herbert Edwardes (*A Year on the Punjab Frontier*, 1851) wrote of new frontiers and of wild places, newly conquered. Missionaries and deeply-involved Christian officers were determined to take the lid off pagan India (Charles Acland, *A Popular Account of the Manners and Customs of India*, 1843). Old-fashioned officials with paternalist leanings painted pictures of an India untouched by the West or sadly damaged by contact

[257]

with it (William Sleeman, *Rambles and Recollections of an Indian Official*, 1844).

All these writers – the travellers and the historians – were critical, in most cases, of India and the Indians. All of what they wrote was primarily designed to influence opinion in Britain. It was from these works that the legislators, and that narrow section of the British people which made up 'public opinion', acquired their image of India. They preferred the evidence for India's depravity and backwardness to the apologetics of such men as Sleeman. One sector of 'Anglo-Indian' literary activity thus helped to create a climate *in Britain* favourable to the consolidation and advance of Western ideas of government and economics in India.

There was also a great deal of fiction written, much of which represented a growing racial consciousness among the British and was without literary merit. There were, however, one or two exceptions. Mrs Sherwood's children's books – *Little Henry and His Bearer* and *The Fairchild Family* (1818) – reveal a great deal about English society in India in the early years of the nineteenth century, as does J. W. Kaye's anonymous novel, *Peregrine Pulteney* (1844). W. B. Hockley wrote *Pandarung Hari* (1826), a picaresque novel set in the times of the Maratha wars, and *The English in India* (1828). Meadows Taylor's *Confessions of a Thug* (1837) is a sort of non-fiction novel based upon the author's experiences in the suppression of Thugee. Taylor's novel contributed – though it was probably not designed to do so – to the general impression in Britain that the moral standard of the Indians was low.

One of the most interesting of 'Anglo-Indian' novels was written (under the pseudonym 'Punjabee') by the poet Matthew Arnold's brother, William Delafield Arnold. This work, *Oakfield or Fellowship in the East* (1853), is more of a tract than a novel, primarily an exposure of the pettiness and – to Arnold – downright evil of most of the British in India. If there was no improvement in the moral standard of the British, India could hope for very little benefit from British rule. Arnold's idea of the Englishman's duty in India was that he should 'help in the work, or try to set it going, of raising the *European Society*, the great influence on Asia, first from the depths of immorality, gradually to a state of Christian earnestness. I am quite

[258]

certain that nothing less than Christianity in the form of Cromwell or some other shape, will have any effect on the awful *vis inertiae* of Asiaticism. The protection of life and property, of which we hear so much, is of course a clear good; hardly, though, a very disinterested boon of ours to this country, for if life and property were insecure, whose throats or purses would go first? But for any purpose beyond protraction to life and property (I for one, will not believe that God gave England the Indian Empire for police purposes only) an eating and drinking, money-getting community is inefficient'.

After 1857 and the taking over of direct rule by the Crown, administrators and soldiers continued the literary traditions of their predecessors. Many of their works were on history and administration, though they occasionally wrote light verse and novels. Among the historians, W. W. Hunter not only explored Indian history but something of the actual scene in the 1870s. The atmosphere of post-Mutiny India is contained in George Otto Trevelyan's *The Competition-Wallah* (1864). In the second half of the nineteenth century, many administrators wrote their memoirs. Few have literary value, but all are of historical and sociological interest. Of officials who could write about their work with style, there were few who could do as well as S. S. Thorburn, whose *Mussulmans and Money-lenders* (1886), though concerned only with the Punjab, is one of the most revealing and humane documents on the state of the debt-ridden Indian peasant. Sir Alfred Lyall, who wrote poetry as well as history, was also a writer of style.

Under the influence of Curzon, there was a revival of interest in the actual life of the British in India, and with his encouragement such works as E. J. Buck's *Simla: Past and Present* (1904) and H. E. Busteed's *Echoes from Old Calcutta* (1908) were written by government officials.

With the considerable growth in the size of the British community after 1860, British society in India took on a life of its own. The business element expanded but new types of English residents – such as journalists and school teachers – also appeared. After the opening of the Suez Canal (1869) the number of 'cold-weather' visitors increased. The English reading public in India was now quite substantial and its needs could not be entirely supplied from Britain.

There grew up a market for verse and fiction about the lives of the British in India. There was also a growing market in Britain for tales about India and for descriptive works about life there. The expatriate community, though it occasionally believed it was menaced by growing Indian unrest, felt – at least till the end of the century – strong enough to laugh at itself. Novels such as H. S. Cunningham's *Chronicles of Dustypore* (1879) took a sly look at the life of the British in their ghetto (known in India as 'the station'). There was also a vague interest in the natives – as servants – as in 'EHA' *Behind the Bungalow* (1901). Most of this kind of work is still readable, and sometimes still amusing. G. Aberigh-Mackay's *Twenty-One Days in India*, first published anonymously in a Bombay newspaper in 1880, contains portraits of such pillars of 'Anglo-Indian' society as the commander-in-chief. 'At Simla and Calcutta the Government of India always sleeps with a revolver under its pillow – that revolver is the Commander-in-Chief. There is a tacit understanding that this revolver is not to be let off; indeed, sometimes it is believed that this revolver is not loaded.'

In this tradition is the Indian work of Rudyard Kipling, who became the laureate of Anglo-India for a larger audience than it could ever have considered possible. Kipling explored the lives of the British in India and reflected some, but by no means all, of their prejudices. The few Indians who appear in such of his work as was written in India are either servants or 'incompetent' educated Bengalis. It was only after leaving India that Kipling was able to write, in *Kim*, what is undoubtedly the best work of fiction about India by an Englishman.

A number of other writers followed Kipling. Among the most interesting was Flora Annie Steel, whose *On the Face of the Waters* (1896) – a novel about the Mutiny – is again concerned with the British. Its Indian characters are merely symbols. No 'Anglo-Indian' writer was able to portray Indians with any sense of life. The journalist Edmund Candler made, perhaps, the first attempt in his *Shri Ram, Revolutionist* (1910).

In the last twenty-five years of British rule two outstanding novelists produced works dealing with British life in India. One, E. M. Forster's *A Passage to India*, though hailed by Indians for its attack on 'Anglo-Indian' society and its prejudices, is just as offensive in its drawing of the Hindu character as its predecessors. Edward Thompson's novels, on the other hand, give an accurate feel of the disintegrating empire of the 1930s.

Many of the British were amateur poets. Much of what they wrote was extremely bad, some reached a fairly high standard of mediocrity. There was a certain amount of humorous verse, but this form was to reach its zenith after the Mutiny. 'Anglo-Indian' poetry reflected the changing attitude of the British both to India and things Indian and towards their own situation. Sir William Jones, as well as making translations, wrote original poems on various Hindu gods which show a real attempt at understanding:

> Wrapt in eternal solitary shade,
> Th' impenetrable gloom of light intense,
> Impervious, inaccessible, immense,
> Ere spirits were infus'd or forms display'd,
>     BREHM his own Mind survey'd,
> As mortal eyes (thus finite we compare
>     With infinite) in smoothest mirrors gaze:
> Swift, at his look, a shape supremely fair
>     Leap'd into being with a boundless blaze,
>         That fifty suns might daze.
>                 *Hymn to Brahma* (1790)

Later work on similar subjects is empty and facile, like the *Hymn to India* (1881) by William Waterfield:

> God of the varied bow,
>     God of the thousand eyes,
> From all the winds that blow
>     Thy praises rise;
> Forth through the world they go
>     Hymning to all below
> Thee, whom the blest shall know
>     Lord of the skies.

[261]

The beginnings of a poetry of exile, of the British spending long years among savage and barbarous peoples, can be found in the melancholy poems of Bishop Heber (author of the well-known hymn 'Brightest and Best of the Sons of the Morning') and John Leyden, who died of fever in 1811 and whose *Ode to an Indian Gold Coin* first stated the theme which was to be taken up by others later in the century. Heber, who also died in India – in 1826, after only three years' residence – expressed his longing for 'Home' in his poem, *An Evening Walk in Bengal*:

> So rich a shade, so green a sod
> Our English fairies never trod!
> Yet who in India's bow'r has stood,
> But thought on England's 'good green wood'?
> And bless'd, beneath the palmy shade,
> Her hazel and her hawthorn glade,
> And breath'd a pray'r (how oft in vain!)
> To gaze upon her oaks again?

There were, however, many writers of light verse, and Kipling's *Departmental Ditties* (1886) are very much in the tradition. Most of this sort of verse was published first (and sometimes only) in newspapers. Much of it was concerned with the 'in' jokes of British society. It is mainly humorous and deliberately imitative of well-known contemporary British poetry:

> 'O grim and ghastly Mussulman,
>     Why art thou wailing so?
> Is there a pain within thy brain,
>     Or in thy little toe?
> The twilight shades are shutting fast
>     The golden gates of day,
> Then shut up, too, your hullabaloo –
>     Or what's the matter, say?'

[262]

That stern and sombre Mussulman,
  He heeded not my speech,
But raised again his howl of pain –
  A most unearthly screech!
'He dies!' – I thought, and forthwith rushed
  To aid the wretched man,
When, with a shout, he yell'd – *'Get out!*
  *I'm singing the Koran!'*
          Anon. *The Poet's Mistake* (1871)

For much of the nineteenth century, the sense of exile and of doing one's duty with suffering remained – it is everywhere in Kipling's Indian work – and it was something expressed with almost pathological melancholy:

My fellow exiles, fill your glasses,
  We'll sing one song before we die;
    The tiger in the jungle-grasses
Has sucked the peasant's life-blood dry.
    W. T. Webb. *The Song of Death* (1884)

For poets of some sensibility like Sir Alfred Lyall, India was the 'Land of Regrets' and the Englishman always a stranger. This attitude, however, did not survive the first world war, when the spread of communications removed the sense of exile, and the growth of nationalism and the constitutional changes lessened the sense of duty. Nevertheless, even as late as 1933, an anonymous poet could still write:

The wheeling months go round
  And back I come again
To the baked and blistered ground
  And the dust-encumbered plain
  And the bare hot-weather trees
And the Trunk Road's aching white;
  Oh, land of little ease!
  Oh, land of strange delight!
          Anon. *Back East* (1933)

[263]

## ii. *The Thug in the Bungalow: Indian Words in English*

As the British established their connections with India they were, not unnaturally, forced to acquire at least some casual knowledge of the languages used by the people with whom they first traded and then came to rule. The British are said to be bad linguists. Though there is little justification for such a *canard* – unless 'bad' is taken to mean 'lazy' – it is nevertheless true to say that very few merchants or administrators in the first half-century learned to speak a local language with any degree of fluency. There were exceptions, of course. Warren Hastings, for example, composed rather bad verses in Persian. But in general the Company's servants relied upon interpreters in their commercial and social relations with Indians.

They did, of course, learn the meaning of a large number of words – commercial, judicial and revenue terms – and mixed them with their normal speech. The Company's records are full of sentences peppered with Indian words in a wide variety of transliterations. Edmund Burke was driven to complain in the House of Commons that this hybrid language was probably 'of necessary use in the executive department of the Company's affairs; but it is not necessary to Parliament. A language so foreign from all the ideas and habits of the far greater part of the members of the House, has a tendency to disgust them with all sorts of inquiry concerning this subject. They are fatigued into such a despair of ever obtaining a competent knowledge of the transactions in India, that they are easily persuaded to remand them . . . to obscurity'. Nevertheless, many of these words made their way into the English language, and not only into the language of poets but into the common speech of everyday life.

The first words to be absorbed into the English language were mainly the names of things, like calico – after the port of Calicut,· from which much of India's cotton cloth was exported to Europe in the seventeenth century – and cummerbund, a waist-sash. Though there were many more (the *Oxford English Dictionary* lists over three hundred words which entered the language from India in the seventeenth century), most have disappeared from normal speech. Such words as mogul, bungalow, pundit, shampoo, and cot have, however, become completely naturalised.

The eighteenth century saw a distinct increase in the number of words relating to political and military affairs – a situation brought about by the changing nature of the role played by the British in India during the collapse of the Mughal power. Of the words which have survived into modern speech, perhaps the most historically pertinent is loot (from the Hindi *lut*, plunder). Another word which indicated the widening of European horizons was 'jungle'. Verandah, bangle and buggy were also imported during the eighteenth century, as was chee-chee, a disparaging term applied to half-castes. The honour of first using it in literature apparently belongs to the journalist Hicky. It appeared in his *Bengal Gazette* in March 1781:

> Pretty little Looking-Glasses,
> Good and cheap for Chee-chee Misses.

Not surprisingly, the nineteenth century brought a large number of Indian words into the English language, particularly words which reflected the growing interest in Indian philosophy and literature. In ordinary English speech, however, such words as 'thug' – which originally meant a particular class of professional robber and murderer, the extent of whose operations was only discovered by the British in the first decades of the nineteenth century – had already taken on the colloquial meaning of 'ruffian' or 'cut-throat' as early as 1839. The use of the word 'damn' in the expression 'don't care (or give) a damn' seems to have originated in the word *dan*, a copper coin of very small value.

The first world war added new words, and new meanings for old ones. This is particularly apparent in army slang. One new word was 'blighty', used to mean 'home' (i.e., Britain) by troops serving abroad. Others were 'cushy' – meaning easy, or comfortable – and 'char', referring to tea. The war gave wider currency to a number of words, including buckshee, puggled (from the Hindi *pagal*, mad or crazy), and wallah.

Although the second world war brought very few new words, it did distribute them widely among the large numbers of British and American troops who passed through India or were stationed there. Among today's survivals are 'phut' ('it went phut', meaning it stopped working or collapsed) which came from the Hindi *phatna*, to burst, and 'dekko' ('let's have a dekko') from the Hindi *dekho*, the imperative of the verb *dekhna*, to look.

★　★　★

The use in literature of words of Indian origin preceded actual contact with India and Indian life. Most of these words – even the word 'India' itself – came via Greek, Latin or French, and were mainly confined to the names of things, such as pepper, beryl, and camphor. The works of English travellers, which began to appear in the seventeenth century, supplied not only colourful and exotic backgrounds and tales, but also some of the language needed to reinforce the exoticism. Strange-sounding place names obviously attracted the poet, John Milton:

> Of Cambulu, seat of Cathaian Can,
> 　　And Samarkand by Oxus, Temir's throne,
> To Paquin of Sinean kings, and thence,
> 　　To Agra and Lahor of Great Mogul.
> *Paradise Lost*, xi, 388

The eighteenth century, with its growing awareness of India and the consequences of establishing British rule in Bengal, brought a number of words into the vocabulary of English men of letters. Some were used precisely, and for a specific purpose, as when Edmund Burke used them in his speeches in the House of Commons; though he complained about them at the same time, he could not avoid using them. Perhaps the most popular Indian word in eighteenth-century literature was 'nabob' (from *nawab*, a Muslim prince), which was applied to returning servants of the East India Company as a term of abuse. Even such words as 'nabobess' and 'nabobry' were invented. Laurence Sterne produced a feminine version of Brahmin ('Bramine') which he applied to Eliza Draper, the wife of a Company servant. Robert Burns seems to have made the first literary use of the word 'toddy' – a mixture of whisky or some other spirit with sugar and hot water – corrupted from the Hindi *tari*, the fermented sap of the palm tree:

[266]

The lads an' lasses, blythely bent,
To mind baith soul an' body,
Sit round the table, well content,
An' steer about the toddy.
*Holy Fair* (1785)

The nineteenth century produced a special category of English literature which is best described as 'Anglo-Indian'. Naturally, writers of this school, who include Edwin Arnold and Rudyard Kipling, utilised a large number of Indian words in their works. Others, such as Jane Austen, Shelley, Carlyle, Dickens, and Robert Louis Stevenson, occasionally used Indian words. Sir Walter Scott went further and wrote a novel about India, *The Surgeon's Daughter*, which displays an accurate knowledge of the meaning of Indian words, acquired apparently from a neighbour, Colonel Ferguson of Huntly Burn. Scott describes him in the novel – under the name of Colonel Mackerris – as 'one of the best fellows who ever trod a Highland moor or dived into an Indian jungle'.

Among other writers, Southey (*The Curse of Kehama*), Byron (*The Giaour*), and Thackeray used Indian words, Southey in particular without much appreciation of their real meaning. Thackeray, however, was born in India and had a wide vocabulary of Indian words although he left the country when he was still a child. He often bent such words in order to make them and the characters who used them objects of fun – as when he used the word 'catamaran' (raft) to describe Mrs Mackenzie in *The Newcomes*: 'an infernal tartar and catamaran'. In the same novel, mulligatawny became a place name. Elsewhere, Thackeray gave characters such names as Mr Chutney (*Vanity Fair*), General Sir Rice Curry, K.C.B. (*A Shabby Genteel Story*), and Colonel Goldmore (*Barry Lyndon*) from the gold *mohur*, an Indian coin.

The present century has produced, in some areas, a greater understanding of India but very little desire to use Indian words for fun. E. M. Forster's *A Passage to India* uses very few Indian words, probably because of the author's inability – in spite of the uncritical praise lavished upon the work – to understand either India itself or the world of the British in India. Edward Thompson's unjustly neglected novels, *An Indian Day*, *Night Falls on Siva's Hill* and *A Farewell to India*, reflect a changing and essentially political vocabulary in which *swaraj* (freedom) and swarajists, *swadeshi* (home-produced) and other such words represent the new world of Indian nationalism.

Among other writers, the words used are mainly taken from Indian metaphysics. They appear in such poems as T. S. Eliot's *The Waste Land*, in the philosophical works of Aldous Huxley, and in the literature produced by the popularisers of yogic exercises. Indian words which still retain their virility in common speech are used without conscious knowledge of their origin. These are examples of genuine cultural penetration. They represent one of the few permanent legacies of the British connection with India.

# NOTES ON SOURCES

## Overture: Shaking the Pagoda Tree

### 1. A Visit to a Factory

| Page | Line | Source |
|------|------|--------|
| 18 | 1 | C. Lockyer: *An Account of the Trade in India* London 1711 |
| 18 | 31 | J. T. Wheeler: *Madras in the Olden Time* London n.d. Vol. 2 |
| 18 | 35 | H. B. Love: *Vestiges of Old Madras* London n.d. Vol. 2 |
| 19 | 2 | Revd T. Ovington: *A Voyage to Surat in 1689* new ed. London 1921 |
| 19 | 16 | Capt. W. Sysson: *A New Voyage to the East Indies* 1720 |
| 20 | 8 | Wheeler op. cit. |
| 20 | 25 | Lockyer op. cit. |
| 21 | 26 | Love op. cit. |
| 22 | 20 | M. L. J. O'H. de Grandpré: *Voyage in the Indian Ocean and to Bengal* Eng. trs. London 1814. Grandpré was writing of the late 18th century. |

### 2. Diplomats, Mercenaries, and Indo-Britons

| Page | Line | Source |
|------|------|--------|
| 24 | 11 | Eliza Draper of John Whitehill 1774 quoted in A. Wright & W. L. Sclater: *Sterne's Eliza* London 1922 |
| 25 | 6 | Quoted in Michael Edwardes: *Glorious Sahibs* London 1968 NY 1969 |
| 25 | 18 | Lord Wellesley, 27 June 1803. Quoted in *Edwardes* op. cit. |

| Page | Line | Source |
|------|------|--------|
| 27 | 36 | Quoted in Edwardes op. cit. |
| 28 | 11 | Metcalfe, quoted in Edwardes op. cit. |
| 28 | 24 | Edwardes op. cit. |
| 31 | 3 | Edwardes op. cit. |
| 31 | 26 | Edwardes op. cit. |
| 33 | 1 | Reginald Heber: *Narrative of a Journey through the Upper Provinces of India from Calcutta to Bombay 1824–1825* London 1829 |
| 34 | 2 | Lord Valentia: *Travels in India 1806* London n.d. |
| 34 | 23 | Emily Eden: *Up the Country* ed E. Thompson. London 1937 |

### 3. The Heathen in His Blindness

| | | |
|------|------|--------|
| 36 | 12 | T. G. P. Spear: *The Nabobs* London 1932 |
| 37 | 31 | Quoted in Love op. cit. |
| 39 | 31 | Henry Martyn: *Journals and Letters* London 1857. The quotes are dated 1806 and 1807 |
| 40 | 12 | William Wilberforce: Speech in the House of Commons London 22 June 1813 |
| 41 | 2 | R. Heber: Hymn: *From Greenland's Icy Mountains.* |

### 4. Nabobs and Nautches

| | | |
|------|------|--------|
| 42 | 9 | T. B. Macaulay: *Lord Clive* 1842 |
| 44 | 7 | Quoted in G. Forrest: *Life of Lord Clive* London 1918 |
| 48 | 31 | James Mackintosh: *Travels in Europe, Asia and Africa 1771–1781* London 1783 |
| 52 | 9 | Maria Graham: *Journal of a Residence in India 1809–11* London 1813 |

### Act One: This Splendid Empire

This and the two following parts consist of edited and revised chapters selected from Michael Edwardes: *Bound to Exile* London 1969 New York 1970

## 1. Her Majesty's Indian Dominions

| Page | Line | Source |
|------|------|--------|
| 58 | 8 | Heber: *Narrative* op. cit. |
| 58 | 24 | J. L. Morison: *Lawrence of Lucknow* London 1834 |
| 59 | 13 | W. H. Sleeman: *Rambles and Recollections of an Indian Official* ed V. Smith. London 1898 |
| 60 | 1 | Victor Jacquemont: *Letters from India* London 1834 |
| 60 | 30 | Morison op. cit. |
| 61 | 13 | Sleeman op. cit. |
| 61 | 31 | Lady Edwardes: *Memorials of the Life and Letters of Major-General Herbert B. Edwardes* London 1886 |
| 62 | 34 | Henry Lawrence: *Essays* London 1839 |
| 64 | 13 | Mrs Postans: *Western India in 1838* London 1859 |
| 65 | 34 | Heber op. cit. |
| 66 | 11 | Emily Eden: *Letters from India* London 1872 |
| 66 | 16 | J. W. Kaye: *The Life and Correspondence of Charles, Lord Metcalfe* London 1854 |
| 66 | 22 | *Private Letters of the Marquis of Dalhousie* ed J. G. A. Baird Edinburgh 1911 |

## 2. Ducks, Mulls and Qui-his

| | | |
|------|------|--------|
| 67 | 24 | Mrs Postans op. cit. |
| 68 | 25 | J. H. Stocqueler: *Handbook to India* London 1844 |
| 69 | 7 | Mrs Postans op. cit. |
| 69 | 19 | Anon: *Life in Bombay* London 1852 |
| 70 | 16 | Mrs Postans op. cit. |
| 70 | 37 | Viscountess Falkland: *Chow-Chow* London 1857 |
| 71 | 19 | *Life in Bombay* op. cit. |
| 71 | 37 | Falkland op. cit. |
| 72 | 19 | Stocqueler op. cit. |
| 73 | 4 | *Life in Bombay* op. cit. |
| 74 | 13 | Mrs Postans op. cit. |
| 74 | 28 | *Life in Bombay* op. cit. |
| 75 | 6 | Stocqueler op. cit. |
| 75 | 26 | *Life in Bombay* op. cit. |
| 76 | 2 | Falkland op. cit. |
| 76 | 28 | *Life in Bombay* op. cit. |

| Page | Line | Source |
|------|------|--------|
| 76 | 35 | Falkland op. cit. |
| 77 | 1 | *Life in Bombay* op. cit. |
| 77 | 8 | Falkland op. cit. |
| 77 | 35 | *Life in Bombay* op. cit. |
| 78 | 18 | Falkland op. cit. |
| 79 | 4 | Stocqueler op. cit. |
| 79 | 24 | *Life in Bombay* op. cit. |
| 79 | 28 | Stocqueler op. cit. |
| 80 | 16 | J. C. Maitland: *Letters from Madras by a Lady* London 1843 |
| 80 | 32 | Captain Bellew: *Memoirs of a Griffin* London 1843 |
| 81 | 29 | Stocqueler op. cit. |
| 82 | 2 | Bellew op. cit. |
| 82 | 11 | Stocqueler op. cit. |
| 82 | 25 | Maitland op. cit. |
| 82 | 37 | Bellew op. cit. |
| 83 | 9 | Maitland op. cit. |
| 83 | 17 | Anon: *Indian Domestic Economy and Receipt Book* Madras 1860 |
| 84 | 4 | Maitland op. cit. |
| 84 | 22 | Sir H. B. Edwardes and H. Merrivale: *Life of Sir Henry Lawrence* London 1872 |
| 85 | 17 | *Life in Bombay* op. cit. |
| 86 | 23 | Maitland op. cit. |
| 87 | 23 | Bellew op. cit. |
| 88 | 3 | Stocqueler op. cit. |
| 88 | 8 | Bellew op. cit. |
| 89 | 6 | Colesworthy Grant: *Rural Life in Bengal* London 1860 |
| 89 | 29 | Bellew op. cit. |
| 89 | 37 | W. H. Carey: *The Good Old Days of the Honourable John Company* Calcutta 1906 |
| 91 | 3 | Bellew op. cit. |
| 91 | 29 | Lord Roberts: *Forty-one Years in India* London 1898 |
| 92 | 16 | W. H. Russell: *My Indian Mutiny Diary* ed M. Edwardes London 1957 |
| 93 | 17 | L. von Orlich: *Travels in India* London 1845 |
| 94 | 19 | Anon: [J. W. Kaye] *Peregrine Pulteney or Life in India* London 1844 |
| 95 | 1 | Stocqueler op. cit. |

| Page | Line | Source |
|------|------|--------|
| 97 | 4 | Sir George Campbell: *Memoirs of My Indian Career* London 1893 |
| 98 | 25 | *Peregrine Pulteney* op. cit. |
| 99 | 10 | Carey op. cit. |
| 99 | 20 | Dalhousie op. cit. |
| 99 | 32 | Eden op. cit. |
| 100 | 12 | Orlich op. cit. |
| 100 | 15 | *Peregrine Pulteney* op. cit. |
| 100 | 29 | Stocqueler op. cit. |
| 101 | 1 | Eden op. cit. |
| 101 | 13 | W. Knighton: *Tropical Sketches* London 1855 |
| 101 | 21 | Russell op. cit. |

## 3. Up the Country and unto the Hills

| | | |
|------|------|--------|
| 102 | 14 | Russell op. cit. |
| 103 | 15 | Stocqueler op. cit. |
| 103 | 37 | Mrs Colin Mackenzie: *Life in the Mission, the Camp and the Zenana* London 1854 |
| 104 | 6 | Richard Burton: *Goa and the Blue Mountains* London 1857 |
| 104 | 33 | Roberts op. cit. |
| 105 | 5 | G. F. Atkinson: *Curry and Rice on Forty Plates* London 1859 |
| 105 | 23 | Grant op. cit. |
| 106 | 8 | Atkinson op. cit. |
| 108 | 20 | 'Punjabee': *Oakfield or Fellowship in the East* London 1853 |
| 109 | 15 | Mackenzie op. cit. |
| 110 | 9 | Atkinson op. cit. |
| 110 | 27 | Stocqueler op. cit. |
| 111 | 5 | Lady Edwardes op. cit. |
| 111 | 30 | Maitland op. cit. |
| 112 | 2 | Falkland op. cit. |
| 113 | 2 | Atkinson op. cit. |
| 113 | 22 | Lady Edwardes op. cit. |
| 114 | 2 | Atkinson op. cit. |
| 114 | 26 | John Lang: *Wanderings in India* London 1859 |
| 115 | 27 | Eden op. cit. |
| 116 | 3 | Russell op. cit. |

| Page | Line | Souce |
|------|------|-------|
| 116 | 8 | Atkinson op. cit. |
| 117 | 4 | Lang op. cit. |
| 118 | 5 | *Life in Bombay* op. cit. |
| 118 | 11 | Burton op. cit. |
| 118 | 37 | Falkland op. cit. |
| 119 | 7 | *Life in Bombay* op. cit. |
| 119 | 15 | Falkland op. cit. |
| 120 | 22 | *Life in Bombay* op. cit. |
| 121 | 13 | Maitland op. cit. |
| 121 | 34 | Sir J. F. Price: *History of Ootacamund* Madras 1908 |
| 122 | 10 | Burton op. cit. |
| 123 | 16 | Anon: [Fanny Parkes] *Wanderings of a Pilgrim in Search of the Picturesque* London 1852 |
| 123 | 31 | Eden op. cit. |
| 124 | 35 | Dalhousie op. cit. |
| 125 | 25 | E. J. Buck: *Simla Past and Present* Calcutta 1904 |
| 125 | 34 | Lang op. cit. |
| 126 | 31 | Mackenzie op. cit. |
| 127 | 10 | Lang op. cit. |

*Entr'acte: The Devil's Wind*

*1. At the Edge of the Abyss*

| | | |
|------|------|-------|
| 134 | 3 | Henry Lawrence: to Lord Canning 18 April 1857 |
| 134 | 23 | George Trevelyan: *The Competition Wallah* London 1895 |

*2. Up among the Pandies*

| | | |
|------|------|-------|
| 137 | 1 | Based on Hugh Gough: *Old Memories* Edinburgh 1897 |
| 141 | 3 | Russell op. cit. |
| 141 | 28 | Anon: [Katherine Bartrum] *A Widow's Reminiscence of Lucknow* London 1858 |

*3. Bloody Assize*

| | | |
|------|------|-------|
| 149 | 15 | J. W. Kaye: *History of the Sepoy War in India* London 1880 |
| 149 | 26 | Michael Maclagan: *Clemency Canning* London 1962 |

| Page | Line | Source |
|------|------|--------|
| 152 | 6 | R. Collier: *The Sound of Fury* London 1963 |
| 152 | 16 | Trevelyan op. cit. |
| 152 | 31 | T. E. Colebrook: *Life of the Hon. Mounstuart Elphinstone* London 1884 |
| 153 | 15 | Kaye op. cit. |
| 153 | 25 | Denis Kincaid: *British Social Life in India* London 1938 |
| 154 | 7 | Trevelyan op. cit. |
| 154 | 13 | M. Edwardes: *The Necessary Hell* London 1958 |
| 154 | 33 | Anon: *Tom Cringle's Letters on Practical Subjects* Bombay 1863 |
| 155 | 13 | Russell op. cit. |
| 156 | 18 | Lt. E. S. Ommanney to Chief Commissioner, Delhi 9 October 1858 |
| 156 | 32 | G. B. Malleson: *History of the Indian Mutiny* London 1880 |

## Act Two: The Queen's Peace Over All

### 1. Mirror of Indigo

| 162 | 27 | S. Gopal: *British Policy in India* Cambridge 1965 |
|------|------|--------|
| 163 | 14 | Trevelyan op. cit. |
| 164 | 16 | B. B. Misra: *The Indian Middle Classes* London 1961 |
| 164 | 26 | Based upon W. M. Reid: *The Culture and Manufacture of Indigo* Calcutta 1887 |
| 168 | 8 | Knighton op. cit. |
| 168 | 14 | Reid op. cit. |

### 2. The Making of a Memsahib

| 169 | 1 | S. J. Duncan: *The Simple Adventures of a Memsahib* London 1893 |
|------|------|--------|
| 169 | 16 | E. C. P. Hull: *The European in India* London 1871 |
| 170 | 7 | Duncan op. cit. |
| 171 | 8 | Hull op. cit. |
| 171 | 29 | Duncan op. cit. |
| 172 | 3 | Hull op. cit. |

[275]

| Page | Line | Source |
|---|---|---|
| 174 | 19 | Duncan op. cit. |
| 175 | 8 | Flora Annie Steel and G. Gardiner: *The Complete Indian Housekeeper and Cook* London 1888 |
| 176 | 8 | Duncan op. cit. |
| 176 | 27 | 'Wyvern': *Culinary Jottings* Madras 1891 |
| 177 | 15 | Duncan op. cit. |
| 178 | 26 | Phil Robinson: *In My Indian Garden* London 1884 |
| 179 | 6 | Steel and Gardiner op. cit. |
| 179 | 11 | Lt. Majendie: *Up Among the Pandies* London 1859 |
| 179 | 24 | Steel and Gardiner op. cit. |
| 180 | 1 | Duncan op. cit. |
| 181 | 1 | Steel and Gardiner op. cit. |
| 181 | 33 | Duncan op. cit. |
| 182 | 25 | Steel and Gardiner op. cit. |
| 183 | 17 | M. Diver: *The Englishwoman in India* Edinburgh 1909 |
| 183 | 28 | G. R. Aberigh-Mackay: *Twenty-one Days in India* London 1910 |
| 183 | 37 | Duncan op. cit. |

## 3. The Day's Work

| 185 | 17 | F. H. Skrine: *Life of Sir W. W. Hunter* London 1901 |
|---|---|---|
| 188 | 21 | Aberigh-Mackay op. cit. |
| 189 | 7 | Mortimer Durand: *Life of Sir Alfred Comyn Lyall* London 1906 |
| 189 | 21 | Trevelyan op. cit. |
| 191 | 8 | T. H. Lewin: *A Fly on the Wheel or How I Helped to Govern India* London 1912 |
| 193 | 27 | Aberigh-Mackay op. cit. |
| 194 | 8 | H. Keene: *A Servant of John Company* London 1897 |
| 195 | 1 | M. Edwardes: *High Noon of Empire: India under Curzon* London 1965 |

## 4. Picnics and Adultery

| 196 | 8 | Diver op. cit. |
|---|---|---|
| 197 | 14 | Buck op. cit. |

| Page | Line | Source |
|------|------|--------|
| 197 | 32 | Lady Dufferin and Ava: *Our Viceregal Life in India* London 1899 |
| 198 | 19 | Edwin Montagu: *My Indian Diary* London 1930 |
| 198 | 23 | Dufferin and Ava op. cit. |
| 198 | 36 | Aberigh-Mackay op. cit. |
| 200 | 4 | M. Edwardes: *High Noon . . .* op. cit. |
| 200 | 18 | Kincaid op. cit. |
| 201 | 19 | Buck op. cit. |
| 203 | 30 | J. C. Oman: *Mystics, Ascetics and Saints of India* London 1894 |
| 204 | 3 | F. Marion Crawford: *Mr Isaacs: A Tale of Modern India* London 1882 |
| 205 | 20 | Dufferin and Ava op. cit. |
| 206 | 5 | Aberigh-Mackay op. cit. |
| 206 | 36 | Rudyard Kipling: *Miss Youghal's Sais*, in *Plain Tales from the Hills* |
| 207 | 20 | Buck op. cit. |
| 208 | 19 | Lepel Griffin, in Buck op. cit. |
| 208 | 28 | M. Edwardes: *High Noon . . .* op. cit. |

## 5. The 'Damned-nigger' Party

| | | |
|------|------|--------|
| 209 | 19 | W. S. Blunt: *India under Ripon* London 1909 |
| 210 | 7 | J. C. Curry: *The Indian Police* London 1933 |
| 210 | 14 | E. Thompson and G. T. Garratt: *Rise and Fulfilment of British Rule in India* London 1934 |
| 210 | 28 | Blunt op. cit. |
| 211 | 20 | Flora Annie Steel: *The Hosts of the Lord* London 1900 |
| 211 | 35 | Aberigh-Mackay op. cit. |
| 212 | 5 | F. A. Steel: *For the Faith* in *The Flower of Forgiveness* London 1894 |
| 212 | 16 | Aberigh-Mackay op. cit. |
| 212 | 30 | *Fraser's Magazine* August 1873 |
| 212 | 34 | Aberigh-Mackay op. cit. |
| 213 | 8 | 'F. Anstey': *A Bayard from Bengal* London 1900 |
| 213 | 17 | W. W. Hunter: *The Old Missionary* London 1889 |
| 213 | 20 | Aberigh-Mackay op. cit. |

| Page | Line | Source |
|------|------|--------|
| 213 | 32 | Lady Betty Balfour: *The History of Lord Lytton's Indian Administration* London 1899 |
| 214 | 34 | *The Times*, London 4 February 1883 |
| 215 | 6 | M. Edwardes: *British India* London 1967 NY 1968 |
| 215 | 29 | Kincaid op. cit. |
| 215 | 33 | *The Englishman* Calcutta 1 March 1883 |
| 216 | 2 | Memorial of 8 March 1883 in C. H. Phillips (ed): *The Evolution of India and Pakistan, Select Documents* London 1962 |
| 216 | 14 | *The Englishman* 6 March 1883 |
| 216 | 34 | *The Englishman* 29 March 1883 |
| 217 | 26 | *The Englishman* 14 December 1883 |

## Act Three: Waiting for the Last Trump

### 1. Everything as before, only different

This chapter owes most to the diaries and reminiscences of 'James Furness', who arrived in India in 1919 and stayed there for more than forty years. Permission for their use was given only on the understanding that the source would not be identified. The pseudonym was chosen by the present author.

| Page | Line | Source |
|------|------|--------|
| 224 | 9 | G. T. Garratt ed: *The Legacy of India* Oxford 1937 |
| 225 | 21 | George Orwell: *Burmese Days* London 1935 |
| 230 | 7 | The description of a Muharram procession and riot is a blending of reminiscences of 'James Furness' who witnessed such a riot in the early 1930s and the description of one in Rudyard Kipling's *On the City Wall* first published in 1880. |

### 2. The Writing on the Wall

This chapter is based upon the experiences of Michael Edwardes during World War II and after.

## Epilogue: After the Sun Set

### 2. Counting the Cost

This chapter is based upon: Michael Edwardes: 'Miss Nightingale and the Imperial Cloaca' *The Twentieth Century* Vol. 154 No. 922 December 1953

### 3. Residues of Empire

This chapter is based upon sections, here revised and extended, in Michael Edwardes: *British India: A Survey of the Nature and Effects of Alien Rule* London 1967 New York 1968

# INDEX